THE FICTION OF THE STATE

STANFORD STUDIES IN JEWISH HISTORY AND CULTURE

Edited by Jessica Marglin and Daniel Schwartz

THE FICTION OF THE STATE

The Partitions of Poland and the Beginning of Modern Jewish Literature

OFER DYNES

STANFORD UNIVERSITY PRESS
Stanford, California

Stanford University Press
Stanford, California

Library of Congress Cataloging-in-Publication Data

Names: Dynes, Ofer author
Title: The fiction of the state : the partitions of Poland and the beginning of modern Jewish literature / Ofer Dynes.
Other titles: Stanford studies in Jewish history and culture (bcp47)
Description: Stanford, California : Stanford University Press, 2026. | Series: Stanford studies in Jewish history and culture | Includes bibliographical references and index.
Identifiers: LCCN 2026007213 (print) | LCCN 2026007214 (ebook) | ISBN 9781503647435 cloth | ISBN 9781503647985 paperback | ISBN 9781503647992 epub
Subjects: LCSH: Jewish literature—Poland—History and criticism | Hebrew literature—Poland—History and criticism | Yiddish literature—Poland—History and criticism | Jewish literature—19th century—History and criticism | Politics and literature—Poland—History—19th century
Classification: LCC PJ5049.P6 D96 2026 (print) | LCC PJ5049.P6 (ebook)
LC record available at https://lccn.loc.gov/2026007213
LC ebook record available at https://lccn.loc.gov/2026007214

Cover design: Susan Zucker
Cover art: Konstantin Matveevich Gribanov, "Kamenets-Podolsk Province," *Album of Geographical Playing Cards of Russia, arranged on 80 cards according to maritime basin (A wonderful and instructive children's game of patience),* (St. Petersburg, 1857). Library of Congress.
Typeset by Newgen in Garamond Premier Pro, 11/15pt

The authorized representative in the EU for product safety and compliance is: Mare Nostrum Group B.V. | Doelen 72 | 4831 GR Breda | The Netherlands | Email address: gpsr@mare-nostrum.co.uk | KVK chamber of commerce number: 96249943

Contents

Acknowledgments

This project originated at Harvard University, where I was privileged to work under the guidance of Ruth Wisse, Ilana Pardes, Joanna Niżyńska, Jay Harris, and David Sorkin. I am deeply indebted to my teachers Peter Gordon, Ajantha Subramanian, Nicholas Harkness, Elaine Scarry, Alison Frank, and Samuel Kassow, whose teaching profoundly broadened my intellectual horizons. My work was continually enriched by the generosity, insight, and friendship of colleagues and fellow intellectual travelers—Adam Stern, Sunny Yudkoff, James Reich, Michaela Pacurar, Ainsley Morse, Vera Koshkina, Andrew Ong, Joelle Abi-Rached, Naor Ben-Yehoyada, Oleh Kotsyuba, Raphaël Koenig, Debra Caplan, Philip Penka, Veronika Kusumaryati, Ariel Evan-Mayse, Sasha Senderovich, Itamar Mann, Iaroslava Strikha, and Marek Majer.

My understanding of the field was shaped by my fellowship Austrian Galicia and Its Multicultural Heritage at the University of Vienna, which provided me with a home away from home in Vienna and sponsored my first archival journey to Ukraine. I am grateful to Christoph Augustinowicz, Philipp Ther, Roman Dubasevych, and Boerries Kuzmany for their mentorship and encouragement, and to Matthias Kaltenbrunner and Elisabeth Janick for their companionship, for our shared adventures in Ternopil,

Brody, and Lviv, and for teaching me how to read *Kurrent.* Further research in Ukraine was made possible thanks to the support and friendship of Sofia Dyak, Vladyslava Moskalets, and Bohdan Shumylovych from the Lviv Center for Urban History. My archival research in Poland was funded through the Thesaurus Poloniae fellowship program.

My vision of Jewish history was further refined through a fellowship at the Center for Jewish History, where I benefited from conversations and feedback from Steve Zipperstein, Glenn Dynner, Britt Trevis, Patrick Koch, Jeffrey Culang, and Sarah Zarrow. As a Posen Fellow, I had the privilege of learning from David Biale z"l, David Myers, and Naomi Seidman, as well as from a remarkable cohort of colleagues—Elisabeth Imber, Gil Rubin, Hadar Samet, Tamar Menashe, Yael Segalovitz, Noemi Duhaut, Wojciech Tworek, and Michael Casper. I am also grateful to the Law and Humanities Workshop for Junior Scholars for providing me with the opportunity to engage in stimulating discussions that helped refine my work.

During my postdoctoral fellowship at McGill University, I was fortunate to be mentored by Gershon Hundert z"l and to learn from Esther Frank, Carlos Fraenkel, Chris Silver, Yael Halevi-Weiss, Daniel Heller, Eric Caplan, Ula Madej-Krupitski, Piotr Kosicki, Jeremy Brown, and Jessica Roda. My subsequent fellowship at the University of Graz benefited from the collegiality of Olaf Terpitz and Daniel Baric.

My tenure as professor of Jewish history at the Hebrew University of Jerusalem afforded me the privilege of working alongside and learning from distinguished colleagues, including Aya Elyada, Israel Bartal, David Assaf, Yonatan Me'ir, Avishai Bar-Asher, David Roskies, Avraham Nowersztern, Marc Volovici, Daniel Mahla, Yanai Israeli, Lilach Netanel, Eli Lederhendler, Chava Turnianski, David Stromberg, Moshe Taube, Scott Ury, Dror Wahrman, Avner Holtzman, Giddon Ticotsky, and Oded Zinger. I also wish to thank Yfaat Weiss and the Dubnow Institute for their generous support.

I am equally grateful to colleagues and interlocutors at other institutions who have shaped my thinking in countless ways: Ada Rapoport-Albert z"l, Samuel Spinner, Yaniv Feller, Adam Teller, Rachel Rojanski, Natalia Aleksiun, Amelia Glaser, Shachar Pinsker, Karolina Szymaniak, Kamil Kijek, Eugenia Prokop-Janiec, Marcin Wodziński, Daniel Hershenzon, Dan Miron, Elik Elhanan, Emanuel Fiano, Guillaume Nicoud, Ma'oz Kahana,

Shmuel Feiner, Olga Litvak, Kenneth Moss, Paweł Maciejko, Hannan Hever, Roni Mazel, François Guesnet, Svetlana Natkovich, Alex Valdman, Uriel Gelman, Gadi Sagiv, Yvonne Kleinmann, and Benyamin Lukin. A heartfelt thank-you to Elly Moseson for the countless hours we spent poring over difficult Hebrew manuscripts.

At Columbia University, my current academic home, I am thankful to my colleagues for their feedback, advice, and support: Irina Reyfman, Jessica Merrill, Valentina Izmirlieva, Adam Leeds, Marina Tsylina, Christopher Caes, Mark Lipovetsky, Aleksander Boskovic, Yuri Shevchuk, Christopher Harwood, Chloë Kitzinger, Tatiana Mikhailova, Liza Knapp, Rebecca Kastleman, Claudia Berger, Agnieszka Legutko, Michael Stanislawski, Elisheva Carlebach, Clémence Boulouque, Catherine Evtuhov, Rebecca Kobrin, Beth Berkowitz, Mark Mazower, Julie Peters, and Jeremy Dauber. Special thanks to the Harriman Institute for Russian, Eurasian, and East European Studies and to the Institute for Israel and Jewish Studies for their generous support.

It is a great pleasure to thank my former and current students—Avraham Oriah Kelman, Tatiana Krasilnikova, Esther Zyskina, Ethan Fraenkel, William Debnam, Myles Garbarini, Samuel Roche, and Eyshe Beirich—for their invaluable insights, as well as the participants in my seminars "Jewish Enlightenment—A New History," "A History of Eastern European Jewry," "The Religious Experience in Yiddish," and "Bible, Literature, Theory," where I tested many of the ideas developed here.

At Stanford University Press, I wish to thank the Stanford Studies in Jewish History and Culture series editors, Jessica Marglin and Daniel Schwartz, as well as editor Genevieve Aoki and editorial assistant Natalie Rovero, for their generosity and patience throughout the process.

This book is dedicated to the memory of my grandparents, Celina (Cynia) Flaksman-Baron z"l, Bolesław (Ben-Tsiyen) Baron z"l, Dora (Dvoyre) Bercovici-Dines z"l, and Marcu (Mordkhe) Dines z"l, and to my father, Tsvika (Herman) Dines z"l. I owe everything to my beloved family, Żanet and Shlomo Bareket, Ziva (Sylvia) Baron-Dynes, Nir Dynes, Or Dynes, and Niv Allon, whose insights and unwavering support accompany me always.

A Note on Place-Names and Transliteration

The challenge of adopting a coherent and historically accurate system of place-names is twofold. First, cities, towns, districts, and provinces in Eastern Europe bore different names in German, Russian, Polish, Ukrainian, Belarusian, Hebrew, and Yiddish, a linguistic plurality thoroughly reflected in the sources in all its complexity and specificity. Second, although the locations examined in this book were divided roughly equally between the Habsburg and Russian Empires, most now fall within the borders of contemporary Ukraine. The war in Ukraine has lent new urgency, and a distinct ethical weight, to decisions about whether to employ Ukrainian place-names.

The guiding principle in this monograph is faithfulness to the sources above all other considerations. Accordingly, when referring to the Habsburg administrative centers of Lemberg and Tarnopol, I use their German names. Russian provinces and district names are transliterated from Russian. Given the book's focus on partitioned Poland as a unifying analytical framework, Polish place names are used where appropriate. For example, Tulczyn, the seat of the Potocki court, is rendered in its Polish form. The transliteration of Bratslav—the seat of Naḥman of Bratslav—follows Naḥman's own usage as it appears in his correspondence with his students. In all of these cases, alternative forms in Ukrainian are noted as necessary. Other locations are transliterated according to their current names. While this solution will likely fully satisfy no one, it offers the greatest clarity for readers, ensuring that place-names appear consistently across the primary sources, the discussion, and the analysis.

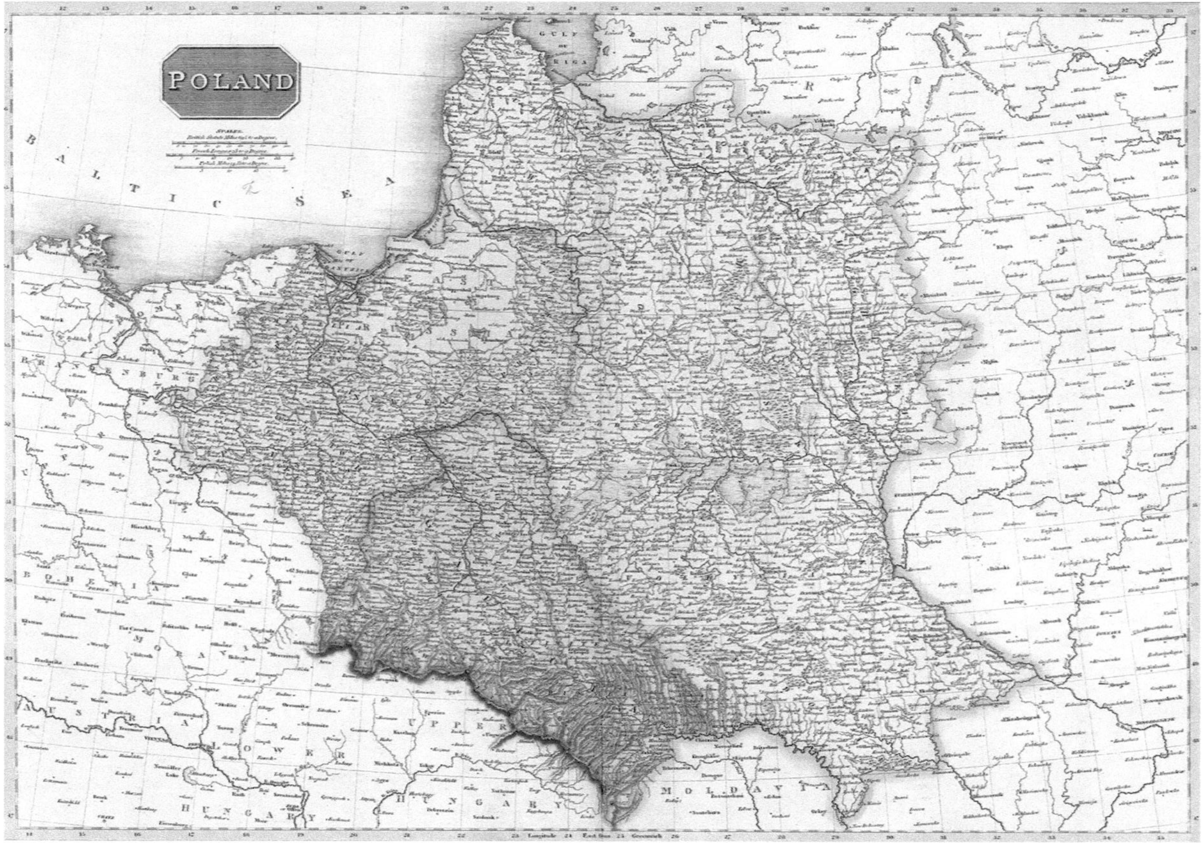

FIGURE 1 Partitioned Poland, 1817. From John Pinkerton and Lewis Hebert, "Poland," in *Pinkerton's Modern Atlas* (Philadelphia: Dobson, 1817), Digital Public Library of America, http://collections.lib.uwm.edu/cdm/ref/collection/agdm/id/26137.

THE FICTION OF THE STATE

INTRODUCTION

From Legibility to Literature

THIS BOOK INVESTIGATES TWO SEEMINGLY unrelated questions. The first pertains to the field of literary history: Why did Jewish intellectuals in Eastern Europe turn to fiction in the first decades of the nineteenth century? The second is rooted in political history and set against the backdrop of the partitions of Poland in the late eighteenth century: How, it asks, did Polish Jews make sense of their encounter with the modern imperial states that took over the Polish lands? These two questions, this monograph argues, are inseparable. The Jewish literary project, it shows, is intimately related to the imperial legibility project, the making of the newly annexed territories knowable, legible, and governable.[1] To introduce this connection and discuss its implications, I turn to a case study: the early literary career of the Hebrew and Yiddish writer Shalom Abramovitsh (1835–1917; pen name Mendele Mokher Sfarim).

In December 1864, Abramovitsh received an official letter from the Chancellery of the Governor-General of Kiev, Podolia, and Volhynia.[2] The letter enclosed a series of questions, initially published in the Kiev-based periodical *Kievlianin*, regarding the cultural and religious life of Russian Jews, their education, and reading practices. It asked Abramovitsh to "take the trouble to examine" these matters in detail.[3] The letter assured Abramovitsh that his response would "contribute significantly to the correct solution"—that is, to formulating governmental policies concerning the Jewish population of the Russian Empire.[4] Upon receiving this letter, Abramovitsh undertook two courses of action. First, he submitted a detailed response to the authorities, for which he received an official acknowledgment that it would be "taken into serious consideration during the discussions of the opinions collected on this important matter."[5] Second, he published his response in the Hebrew periodical *Ha-melits*, and later expanded it into a book he titled *ʿEin mishpat* [Fountain of Justice].[6] Abramovitsh incorporated into *ʿEin mishpat* his correspondence with the Russian authorities, the document he supplied to them, his reflection on this correspondence, as well as an article devoted to his assessment of the nascent Hebrew literature. In this sui generis genre, Abramovitsh's review and evaluation of Hebrew publications doubled as a survey of the Jewish cultural and religious intellectual landscape for the Russian authorities.

The lengthy subtitle of the book lists its two components: "the first judges [*ʿorekh din*] contemporary Hebrew literature . . . and the second properly responds to the governmental inquiry," and underscores the synergy between them, which Abramovitsh, in an evocative phrasing, likened to "brothers bound together" (*meshulavim ʾish ʾel ʾaḥiv*). In so doing, he articulated a vision that brought together the Russian governmental project of gathering information on the Jewish population, the rise of a new mode of Jewish expression, and the inception of his own writing. This vision culminated in Abramovitsh's proposal to reform Hebrew literature by means of governmental engagement and supervision:

> The benevolent government, in its magnanimity, would establish a dedicated committee . . . endowed with funds drawn in part from the candle tax . . . and entrust it with the responsibility of supporting Jewish writers. This body would allocate subsidies and oversee the dissemination of beneficial literature across a broad spectrum of disciplines.[7]

Abramovitsh's choice to title the entire project "ʿEin mishpat," reveals the extent of his optimism regarding the transformative potential of his literary-political enterprise, which he envisioned as a flowing source—*ʿayin* in Hebrew—of fairness, laws, and judgment, the three possible meanings of the Hebrew *mishpat*.

While Abramovitsh's introduction to *ʿEin mishpat* has been examined and discussed in the classical surveys of his work, the broader questions it raises are yet to be explored.[8] What should we make of the fact that a seminal figure in the Jewish literary and cultural pantheon wrote a book in dialogue with the Russian imperial authorities? What does it mean that a foundational text of Hebrew literary criticism incorporates official correspondence between a Jewish writer and a Russian official? What does it tell us about the intersection of Hebrew and Yiddish prose and bureaucratic prose? What kind of literary history emerges from these poetic-bureaucratic entanglements?

This historical episode encapsulates several of the central phenomena that this monograph recovers, contextualizes, and theorizes. First, it sheds light on a case in which the Jewish encounter with the modern state and its institutions informed the formation of Hebrew and Yiddish literature. In Abramovitsh's case, a letter from the authorities was, quite literally, the inspiration for putting pen to paper. Second, it demonstrates how Hebrew and Yiddish prose intersected with a governmental survey project. *ʿEin mishpat* was simultaneously a document commissioned by the Russian government to gather information about the Jewish population of the southwestern gubernias, Kiev, Podolia, and Volhynia, and a Hebrew book that informed Jewish readers about the Russian state and its interest in its Jewish subjects. The insights it offered into the cultural, religious, and literary life of the Jewish community functioned both as a bureaucratic record for the provincial administration and as a text that conveyed to Hebrew readers how they were perceived by the state. Finally, this monograph advances the premise that the production of Jewish literature in nineteenth-century Eastern Europe should be situated within a wide-ranging network that encompasses not only authors, publishers, and printing houses but also state bureaucrats, censors, Jewish converts, police officers, and spies.[9] In this context, *ʿEin mishpat* serves as a particularly revealing case study, shedding light on the numerous administrative actors who were implicated in its creation.[10]

While the Hebrew text refers to the Russian authorities using the impersonal collective noun *ha-memshala* (the government), the Russian letter identifies the sender by name: V(ladimir) Fedorov, head of the Chancellery of the Governor-General of Kiev, Podolia, and Volhynia. Many within

Abramovitsh's circle were aware of Fedorov's background: born Hirsh Grinboym, he had converted to Christianity in 1843 and was subsequently appointed as an "expert Jew."[11] Fedorov's official role was to interpret Jewish religious laws and customs to assist in drafting the administrative policies toward the provinces' Jewish population. Fedorov's engagement with the production of *ʿEin mishpat* was part of a broader, long-standing relationship he maintained with Hebrew and Yiddish writers after his conversion. First, in addition to Abramovitsh, Fedorov contacted other Hebrew writers, most notably Uri Kovner.[12] Moreover, the letter Fedorov addressed to Abramovitsh was not a singular act of communication. While preparing his manuscript for publication, Abramovitsh had approached Fedorov, who subsequently granted permission for his letters to be reproduced as a preface to the volume.[13] When Fedorov was later appointed as Warsaw's censor of Jewish publications, he routinely invited Hebrew publishers to his home to discuss their works.[14] A decade after the publication of *ʿEin mishpat,* Fedorov translated Moses Mendelssohn's *Jerusalem* into Hebrew, thereby making his own contribution to the world of Hebrew letters. He did so under the telling Hebrew pseudonym Doresh Tov le'Yisrael, "A Seeker of Israel's Welfare."[15]

The overwhelming majority of the studies *ʿEin mishpat* overlook the impetus for its inception. The letters appended to *ʿEin mishpat* are not incorporated in the robust collection of Abramovitsh's correspondence.[16] Some of the most insightful studies of *ʿEin mishpat* omit any mention of Vladimir Fedorov: his name, bureaucratic position, biography, or contribution to the creation of the book.[17] One explanation for this omission lies in *ʿEin mishpat*'s favorable vision of the Russian authorities, which stands in sharp contrast to some of the most celebrated publications in Abramovitsh's career. For this reason, the Hebrew critic Yaʿakov Fichman called this work a "prehistory" to Mendele's long literary career.[18] "How markedly different," wrote Klausner in his analysis of *ʿEin mishpat,* is Abramovitsh's positive vision of the Russian government, compared to the "Abramovitsh of later years."[19]

Yet the publication of *ʿEin mishpat* did not mark the conclusion of Abramovitsh's career as an author-collaborator. In 1869, he published a Yiddish play titled *Di takse, oder di bande shtot baley-toyves* [The Tax, or the Gang of the Town Benefactors], which represented a further development of the writer's bureaucratic-literary vision. The plot of *Di takse* takes place in Glupsk, where the corrupt community leaders have transformed the *koroba* (kosher meat tax) from a communal levy into a source of personal gain. Abramovitsh dedicated *Di takse* to Nikolai Novoselskiy, the mayor of Odessa, addressing him with the following words:

> In the speech delivered by Your Excellency on June 13, 1868, at the opening of the meeting of the members of the Odessa Jewish Society, you . . . pointed out the hardships caused to the poor class of Jews by the kosher meat tax and expressed a very just thought—that our society must oppose this evil.
>
> In this work in Yiddish, titled *The Tax*, I have tried, to the best of my ability, to depict all the hardships endured by the poor class of Jews due to the kosher meat tax. Filled with deep gratitude to Your Excellency for raising this issue, I dare to dedicate my humble work to your name, which will always be associated with the memory of the abolition of this burdensome levy for the people. The gracious attention of Your Excellency will be the best reward for my modest labor.[20]

As Ruth Wisse has noted, the dedication of *Di takse* to the Odessan authorities accords with the play's sympathetic depiction of the informer and its broadly positive view of denunciation.[21] When the protagonist, Shloyme Veker, asks why Jews refrain from filing a formal complaint against the Jewish community's corrupt leaders, his friend Gedalye Pikholts replies that whenever Jews complain, "people call them snitches. A town full of people, thousands of homeowners are snitches!"[22] As the reader discovers later, Veker himself professes he made a formal complaint to the local mayor.[23] Thus, at the very outset, *Di Takse* sought to influence Jewish attitudes toward the state by promoting a conception of legality and the rule of law and encouraging appeals to the authorities. Furthermore, I contend, its publication was, in and of itself, an act of denunciation.

As scholars have often noted, *Di takse* was a thinly veiled roman à clef, which was meant to unmask the corruption of a number of recognizable figures among the Jewish communal leadership in Berdichev (Polish: Berdyczów, today Berdychiv, Ukraine), where Abramovitsh resided between 1858 and 1869. That some individuals portrayed in the play felt compelled to defend themselves against its accusations underscores the seriousness with which it was received.[24] In dedicating the play to a Russian official, Abramovitsh was not merely offering "a confirmation" of his "faith in the government," as Wisse suggested. The dedication, written in Russian, arguably signaled the author's proximity to, or alignment with, the Russian authorities. The protagonist's confession to having informed the authorities about the corruption of the Jewish community's leaders may have been read by audiences as a veiled admission by Abramovitsh himself—that he had once done the same and might do so again.

The introduction to *Di takse* also illustrates another central argument of this monograph: Jewish fiction was crafted not only to shape Jewish attitudes toward the state but also, oftentimes, as a means to influence the state's perception of Jews. Abramovitsh's expressed desire to attract "the gracious attention of Your Excellency" identifies Nikolai Novoselskiy, the mayor of Odessa, as the ideal reader of the play, and perhaps also as an actual reader. As the publication of *ʿEin mishpat* exemplifies, by this time, there was already a network of Jewish experts in place who could translate Hebrew and Yiddish texts for the use of the authorities. Indeed, *Di takse* was eventually translated into Russian in 1884, potentially extending its reach well beyond the Yiddish-reading public.[25]

Finally, whereas in *ʿEin mishpat* Abramovitsh was recruited by the Russian authorities to supply information, in *Di takse,* he voluntarily offered information to the state. The writing of literature functioned in this case as a site for producing "affective knowledge," to borrow Christopher Bayly's term, knowledge that "derived from the creation of moral communities within the colonial society by means of conversion, acculturation, or interbreeding."[26] In the 1860s, Abramovitsh and his circle were ready to volunteer incriminating information against other Jews for moral reasons rather than financial remuneration (thus constituting a "moral community"), in hope that the authorities would intervene.

THE PARTITIONS OF POLAND AND THE RISE OF HEBREW AND YIDDISH PROSE

So far, I have demonstrated how Abramovitsh's early literary career provides a lens for understanding the relationship between the Jewish author and imperial power. My further argument situates this dynamic within the broader historical context of the Partitions of Poland (1772–1795) and their aftermath (fig. 1). At first glance, the decision to begin a monograph that centers on the Polish partitions with the figure of Shalom Abramovitsh is not self-evident. Born in 1835, four decades after the dissolution of the Polish-Lithuanian Commonwealth, Abramovitsh's literary career appears, at least ostensibly, to be chronologically removed from the historical events of the partitions. Moreover, the Polish dimension is not immediately apparent either in *ʿEin mishpat* nor *Di Takse.* Notwithstanding, I argue that Abramovitsh's early career must be understood in relation to the emergence of Hebrew and Yiddish literature in the Polish lands, and his erasure of the Polish context was deliberate, aligning with Russian imperial policy.

The questionnaire addressed to Abramovitsh in 1864 originated in the Chancellery of the Governor-General of Kiev, Podolia, and Volhynia—the gubernias encompassing the former Polish territories annexed by the Russian Empire in the final quarter of the eighteenth century. A year earlier, in 1863, the local Polish nobility in these provinces had joined forces with rebels across the historical Polish lands, in what would later be known as the January Uprising, an attempt to restore Polish political autonomy. The project of collecting information about the Jewish population in the Polish gubernias was one of several Russian imperial initiatives aimed at strengthening control over the historical Polish lands, alongside efforts to curb the influence of the Polish nobility as a measure to prevent another local insurrection.[27]

In response to the insurrection, Governor-General of Kiev, Podolia, and Volhynia Nikolai Annenkov undertook various measures to suppress the movement for Polish independence. Among these was the establishment of the Russian-language journal *Kievlianin*, as a means "to watch over native Russian interests" and to counter "the illegal and irrational encroachments of Polish propaganda" in these formerly Polish lands.[28] Fittingly, *Kievlianin*'s motto was "This land is Russian, Russian, Russian!"[29] As noted, it was on the pages of *Kievlianin* that the questionnaire addressed to Abramovitsh, among other Jewish intellectuals, was first published and discussed.

Two years after the publication of *ʿEin mishpat*, Abramovitsh, together with Osip Levin, attempted to establish a Yiddish journal in Zhitomir (today Zhytomyr, Ukraine), with the intention to further "the efforts of the authorities to popularize among the Jews a sense of Russian belonging (*dos gefil fun rusen*), the learning of the language of the land, and thereby to integrate them with the local population," as well as "to combat German and Polish influence on the Jewish masses."[30] The erasure of any discussion of the Polish context was thus part and parcel of a progovernment maskilic agenda.

Abramovitsh wrote *'Ein mishpat* very much with an eye to the government's Russification policies in the Polish lands. Tellingly, the term "Polish Jews" appears in the book solely in reference to a distant past.[31] As a result, a contemporary reader of *'Ein mishpat* would not be aware of its Polish context and, when reading *Di takse*, would have no way of knowing that Berdichev, the location of the plot, was a private estate owned by the Polish noble Tyszkiewicz family. As Israel Bartal has observed, the same holds true for Abramovitsh's prose in the 1860s and 1870s: the Polish nobility, which was central to the works of Nahum Meir Schaikewitz, pseudonym Shomer (1858–1911) and Peretz Smolenskin (1842–1885), is entirely missing.[32] And yet, it was during his residence in Berdichev that Abramovitsh witnessed the Polish Insurrection led by the local nobility in January 1863. The Polish-Lithuanian Commonwealth was a matter not only of the past but of pressing contemporary urgency.

This is not to suggest that the specters of the Polish-Lithuanian Commonwealth were entirely erased from Abramovitsh's prose. Rather, they were relegated to the status of a vestige of the past, an anachronism invoked by traditional Jews. In 1865, around the same time he started corresponding with the Russian authorities in response to the above-mentioned questions, Abramovitsh created his famed fictionalized figure of Mendele Moykher Sforim, Mendele the Book Peddler, which would serve as his pseudonym for the rest of his literary career. This is how Mendele presents himself to the reader in his introduction to the 1865 *Dos kleyne mentshele* (The Little Man):

> I was born in Tsviatshits and my name is Mendele the Book Peddler. Most of the year, I'm on the road, traveling from one place to another, so people know me everywhere. I ride all over Poland with a full stock of books printed in Zhitomir, and apart from that, I carry prayer shawls, fringed undergarments, tassels, shofars, tefillin, amulets, mezuzas, wolf tooth charms, and sometimes you can even get brass and copper goods from me.[33]

Strikingly, when speaking in the voice of a traditional Jew, Mendele describes the territories which were annexed to Russia more than half a century prior as "Poylen," Poland.[34] This striking reference was expunged from the text a decade later. In 1879, when revising *Dos kleyne mentshele*, Abramovitsh erased Poland from the introduction. In this new version, Mendele, the traditional Jew, referred to the very same territories by their Russian administrative names and described himself as a man of long Muscovite pedigree.[35]

As this case study demonstrates, as late as the 1870s, the long shadows of the Polish-Lithuanian partitions continued to shape the Jewish literary enterprise. During the first two decades of his literary career, Shalom Ya'akov Abramovitsh projected the Russian imperial political imaginary onto the partitioned Polish lands, thereby participating in the bureaucratic project that this monograph terms the "fiction of the state."

THE FICTION OF THE STATE

Abramovitsh's writing holds a privileged position in Jewish literary historiography. As the "founder of modern artistic prose in Hebrew and Yiddish," to cite Dan Miron, the multiple directions he took in his career are often cast as a symbolic focal point for theorizing the emergence of modern Jewish literature. Scholars such as Gershon Shaked, Amir Banbaji, Irene Tucker, Todd Hasak-Lowy, Lilach Nethanel, Naomi Seidman, and Yigal Schwartz, among others, have positioned Mendele as a symbolic departure point for the study of nationalism in Hebrew literature, the revival of the Hebrew language, the creation of modern Hebrew literary language, Jewish bilingualism, or the rise of modern Yiddish literature.[36]

The Fiction of the State supplements this list. The image of Jewish literary creativity it recovers differs significantly from the figure of the Yiddish writer as a "traveler disguised," to use Dan Miron's term, a modern enlightener who conceals himself as a traditional Jew. It also diverges from the figure of the Hebrew maskilic watcher over the House of Israel, which Hannan Hever, drawing on the Galician Hebrew author Yitzḥak Erter, describes as embodying "the sovereign power of the Jewish Enlightenment."[37] Rather, a different symbolic imagery emerges: that of a writer who serves as a watcher over the House of Israel in service of the empire, a figure who is not a traveler disguised, but a bureaucrat or a spy in disguise. Viewed from the historical perspective of the partitions, *'Ein mishpat* and *Di takse* are not only, in David Frishman's terminology, a "prehistory" of Hebrew and Yiddish literary modernity; they are among the final chapters in an anthology of literary texts written in response to the partitions and the imperial transformation of the Polish lands, extending from the partitions to the 1860s.

The Fiction of the State recovers this library of texts, situating Hebrew and Yiddish literature within a broader framework of writings that documented the state's newly acquired territories and populations, and tracing its trajectory from the partitions through the mid-nineteenth century. The first chapter, "Between the Court of Polish Nobles and the Russian Tsar: The Hebrew Panegyric Poetry of Moshe Elḥanan 1789–1811," centers on the Jewish experience of the legal shift occasioned by the partitions, from Polish feudal-like noble rule to direct subjection to a centralizing state. It offers a historically informed analysis of a particular literary genre: Jewish praise poems dedicated to rulers. The case study I bring is the panegyric poetry of Moshe Elḥanan (1769–1810), which was authored when Elḥanan was a resident of the Polish Potocki noble court of Tulczyn. This chapter shows how Hebrew poetry participated in a larger cultural project the Potocki family had initiated, which was meant to reimagine the meaning of Polish noble culture after the dissolution of the Polish-Lithuanian Commonwealth.

The second chapter, "Arresting Stories: The Rise of State Law in Partitioned Poland and the Beginning of Haskalah Literature, 1811–1819," further lays out my argument about the connection between the beginning of Jewish literature in Eastern Europe and the rise of the modern centralized state, shifting from Russia to the Habsburg Empire, and from panegyric poetry to maskilic prose. Here, I show how the earliest Hebrew and Yiddish maskilic parodies from Galicia responded to the rise of a new concept of state law. In Austria, the year 1811 saw an empire-wide project to create a homogenized civil law and to popularize legal knowledge among the residents of the empire. Jewish enlighteners, I argue, wished to join forces with state officials and disseminate legal knowledge among their coreligionists. Fittingly, maskilic literary narrative served as a vehicle to naturalize the logic of the imperial state and propagate legal knowledge. Thus, rather than an end in and of itself, maskilic critique of Hasidism was one component of a much larger project to legitimize the logic of the centralized state among the Jewish population.

The third chapter, "Naḥman in Bratslav: The End of the World and Beginning of Hasidic Literature, 1802–1810," continues within the same time frame and in the same geographical region as the first chapter, shifting our focus from the court of Tulczyn to the neighboring town of Bratslav. "Naḥman in Bratslav" revisits Naḥman of Bratslav's turn to storytelling in 1806 in the context of his Bratslav residency period (1802–1807). Naḥman's sanctification of Bratslav as a center of the Hasidic universe, I argue, was inspired by the Russian imperial project to elevate the status of the town as a bureaucratic and religious capital, as an alternative to the neighboring, noble-owned Tulczyn. Drawing on a new, archivally informed history of the town, I show how, in his tales, Naḥman allegorized the political transformation that he and his followers experienced under Russian rule, offering a narrative that defers the imperial promise for justice to the world to come. Recovering the political dimension of the tales in its localized and historical specificity, this chapter demonstrates, is central to our interpretation of their theological message.

The final chapter, "Discipline and Publish: The Hebrew Epistolary Novel and Other Intelligence Technologies, 1815–1845," extends my inquiry into the Jewish participation in the imperial legibility project, covering the intersection of Jewish literary creativity and state secret surveillance. "Discipline and Publish" explores the response of Jewish intellectuals to the rise of political surveillance in post-1815 Europe. Jewish enlighteners, I argue, sought to integrate themselves into the state's surveillance apparatus. By collaborating with the secret police, they facilitated the transmission of internal Jewish community affairs to the imperial authorities. Simultaneously, they also produced works of fiction that conveyed to the Jewish population the way it was viewed from the perspective of the secret police. During the Napoleonic Wars, the Austrian Secret Services started intercepting Yiddish and Hebrew letters and translated them into German with the help of maskilim. In their Hebrew and Yiddish epistolary prose, I show, the same maskilim combined fictionalized letters with citations from intercepted Hebrew letters. In so doing, I argue, they trained their readers to imagine Jewish society from the point of view of the Austrian police state.

The title of this monograph, *The Fiction of the State,* aims to offer a useful idiom that thematizes the different ways state building and fiction writing intersect. First, it seeks to highlight state building and empire building as forms of "collective fiction," to adopt Pierre Bourdieu's term—a project that is grounded primarily in a widely shared set of political imaginaries.[38] The transformation of the Polish territories in the first two decades of the nineteenth century is a striking example: The rise of Hebrew and Yiddish literature around the year 1815 was cast against the background of weak imperial reach and sparse state bureaucratic apparatus. The presence of the new imperial states was, to a great degree, symbolic, while very little change was actually implemented on the ground. It was not fictitious, to rephrase Bourdieu's argument; however, its perception required a great deal of imagination.

Second, the title is meant to place Hebrew and Yiddish fiction in tandem with the fiction of the state, which, in this sense, refers to the body of prose produced by state bureaucrats. This new literature, generated by the imperial authorities, evoked what Larry Wolff has termed a "fantasy of enlightened statecraft," of "perfect displacement of old forms and institutions by new."[39] Hebrew and Yiddish maskilic literature, this monograph argues, aligned with these imperial projects aimed at making the state visible, tangible, knowable, and imaginable. In their fiction, the maskilim sought to produce a literary effect that would amplify the so-called state effect, the organizational practices and political representations that "create the effect of an enduring structure," to quote Timothy Mitchell.[40] As chapter 3 shows, Hasidic fiction, in contrast, portrayed the state as a malicious deception, and state practices as "the pranks of the state" (Hebrew: *ha-katoves shel ha-medina*). In Naḥman's metaphoric language, the fiction of the state is, indeed, pure fiction, a falsehood, a malicious deception, a scam.[41]

Finally, by framing the monograph as a study of fiction, I draw attention to what I consider the most salient shared characteristic of the texts I analyze—their capacity to generate a fictional world. Fiction, according to Lubomír Doležel, possesses the power to evoke "possible worlds," that is, "ensembles of nonactualized possible states of affairs" that are partially congruent with the actual world.[42] This quality of fictionality, in turn, encourages readers to reconsider the reality they inhabit.[43] In the context examined by this monograph, the turn to fictionality allowed Jewish intellectuals to sensitize their audience to the political transformation of the Polish lands and its potential implications. Examining Hebrew and Yiddish literature from this perspective allows us to study a highly heterogeneous group of texts that depict the same territories and political regimes in radically different ways within the same analytic framework. The study of fiction, according to the model this book proposes, is a bifocal enterprise: identifying each text's ideological dimension and reconstructing the emerging political reality it engages. Accordingly, each chapter begins with an archivally informed historical account—recovering, for instance, the shifting meanings of law and legality for Polish Jewry or tracing the ways in which Polish Jews became politically suspect during the Napoleonic Wars, in tandem with an analysis of the literary works that refracted this political context. Thus, by approaching Jewish fiction as an anthology of possible worlds, this book positions Hebrew and Yiddish fiction at the center of Jewish literary history, Eastern European political history, and Jewish political thought.

ONE

Between the Court of Polish Nobles and the Russian Tsar

The Hebrew Panegyric Poetry of Moshe Elḥanan, 1789–1811

> **The persons who think Panegyrics are nothing but flattery, appear not to know with what design this kind of writing was invented by men of great sagacity . . . By having the image of virtue put before them, bad princes might be made better, the good encouraged, the ignorant instructed, the mistaken set right.**
>
> **[ERASMUS, EPISTLE 177][1]**

> **Praise is, above all, a ritual activity, which produces a "hierarchical intimacy" between the worshipper and the worshiped . . . The ritual practice, though intimate, is performed for others to see; it is meant to be observed and evaluated by onlookers.**
>
> **[BERNARD BATE, "POLITICAL PRAISE IN TAMIL NEWSPAPERS: THE POETRY AND ICONOGRAPHY OF DEMOCRATIC POWER"][2]**

PANEGYRICS AND THE PARTITIONS

This chapter examines one of the earliest literary forms to emerge after the first partition of Poland (1772): Jewish panegyric poetry dedicated to rulers. It investigates Hebrew panegyrics as a transitory literary form and probes what insights they offer into Jewish experiences of the gradual dissolution of the Polish-Lithuanian Commonwealth.[3] To this end, the chapter focuses on a specific case study: the panegyric poetry of Moshe Elḥanan (c. 1769–1822), a rabbi and occasional poet living on the Potocki estate in Tulczyn, who authored two praise poems—one addressed to Stanisław August Poniatowski (1732–1798), the last king of Poland, and the other to Tsar Alexander I (1777–1825) of Russia. First, I reflect on the emergence of Eastern European Jewish panegyrics in partitioned Poland and theorize the political world that this genre evoked. I then turn to a reconstruction of Moshe Elḥanan's biography and his relationship with the Potocki court. Building on my theoretical intervention and historical reconstruction, I conclude with a close reading of Moshe Elḥanan's panegyric poetry, guided by two questions: What do the poems reveal about the conceptual world of the author? And how did the composition of poetry relate to other political practices?

Panegyric poetry as a genre of Jewish political expression is intimately associated with the period of the partitions. Before 1772, Polish Jews were not involved, by and large, in writing panegyric poetry. Rather, scattered evidence suggests that it was customary on the occasion of royal visits to print a Polish translation of the traditional prayer for the well-being of the government, *Ha-noten teshuʿa le-melakhim* (He who gives salvation to kings).[4] In Russia, since the reign of Peter the Great (1672–1725), panegyric writings became a central genre through which the new discourse of empire was propagated, serving, in the words of literary historian Harsha Ram, as "a powerful tool for the festive propagation of Petrine ideology."[5] Following the First Partition (1772), Polish-Jewish communities under Russian rule, seeking to use panegyric poetry for political purposes, often turned to Hebrew poets from Central and Western Europe. In 1780, Jewish communities were preparing for the visit of Catherine the Great, who planned to tour the newly annexed Polish territories. Prior to her visit, local ethnic and religious communities were encouraged to prepare praise poems for their new ruler.[6] Three Jewish communities—in Polotsk, Shklov, and Mogilev (now Polack, Škłoŭ, and Mahilioŭ in Belarus)—participated in the publication of panegyrics dedicated to Catherine. All three outsourced the writing of these poems to Western European Jewish enlighteners (maskilim).[7]

In contrast to their counterparts in partitioned Poland, Jews in Prussia possessed substantial experience in the composition of panegyric poetry. According to Moshe Pelli, 10 percent of the poems in *Ha-me'asef*, the journal of the German Haskalah movement, were panegyric poems. Small wonder, then, that Hebrew panegyric poetry was associated with the Prussian Haskalah.[8] Accordingly, two of the three aforementioned communities, Mogilev and Shklov, commissioned their panegyrics from leading figures of the Prussian Haskalah: the Hebrew version from Naphtali Herz Wessely (1725–1805) and the German translation from Moses Mendelssohn (1729–1786).[9] The Polotsk community resorted to hiring a maskil from Königsberg, Prussia (now Kaliningrad, Russia). Since all three poems were published anonymously, this decision to enlist Prussian maskilim was evidently not driven by a desire to enhance communal prestige. Rather, it stemmed from a genuine necessity, as the leaders of these communities could not find a suitable local candidate. Remarkably, this practice of commissioning occasional poetry from Western European Jewish communities persisted into the nineteenth century. As late as 1801, the same communities that had engaged Wessely to compose a poem honoring Catherine the Great's visit turned again to the Prussian poet, this time to celebrate the coronation of her grandson Alexander I.[10]

The emerging genre of Hebrew panegyrics offered a novel conceptual vocabulary for articulating the Jewish communities' relationship with their new sovereigns. At the heart of the panegyric genre lies an imagined intimate and direct relationship between subject and ruler. Arjun Appadurai described this imagined dialogical connection as "hierarchical intimacy," a paradoxical notion that rulers were both deeply engaged in the lives of their subjects and simultaneously separated from them by an unbridgeable hierarchical divide. For instance, the Shklov community appealed to Tsar Paul I as both a revered sovereign and a compassionate "father who has mercy on his children" (*ke-raḥem 'av 'al banim*). Despite living thousands of miles away in distant St. Petersburg, the Russian Tsar was thus portrayed as a figure of the closest kinship.[11]

Strikingly, in the Polish territories which fell under Russian rule, Hebrew panegyric poetry was also adopted as a new means to articulate the centuries-old relationship between Jews and the Polish nobility. Comparing a poem dedicated to the Russian Tsar with one addressed to a Polish noble reveals both the shared political vocabulary used to express these relationships and the key differences in how they were experienced and conceptualized. To date, I have been able to locate only one Jewish panegyric dedicated to a Polish noble, Mendel Lefin's manuscript "Expression of Gratitude" (Divrei toda). The accidental manner in which the poem survived, a hurriedly written personal copy Lefin scribbled on the lower portion of a personal letter, suggests that other occasional poems of this kind may have existed but did not come down to us, since, unlike poems dedicated to the Tsar, they were not reproduced in print.[12]

Similar to the communities of Shklov, Polotsk, and Mogilev, the writing of this poem was also occasioned by an official visit. In 1805 Mendel Lefin (1749–1826), a Podolian maskil residing in Mikołajów (today Mykolaiv, Ukraine) under the patronage of Prince Adam Kazimierz Czartoryski (1734–1823), composed a poem on behalf of the local Jewish community to commemorate a visit by the prince's daughter Izabella Czartoryska (1745–1835). For the aforementioned Shklov community, proximity to the ruler had conveyed a largely symbolic significance. Even during the town's reception of Empress Catherine the Great in 1780, Wessely's poem indicates that most community members expressed respect through a ceremonial bow (*yishtaḥave ʿam dal*), while only select dignitaries (*roznim*) were permitted to behold her face (*yeshaḥaru ʾet panayikh*).[13] In contrast, Lefin's poem "Divrei toda" culminates in a much more intimate vision of the entire Mikołajów Jewish community beholding Princess Czartoryska's beauty. "Your many lovers who are close to you" (*revavot ʾohavayikh ha-kerovim ʾelayikh*), we read, shall witness "your beauty" and "engrave the image of your portrait within their hearts" (*laḥuk demut deyokanekh be-kirot levavam*). These words convey a tangible proximity between the community and Czartoryska. Strikingly, the poem refers to the Jewish townsfolk as Czartoryska's *kerovim*—a term connoting both kinship and physical nearness. Wessely's poem, by contrast, concludes with the aspiration to be "servants" (*ʿavadim*) of the empress, highlighting a more distant, subservient relationship.[14] This comparison reveals how the gradual domestication of praise poems among Jews in the Polish lands reflected an ongoing negotiation of the processes of centralization. In Lefin's case, it involved projecting imperial panegyric tropes onto the relationship between Jews and town owners. Thus, the composition of laudatory poems—whether for local nobles or sovereign rulers—formed part of a broader assimilation of the new political language of direct subjecthood.

Analysis of Jewish panegyric poems is hindered by the paucity of evidence concerning the contexts in which they were composed. This lack limits our ability to reconstruct the complex and nuanced political experiences behind the hyperbolic and hackneyed language of flattery. For example, when Wessely wrote his poem in honor of Catherine the Great's visit to Shklov, the town was in the midst of a radical political transition. Since 1731, it had been the private property of the Czartoryski family. Yet once it fell under Russian sovereignty in 1773, the owner, Michał Czartoryski, refused to pledge allegiance to the Russian sovereign and thus lost his latifundium.[15] To what extent was Wessely aware of these historical developments? What relationship does his ode bear to the actual lived experience of the Jewish community of Shklov at the time it received the empress? Given the lack of archival documentation, these fundamental questions remain open to speculation.

The case study examined in this chapter, the panegyric poetry of Moshe Elḥanan, is a rare exception. The analysis is supported by a particularly rich body of evidence: the panegyrist's own autobiographical account, alongside documents from state archives, noble archives, contemporary memoirs, and even an oil painting, among other sources. The case is exceptional in another respect: Moshe Elḥanan composed not one panegyric but two—one dedicated to the Polish king and the other to the Russian Tsar.

Drawing on this exceptional wealth of evidentiary record, the chapter offers a novel perspective on the formation of modern Jewish literature, situating it within the supranational cultural landscape of a Polish noble court as it transitioned from the Polish-Lithuanian Commonwealth to the Russian Empire.

MOSHE ELḤANAN EXPLAINS HIS HIGH CALLING (ST. PETERSBURG, 1820)

Moshe Elḥanan, the protagonist of this chapter, is a relatively marginal figure in the history of Eastern European Jewry. As the first Jewish librarian at St. Petersburg's Imperial Public Library, he has merited a few brief biographical notices in Russian reference materials. The 1995 *Biographical Dictionary of Employees of the Russian National Library* includes the following entry:

> Elkan, Moshe (Yosefovich) (?–January 31, 1822, St. Petersburg). [Received] an honorary appointment in 1820. [Formerly] rabbi in Tulczyn (Russian: Tulchin, today Tul'chin, Ukraine). On April 10, 1820, A[leksandr] N[ikolayevich] Golitsyn, Minister of Education and Religious Affairs, proposed to A[leksei] N[ikolayevich] Olenin [the director of the Imperial Public Library] that Elkan be hired to catalog [the library's] Hebrew books. On April 11 Olenin responded that, due to the small number of books, this position was unnecessary. On June 23 A. N. Golitsyn turned to A. N. Olenin with a request to appoint Elkan as an honorary librarian. Elkan was notified [of this appointment] on June 30, 1820. In 1811 he wrote a hymn honoring Alexander I (in Hebrew and French, with commentary).[16]

The entry draws on Moshe Elḥanan's personal file at the Imperial Public Library. As such, it appears fragmentary and incomplete, containing almost no substantive information on the subject's life before his appointment as honorary librarian. How, one wonders, a rabbi from Tulczyn in distant Podolia came to be recommended for a position as Hebrew librarian in St. Petersburg at a time when Jews were officially barred from living in the city. How did he develop a relationship with the Russian Minister of Education and Religious Affairs Aleksandr Golitsyn (1773–1844)? Why was he granted the honorary (and salaried) position if his services were not needed? The entry concludes with Moshe Elḥanan's single publication, an 1811 hymn dedicated to Alexander I. How, one wonders, is this politico-literary publication related to the author's career shift from rabbi to librarian?[17]

This chapter connects some of the dots, bridging the gaps between Moshe Elḥanan's career in Tulczyn, his 1811 poem, and his 1820 appointment. A starting point is provided by the archival discovery of a seven-page autobiographical letter Elḥanan wrote to his family in Belgard, Prussia (now Białogard, Poland) in July 1820.[18] His letter is a notable historical document, one of the few surviving autobiographies documenting Jewish experience during the period of the Partitions. To date, only two other such witnesses are known to scholars: the memoirs of Dov Ber Birkenthal (1723–1805) of

Bolechów, which fell under Austrian rule, and the autobiography of Moshe Wasserzug (c. 1760–1832) of Płock, which was annexed by Prussia. With Moshe Elḥanan's autobiography we now have a document originating from the Russian Partition as well.[19]

Elḥanan's entry in the Russian *Biographical Dictionary* sheds light on the immediate context in which he wrote his short autobiography. The date of the latter is July 1820—less than a month after he had received the news about his appointment at the library. The autobiographical letter thus reflects Elḥanan's reinterpretation of his life events in light of his recent hiring as a public servant. In the letter he shares the good news with his family and apologizes for not being able to travel to pay them a visit:

> I have no leisure time; my work as a librarian in the Imperial Public Library [Öffentliche kaiserliche Bibliothek] occupies my every moment. Nor have I any time to elaborate. By the grace of God I expect more great things to come, for God has made me an important man among all the ministers, senators, and generals.
>
> [*U-mi-ḥamat she-'ein li pnai she-'ani mutrad gadol ba-bibilotek she-yesh li hitmanut ha-nikra' in der efentleche kesarliche bibliotek, ke-biblioteker, ve-'eyn li shum pnai le-harḥiv ha-dibur, ve-'od ḥazon la-mo'ed 'im yirtse ha-shem, ve-ha-kaba higdil 'alay she-ḥashuv 'ani 'etsel kol ha-ministerim ve-senatorim ve-yeneralim.*]

As suggested by his personal file at the Russian Imperial Public Library, however, Moshe Elḥanan was actually not very busy, or at least not with Hebrew books. The six hundred Hebrew books in the library's collections had already been cataloged, according to the director Alexey Olenin, prior to his move to Saint Petersburg.[20] In emphasizing the significance of his current position, then, Elḥanan structured his autobiographical text not as a nostalgic memoir (even if that sentiment is certainly evident as well), but rather as a testament, a manual for achieving success. By means of this letter he shared with his family back in Prussia how he had been able to achieve such a prominent position and therefore socialize with "ministers, senators, and generals." Later in his letter, Moshe Elḥanan offered an additional justification for his inability to undertake a journey to visit his family. Recently, he confided, he had recovered from a serious illness:

> I was gravely ill, and my power had weakened, and my internal organs had become swollen, as a result of the excessive strain and little sleep to which I had subjected myself as a youth due to the intensity of my studies.
>
> [*She-hayiti ḥole gadol ve-neḥlash koḥi ve-higdil ha-nafuaḥ, mi-ḥamat ha-yegiʿot shel ha-limud meʿat shnati mi-neʿuray.*]

As a man in his fifties, Elḥanan probably worried that he was no longer in fit shape to embark on a journey from St. Petersburg to Pomerania, a journey of nearly a month. Indeed, he would never see his family or his hometown again. Elḥanan died in St. Petersburg in 1822, two years after writing the autobiographical letter. Meanwhile, his relatives in Prussia did not fail to recognize the importance of this record. They appended to the Hebrew manuscript a German translation transcribed in fine Hebrew letters, thus making the text more accessible for future generations. They carried the letter with them when they moved from Belgard to Berlin in the late nineteenth century. In 1939 Yehuda Lewi (1878–1950), the grandson of Moshe Elḥanan's elder brother, and his wife, Johanne Frank, took the letter with them when they fled from Nazi Germany to Mandatory Palestine. Shmuel Lewy, their son, donated the extensive family archive to the Central Archives for the History of the Jewish People in Jerusalem, where it remains today.

The fact that Elḥanan wrote the autobiographical sketch at this particular moment in his life, after he had been appointed a state librarian, represents both an advantage and a challenge for the historian. His appointment clearly colored the way he understood and interpreted his life events, personal relations, and career choices. His autobiography is narrated from the point of view of a person who has completed the transition from living under Polish noble rule to residing in the Russian capital as an employee of the Russian imperial state.

FROM ST. PETERSBURG TO PRUSSIA AND BACK

As his autobiography suggests, Elḥanan enjoyed elaborating on his life in St. Petersburg: the generous governmental stipend he received, five hundred rubles a month, or the difficulty in purchasing kosher meat in a city where most Jews were not allowed to live. His colleagues at the Imperial Public Library were some of the finest Russian intellectuals of the time, including, among others, Ivan Krylov (1769–1844), Russia's best-known fabulist, and Konstantin Batyushkov (1787–1855), a famous poet and translator. Elḥanan's autobiography reports experiences of entertaining important guests with pastries (*kondituryes*) and expensive wines; the joy of buying new, fancy clothes before his meetings with the Tsar and his ministers. In comparison, the Poles he had known all seemed "wild and lacking any manners at all" (*pere' 'adam, meno'arim mi-kol derekh 'erets*).

Moshe Elḥanan also reflected on the beginning of his professional life, sharing memories of his childhood studies and first rabbinic appointments. At the age of eight he had been sent to the Prague yeshiva, where he was a student of Yechezkel Landau (1713–1793), the Noda' bi-Yehuda (Renowned in Judah). As another memoirist, Isaac Hirsch Weiss, wrote, "The eyes of most young men who dedicated themselves to study the Torah were set toward Prague."[21] At fourteen, Elḥanan complemented his yeshiva education with study of "medicine and other wisdoms and languages" (*refu'ah u-she'ar ḥokhmot u-leshonot*). As a successful graduate of the Prague yeshiva, Moshe Elḥanan was preparing himself for a lifelong career as a rabbi. Some of the most famous graduates of Landau's yeshiva came to occupy rabbinic positions in Bohemia, Moravia, and Hungary.[22] Yet Elḥanan moved eastward to the Polish-Lithuanian Commonwealth, and at the age of seventeen he was appointed rabbi in Kutno. According to his own account, at the age of nineteen he was then "accepted as a doctor of the Polish king in Warsaw" (*u-khe-she-hayiti tish'ah 'asar shanim, nitkabalti le-'asa 'etsel melekh polania be-varshoy*). In 1789, after less than two years in Warsaw, Moshe Elḥanan was "ordered," to adopt his own phrasing to take up the position of rabbi in Tulczyn, Podolia, the so-called capital of the Potocki family's immense estates:

> When I was twenty-one years and a few months old, God increased his mercy upon me, and I was given by order of the king and his ministers, chief among them the military commander [Szczęsny] Potocki, head administrator of the Ruthenian voivodeship (voivod ruski), a letter of appointment as rabbi and [Jewish] provincial judge.
>
> [*U-khe-she-hayiti shenat 'aḥad ve-'esrim ve-'ezeh ḥodashim, higdil 'adonay ḥasdo 'alay, ve-nitan li 'al-pi tsivuy ha-melekh ve-sarei ha-partemei u-ve-rosham ha-sar tsava' pototski voyevud ruski, konsens lihyot rav ve-'av bet din de-ha-medina.*][23]

The personal relationship between Moshe Elḥanan and his benefactor Szczęsny Potocki brings to mind other formal relationships between enlightened Polish nobles and exceptionally gifted Jews. The most celebrated case was the aforementioned relationship of Mendel Lefin with the Czartoryski family. It is worth noting, though, that Mendel Lefin received a monthly pension from the Czartoryskis, which suggests a greater degree of patronage and support. By contrast, Moshe Elḥanan remained an employee, even if a privileged one.

By the age of twenty-one, Moshe Elḥanan had already become a "provincial rabbi" (Hebrew: *rav de-ha-medina*; Polish: *rabin generalny*), with responsibility not only for Tulczyn but also for its neighboring villages. The Kiev archive of the Potockis of Tulczyn preserves a large file documenting his tenure there. Elḥanan is revealed to be a confident young man, able to judge with great mastery and authority even complex juridical and financial matters.[24] After his relocation to Tulczyn, Moshe Elḥanan continued cultivating his connections at the Polish court. Sometime between 1789 and 1793, Moshe Elḥanan authored his first panegyric poem, which he dedicated to the Polish king, Stanisław August Poniatowski.[25]

The poem is structured as an acrostic of the Polish king's name in French (Stanislas). In brief, two-word lines Moshe Elḥanan allegorized his relationship with Stanisław August as an encounter between a famished Jewish scholar and a fruitful tree. The tree provides nourishment, and the scholar, in gratitude, lavishes praise, which he immortalizes in this poem. The most striking autobiographical allusion in this poem is the portrayal of the favor the Polish king bestows upon the Jewish scholars as *tuv mitsrayim* (the good of Egypt). The idiomatic expression *tuv mitsrayim* (Genesis 45:19) evokes the privileged relationship between Pharaoh and Joseph and the former's generosity toward the latter. In so doing, Moshe Elḥanan paralleled his own eastward migration from the German lands to the Polish-Lithuanian Commonwealth, and the success he achieved there, with Joseph's descent to Egypt and his subsequent integration into the Egyptian court. Comparing Poland to Egypt may also have implied that Moshe Elḥanan saw his stay there as a form of exile. As Joseph longed for the Land of Israel, Moshe Elḥanan may similarly have longed to return to Prussia. To be sure, the privileged relationship with the Polish court the poem portrayed was not purely a matter of poetic fancy. Avigdor of Pinsk, who met Moshe Elḥanan in Warsaw in 1791, describes the latter in the following words:

"He is a great scholar and close to the king and his ministers, such that almost throughout all of Poland and Ashkenaz there is no one like him; his hand is in all branches of knowledge and languages."[26]

The description of the wealth of the Polish king, "your water is pure, the goodness of Egypt" (*meimekha tselulim, tuv mitsrayim*), is followed by an obscure reference to Poland's political situation: "Your army is all around" (*tseva'akha sovevim*), which reflects a certain awareness of an external threat. The poem concludes with an extended wish for the Polish king's prosperity and the enduring stability of the Polish throne, which Moshe Elḥanan likens to a firmly rooted, blossoming tree. Alas, this prophecy went unfulfilled. Shortly thereafter, in 1793, Russia annexed the province of Podolia during what became known as the Second Partition.

Once Tulczyn fell under Russian rule, Moshe Elḥanan lost his rabbinic position for good. While he signed his 1820 autobiographical letter using the title "provincial rabbi," by this point it was a mere honorific and did not denote any actual appointment.

A SMALL KINGDOM AND A BIG SALARY

The shift from Polish to Russian imperial rule carried dramatic personal consequences for Moshe Elḥanan. As a result of the Second Partition, in 1793 Tulczyn was annexed by the Russian Empire, rendering the relationships Elḥanan had cultivated with the Polish king and his court effectively worthless: "When the province [of Podolia] was taken from Poland" (*ke-she-nilkeḥa ha-medina mi-polaniya*), wrote Elḥanan in his letter, "my detractors denounced me . . . telling the governors that I had 'a small kingdom and a big salary'" (*'okhley kurtsi bi . . . be-'amram la-gubernatorim she-yesh li melukha ketana ve-hakhnasa gedola*). The upshot of this event was that Elḥanan lost his rabbinic appointment. Thus, his initial encounter with the Russian authorities turned out to be a decidedly negative experience. In stark contrast to the Tsar—whom he characterizes as "a wise man like King Solomon, a pious individual of exemplary righteousness"—and the ministers in St. Petersburg, whom he regards as "pious sages" (*tsadikim ve-ḥakhamim*), the local authorities in Podolia are depicted as deeply enmeshed in corruption.

In his autobiography Elḥanan chose not to divulge the identity of the informers, leaving the reader to speculate. We may note, however, that the province of Podolia, where he found himself after his brief stay in Warsaw, was in fact the heartland of Hasidism. One wonders how well the Prussian-born, Western Yiddish–speaking rabbi, with his Central European rabbinic education, was equipped for navigating communal tensions surrounding the rapid spread of Hasidism. Was he aware upon accepting the appointment, for instance, that Tulczyn already had a highly powerful and very well-connected local rabbi, a grandson of the Ba'al Shem Tov by the name of Barukh ben Yechiel (Barukh of Międzybóż)?[27] It appears that around the time Moshe Elḥanan came to Tulczyn to take up his rabbinic appointment Barukh ben Yechiel left for Międzybóż.[28] One can only imagine the nature of the relations between the German rabbi appointed by the Polish landowner and the local Hasidic rabbi.[29]

There is another reason to suspect that Moshe Elḥanan was fighting against the nascent Hasidic movement. As noted above, Moshe Elḥanan was an associate of Avigdor ben Haim (also known as Avigdor of Pinsk), a fiery opponent of Hasidism. In 1793, following the Second Partition, Hasidic leaders exploited the political upheaval to denounce several misnagid rabbis in Vilna and Pinsk to the Russian authorities, leading to Avigdor ben Haim's dismissal from his rabbinic post. It stands to reason that the denunciation of Moshe Elḥanan also formed part of the same campaign.[30]

We can only speculate as to why Moshe Elḥanan chose not to mention Hasidism in his letter. One plausible explanation is the specific context in which it was written. By this time, he probably did not find any reason to warn his Prussian family of the dangers of this largely Eastern European movement. Of much greater concern was the Prussian Haskalah movement. Elḥanan was a student of Yechezkel Landau, who famously argued against Naphtali Hertz Wessely, and he accordingly warned his nephews, "The most important thing is to distance yourself from the sect of good-for-nothings called the 'enlighteners'" (*Ha-'ikar—tihyu reḥokim mi-kat ha-ḥadelim ha-keru'im 'ufgeklerte*).

AT THE COURT OF THE POTOCKIS

Losing a rabbinic appointment often resulted in significant financial loss. "I have been so greatly impoverished that I have been forced to sell all my possessions," wrote Avigdor ben Haim in one of his appeals to Paul I.[31] It is possible that Moshe Elḥanan encountered similar difficulties. In his autobiography Moshe Elḥanan was reluctant to reflect on his twenty-five years in Tulczyn after losing his position. He summed up this long period in two anecdotes, both related to financial difficulties. First, he recounted how, after losing his rabbinic position, he had to return to work as a physician, a profession he found not very profitable. Tulczyn already had two established physicians, the court doctor and the Potocki family's private doctor, which likely limited Elḥanan's prospects for profitable practice.[32] To make ends meet, he also invested in several business ventures, though, by his own account, with little success.

Despite these troubles Moshe Elḥanan chose to stay in Tulczyn rather than to return to his family in Prussia or to Vilnius, where his wife, Sara née Horowitz, had family.[33] The autobiography offers no explicit explanation for this decision. To understand it, one must instead consider Tulczyn's rapid transformation in the wake of the partitions of Poland. Between 1796 and 1805 the owner of the estate, Elḥanan's patron Szczęsny Potocki, spent fifteen million zlotys to construct a park on his estate he called Sofijówka, after his wife Sophia. Potocki employed a small army of gardeners and architects, including French, British, and Italian experts. After the garden was completed, it attracted visitors from all over Europe.[34] It served as a major attraction even for Naḥman of Bratslav, who rhetorically asked his students, "Can one go to Uman and not go to the Sophia Garden"?[35] According to August Lagarde, a Russian diplomat who visited Tulczyn in 1811, the town functioned as "the capital . . . of the vast domains possessed by the head of the family of the Potocki," and the Potocki residence itself ranked among "the most splendid edifices of Europe."[36] The family's library contained seventeen thousand antique books, many of them extremely rare, and their art collection boasted originals of Raphael, Rubens, Titian, Johann Baptist von Lampi the Elder, and Van der Helst.[37]

Having spent two years in Warsaw, in the proximity of the Polish royal court, Moshe Elḥanan surely valued his connection to the thriving court of the Potocki family, with the political and economic opportunities it presented. During the French Revolution, the court of the Potocki family became a safe haven for all kinds of people who had lost a state, a position, a title, or a piece of land. Several French aristocrats chose to take refuge in Tulczyn: Yolande-Gabrielle, duchess of Polignac (1749–1793); Pierre-Louis-August Ferron, count of the Ferronnays (1777–1842); and Jean-Louis-Henri de Bancalis de Maurel, marquis d'Aragon (1763–1848).[38] When Napoléon invaded Italy, Italian aristocrats also flocked to this island of safety and calm, for example, Queen Marie-Caroline de Bourbon-Sicile (1752–1814), the older sister of Marie Antoinette.[39] "In Tulczyn, you always wait for someone [important]" wrote Jean Potocki, the author of *A Manuscript Found in Saragossa*, who resided in the court intermittently.[40]

Tulczyn also furnished a place of refuge for Stanisław Trembecki (1739–1812), Poland's former royal poet. When the last Polish king, Stanisław August Poniatowski, died in exile, Trembecki was left to his own devices and had to move from one noble estate to the other. He finally settled in Tulczyn, where he spent the last decade of his life, relying on the hospitality of the Potocki family.[41] Among all the distinguished guests in Tulczyn, Trembecki was perhaps the most comparable to Moshe Elḥanan in terms of his position. Both Moshe Elḥanan and Trembecki had enjoyed prior associations with the Polish court, albeit to varying degrees of intimacy. Both wrote panegyrics for Stanisław August; whereas Trembecki's verses are appreciated to this day, Moshe Elḥanan's are largely forgotten. In Tulczyn, both had to maintain favorable relations with the Polish nobility while also navigating the need to establish connections with the new Russian authorities. As I will show, there was a period in which the two figures once again became associated with each other through the medium of panegyric poetry.

In his autobiography, Elḥanan emphasized his ties to the Potocki family but made no mention of interactions with guests of the Tulczyn court. Lucky for us, at least one of the visitors did leave an account of Elḥanan—the aforementioned Auguste Lagarde (1785–1853). Lagarde was a guest at the Tulczyn court in 1811. In July of that year, he documented an invitation to attend the wedding ceremony of Moshe Elḥanan's son Yekutiel Grunem:[42]

> This evening, we went to the nuptial ceremony of one of Rabbi Elkana's sons. We were greatly amused. The bizarre scenes that happened there are beyond description, but they inspired the imagination of our young Scottish painter, who wants to paint two drawings that would be of great local interest. At supper all the Rabbis sat round an immense table in their imposing and picturesque costume; they looked like the old patriarchs. Dancing commenced after the repast . . . What you probably have never seen is the Jewish clown, a type of jester, a personage

> whose presence is an indispensable appendage of the nuptial festivities observed among the Polish Jews. His grotesque attitudes and disgusting contortions, which seem to be considered as the greatest achievement of his profession, made the younger ladies run away, terrified.[43]

This paragraph is significant, as it offers crucial information regarding the decade Moshe Elḥanan omitted from his autobiography. First, it indicates that he was able to retain his honorable title of "provincial rabbi," decades after he had ceased to serve as the rabbi of Tulczyn. From the context of the paragraph, it is clear that the "we" at the beginning of the paragraph included, in addition to Lagarde, Sophia Potocki (the widow of Szczęsny Potocki), other "ladies" from the Potocki court, and a Scottish painter. There was only one Scottish painter in Tulczyn at the time: William Allan (1782–1850).[44]

Lagarde's memoirs record Allan's plan to depict the wedding scene, a plan the painter carried out upon his return to Edinburgh. The result was a small oil painting Allan titled *Jewish Merrymaking Prior to the Celebration of the Wedding: Scene in Poland*.[45] While the painting itself appears to be lost, an old black-and-white reproduction survived (fig. 2). John Gibson Lockhart (1794–1854), a Scottish writer, saw this drawing while visiting Allan's house and was highly impressed. In a letter to his family, Gibson produced a lengthy description of *Jewish Merrymaking*: "This piece is small . . . a cluster of happy faces, grouped above, below . . . rustic musicians . . . near a window . . . a grave small group of the Elders of Israel."[46] The reproduction itself shows a traditional Jewish household, with the image of a *mizraḥ*, a decorative Jewish item placed on the wall. The painting is divided into equal segments. To the left, the Jewish guests, mostly men, including three seated at a table, are signing the engagement agreements. It would appear that Elḥanan is the man with the impressive white beard seated at the table, presiding over the entire event. His wife, Sara, may be one of the two women standing to his right. At the center of the image is the *badḥan*, or professional entertainer. To his right is a group of women, most likely visitors from the Potocki court, accompanied by a traditionally dressed elderly Polish man, recognizable by his mustache.

Inviting members of the Tulczyn court to his son's wedding was surely part of a larger series of interactions between Moshe Elḥanan and the Tulczyn court and was probably motivated by some hopes of political or economic gain on his part. The invitation to the wedding also served the interests of the

FIGURE 2 William Allan, *Jewish Merrymaking prior to the Celebration of the Wedding: A Scene in Poland*, c. 1815. Moshe Elḥanan is presumably third from left. Image courtesy of Agnew's Gallery, London.

court, that is, of Sophia Potocki. This was one of the ways for her to amuse her guests with some of the curiosities of her estate—in this case, a Jewish wedding—alongside other, more traditional forms of entertainment, such as evening balls and a quasi-professional French theater.[47] She likely derived satisfaction from the fact that both Lagarde's memoirs and Allan's painting made use of the Jewish wedding that had taken place on her estate.

THE FAMISHED TALMUDIC SCHOLAR AND THE RUSSIAN TSAR

Like Elḥanan's autobiography, Lagarde's memoirs are highly selective. Although he implies that their interaction was limited to the wedding night, their relationship in fact extended well beyond that occasion. When Elḥanan wrote another panegyric, titled *Shir ve-shevaḥ la-'adonenu ha-keysar shel ḥesed mi-kol rusiya yerum hodo 'aleksander pavlovich ha-rishon* (A Praise-Poem to Our Master, an Emperor of Grace Ruling over all Russia, May His Glory Be Exalted, Aleksandr Pavlovich I), Lagarde was tasked with translating it into French. In addition, during his 1811 stay in Tulczyn Lagarde translated another work into French of a considerably greater renown, a Polish poem by the aforementioned former royal poet Stanisław Trembecki. Trembecki's poem *Sofijówka* (1806) depicted the eponymous gardens of the Potocki estate.[48] It featured extensive panegyrical passages extolling the creator of the gardens, Szczęsny Potocki, who is described as a man who "bear within himself a greatness above all others . . . and all that he did for his country, all he did for his compatriots" (*Potocki nad innych wyższość w sobie niesie . . . i co dla swego kraju, co czynił dla ziomków*) (lines 41–52). It also includes praise of Catherine the Great, "immortal through her deeds" (*przez czyny nieśmiertelna swoje*) (line 27) and her grandson Alexander I, who was celebrated as a "great monarch, granted to us by fortunate fate, who, with a nod, can move the greater part of the earth" (*wielki monarcha, losy dany nam szczęsnem skinieniem zdolny ruszać część największą ziemi*) (lines 319–20).[49] Trembecki's *Sofijówka* was published in 1815 in a bilingual Polish-French edition, which included drawings of the gardens by William Allan, the aforementioned Scottish painter. Lagarde, Elḥanan, and Allan thus all formed part of the same cultural network associated with the Tulczyn court.[50]

Trembecki's *Sofijówka* is now considered "[one of] the most celebrated Polish poem[s] of the time," to quote the historian Daniel Beauvois, and it has received substantial scholarly attention.[51] Elḥanan's poem, by contrast, has been completely forgotten. In many respects, the two works are not truly comparable. *Sofijówka* is a lengthy poem, 526 lines according to the latest scholarly edition.[52] Elḥanan's panegyric is short: a mere forty lines. *Sofijówka* builds both on an eighteenth-century Polish literary tradition of writing about gardens and on an impressive variety of Latin and Greek literary references. Elḥanan's panegyric dedicated to the Tsar, similar in this respect to his poem addressed to the last Polish king, draws mostly on kabbalistic imagery and biblical and Talmudic sources. Nevertheless, the two works, *Sofijówka* and *Shir va-shevaḥ*, are intimately connected in their political and social history. Both emerged from the intensive cultural life of the Tulczyn court, and both played a similar role within the multilinguistic, multicultural culture that thrived in Tulczyn. Finally, both deploy botanical metaphors and panegyric conventions to project a vision that conjoins two allegiances: loyalty to the Polish nobility and loyalty to the Russian sovereign.[53]

Moshe Elḥanan's poem is cryptic and esoteric, yet its general meaning is clear thanks to his autobiography, which helps us unpack its personal dimension, and to his own explanations, which clarify its symbolic language. The first clue to the interpretation of the poem, according to Elḥanan, is the inspiration he found in an eschatological interpretation of Isaiah 9:6–7:

> For the abundance of authority and for peace without end, upon David's throne and upon his kingdom, to establish it and to support it with justice and with righteousness from now and forever; the zeal of the LORD of Hosts will do this.
>
> [*Le-marbe ha-misra u-le-shalom 'eyn-kets 'al-kise david ve-'al-mamlakhto le-hakhin 'otah u-lesa'ada be-mishpat u-vi-tsedaka me-'ata ve-'ad'olam kin'at YHWH tseva'ot ta'ase zot.*][54]

In the original Hebrew text, the second letter of the first word (לםרבה, "for the abundance") represents a scribal corruption or curiosity. The letter is given as a final, closed mem (ם) instead of a regular one (מ). The closed mem, writes Moshe Elḥanan, brings peace and success, "as is known to kabbalists and to those people who know the reason behind the forms of the Hebrew letters." The kabbalistic tradition he had in mind is documented in a verse from the Zohar (III:157b). There we read that the mem was closed as a result of the destruction of the Temple, and that it will open again when the Messiah arrives. Accordingly, every two words in Elḥanan's mystical poem end with a closed mem. This literary device creates a repetitive grammatical rhyme, provides a strong rhythmic structure, and, on the mystical plane, "bring(s) peace and success" (to use Elḥanan's own words) by associating Alexander I with messianic expectations.

The second key, according to Elḥanan, is recovering the politico-botanical imagery in the poem. The imagery of trees, Elḥanan explains, is associated in traditional Jewish sources with dignitaries and wise men, and especially with King David, who is depicted as a "tree planted beside streams of water" (*'ets shatul 'al palgei mayim*), following Psalm 1:3.

As these examples indicate, in composing a panegyric for the Russian Tsar, Moshe Elḥanan employed politico-religious tropes similar to those he had used two decades earlier for the Polish king, adapting them to the new political context.

The first line of the 1811 poem roughly translates as follows: "A wise man / wise as the scholars of the Babylonian (Talmud) / hungry for bread / thirsty for water" (fig. 3). In the following lines, the poem describes the wise man relocating to a place in which the "trees that are moist" (*laḥ alonim*), thanks to their location next to a source of water (*shatul 'al mayim*). The wise man selects one tree among the many trees (*baḥar 'alonim*). In gratitude for the nourishment he has received, the wise man offers words of praise, blessing the tree (*'akdim shevaḥ shvaḥim . . . shalaḥ 'anafim*). The tree, revealed to symbolize the Tsar (*keysar*), responds by singling out the wise man (*baḥar 'ishim*), presumably providing him with additional sustenance and support. The poem concludes with a laudatory description of the Tsar as a king who "rules over other kings" and with a blessing of longevity (*rada melakhim / 'arikh yamim*).

The similarities between the poems addressed to the Polish King and the Russian Tsar are striking. Both follow the overarching narrative of a Jewish wise man encountering a fertile tree. Both are composed as an acrostic of the ruler's name. They also share a distinctive literary technique: each line contains four sentences, and each sentence consists of two words. In both poems,

FIGURE 3 Moshe Elḥanan, excerpt from panegyric to Tsar Alexander I (1811). From Moïse Elkana, *Hymne addressée à sa Majesté l'Empereur Alexandre I*, 3.

the rhyme scheme relies on the repeated use of the Hebrew suffix -mem or -yud-mem. At the same time, the two poems also manifest a marked difference in terms of the political system they allegorize. In addressing the Polish king, Moshe Elḥanan presents himself as an "expert in spells" (*bin leḥashim*), presumably of kabbalistic wisdom. In his poem to Alexander I, this allusion to esoteric knowledge is expanded to represent a messianic vision of the Russian throne and an engagement with eschatological calculations. Both poems open with an image of a famished, thirsty scholar who encounters a tree. While the "Polish" poem featured one tree, in the poem to Alexander I, this image extends to incorporate a group of trees, and, within them, one tree that is superior to all. Bringing the author's autobiography and his symbolic language together, it appears that the multiplicity of trees represents Elḥanan's association with the Polish nobility, while the turn toward the single tree his aspiration for protection under the Russian monarch. Finally, the poem addressing Alexander I recalls the immediate historical context, the Napoleonic Wars raging across Europe. In so doing, it intertwines a narrative of European political salvation with a story about personal salvation. On a global political level, it presents Alexander I as the savior of Europe, envisioning his military victory over a host of other European kings (*rada melakhim*) in messianic terms. On a personal level, the poem imagines an encounter between the famished scholar Moshe Elḥanan and the Tsar, his savior, who provides shelter and nourishment, a depiction that may reflect the author's wish to be in closer proximity to the Tsar's court.

As Rebecca Gould noted, "When the object of praise is generic and controvertible with other patrons, the referent's emptiness leaves greater scope for literary invention."[55] In both of Moshe Elḥanan's panegyric poems, the formulaic and readily transferable portrayal of the ruler, whether a Polish king or the Russian Tsar, as a fertile tree enables a marked amplification of the poems' personal and biographical resonances. A comparison of the two works demonstrates, on the one hand, the malleability of the panegyric narrative of salvation, which can be seamlessly adapted to markedly different political contexts. At the same time, setting the two poems side by side highlights the degree to which texts that appear formally similar diverge substantially once their political and autobiographical dimensions are taken into account. This observation, I contend, should inform the analysis of other panegyric compositions from the same period.

Finally, both poems were accompanied by a translation. The anonymous French translation of the poem dedicated to Stanisław August offers a pedestrian summary of the overarching narrative:

> A Talmudic sage, being in the greatest necessity, found a beautiful tree . . . after having satisfied himself, gratitude inspired him to cry out in ecstasy: tree, tree, how could I bless you? . . . I therefore wish that you may exist for many years and that your branches may multiply from day to day.
>
> [*Un sage Talmudique étant dans la plus grande nécessité, trouva un bel arbre . . . Après s'être rassasié, la reconnaissance l'inspira à s'écrier avec extase: arbre, arbre, comment pourrai-je te bénir? Je souhaite donc que tu puisses exister nombre des années et que tes branches se multiplient de jour en jour.*]

This modest anonymous rendition recast the Hebrew poem as a continuous prose narrative, thereby rendering its overall contours accessible to a French readership. By contrast, Lagarde's French translation of the panegyric addressed to Alexander I constituted a significantly more ambitious literary adaptation. First, it compensated for the lack of kabbalistic references with high diction and adherence to meter and rhyme, lending the text an air of classical poetry:

> A Talmudic scholar, exhausted by hunger,
> Near a stream encounters a solitary palm tree . . .
> Shall I fill with sap the water that adorns you?
> Or may I increase the ambrosia of your fruits?
>
> [*Un Savant Talmudiste épuisé par la faim*
> *Près d'un ruisseau rencontre un palmier solitaire . . .*
> *Remplirai-je de suc l'eau qui vient t'embellir*
> *Ou puis-je de tes fruits accroître l'Ambroisie.*][56]

As this excerpt demonstrates, the translation further developed the vocabulary and imagery related to nature: In the French, the imagery of the natural world encompasses multiple parts of the tree—fruits and roots—as well as other parts of the physical landscape, such as the stream. Moreover, Lagarde's French translation draws heavily on references to Greek mythology. This addition, I argue, should be interpreted not only as poetic license but also as a political statement. As a cultural product emanating from the Potocki estate, the French translation invites the conclusion that the garden in question is

Sofijówka and that Lagarde was drawing on the lexical and thematic repertoire of Trembecki's poem.[57] This argument is further supported by the fact that Elḥanan's poem describes the tree in general terms (*'alon*), while Lagarde's translation presents it as an exotic palm tree, "the ornament of the desert" (*ornement du désert*). The gardens of Sofijówka were known for their collection of plants originating from distant regions. In the summer, greenhouse trees were presented to the public, among them palms, figs, pineapples, and lemons.[58] In *Sofijówka*, Trembecki highlights this global provenance, celebrating specimens "brought from afar . . . Lebanon, the Atlas, and the antipodes" (*z daleka przyniesione . . . z Libanu, z Atlasu, z antypodów*) (lines 118–120). Similarly, an anonymous Russian poem of 1804 praised the gardens for their "American flowers."[59] Another indication of the association Lagarde draws between the French translation and the gardens is his extended reference to fruit consumption. Whereas Elḥanan's poem emphasizes the tree as a source of protection and shade, Lagarde's poem presents it as a source of delectable nourishment, which he describes as "ambrosia." This may allude to the gardens' renown as a source of exotic fruits.[60] In this respect, Lagarde offered a literary text that negotiated two forms of political loyalty: to the "noble" gardens of the Potocki family, and to the "palm tree" within it, that is, the Russian Tsar. As the panegyric dedicated to Stanisław August reveals, Moshe Elḥanan had developed the image of the ruler as a tree independently, prior to the creation of the gardens. For this reason, the association of the 1811 *Shir va-shevaḥ* with Sofijówka is in all likelihood a novel interpretation that Lagarde introduced in his French translation.

The hypothesis that the French translation alludes to the Sophia Gardens finds further support in the following evidence. In 1813 the Polish writer Michał Konarski (1784–1861) described his meetings with the aforementioned Polish poet Stanisław Trembecki while the latter resided in Tulczyn. Apropos Trembecki's poem about the gardens there—Sofijówka—he wrote in a letter:

> Speaking of Sofijówka, I forgot to add that there is in Uman a certain Jewish woman, a scholar, who knows all kinds of languages, even Greek, who, having returned from a trip, described Sofijówka in French—I don't know if in prose or in poetry.[61]

Konarski's commentary illuminates Elḥanan's involvement in the cultural production of the Polish court. On the one hand, Elḥanan's poem was specifically solicited for inclusion in a local "anthology" of works depicting the gardens. Konarski's analysis offers a relatively precise account of the poem's narrative, based on its French translation. On the other hand, due to the rendering of the author's name as *Elkana* in French, Konarski mistakenly assumed the poet to be female. While Elḥanan's poem formed part of the multilingual circulation of texts celebrating noble culture, he himself remained at the periphery of this cultural sphere, his authorship largely unrecognized even by some of the court's guests.

Moshe Elḥanan himself understood his access to the Russian Tsar as a product of the personal relationship he cultivated with Peter Wittgenstein (1769–1843), a Russian field marshal who was stationed in Tulczyn.[62] It is unclear whether he was aware of the fact that, thanks to Lagarde's connections, the panegyric was gifted to Aleksandr Balashov (1770–1837), a member of the Russian state council and the minister of police, and, through him, made its way to the Russian court. In a letter Balashov extended his gratitude both to Elḥanan and to Lagarde, writing that Alexander I had enjoyed the beautiful translation. While these could be just empty verbiage, it is at least clear that the name of the rabbi of Tulczyn had come to the attention of some prominent figures in St. Petersburg. In this respect, the poem also served another practical end. It constituted a vehicle for Moshe Elḥanan to demonstrate both his support of Alexander and his erudition and expertise in Jewish sources. At a time when the Russian government was looking for experts on Jewish matters, the knowledge he possessed could be deemed very useful.[63] Five years after Tsar Alexander I read the poem, his younger brother, Nicholas Pavlovich (later known as Nicholas I), traveled to Scotland and visited, among other places, William Allan's studio in Edinburgh.[64] At the studio, the aforementioned painting depicting Moshe Elḥanan hosting his son's wedding in Tulczyn (see fig. 2) was on display. We can only speculate whether Allan discussed the painting with his Russian visitor, perhaps reminiscing about his own days in Tulczyn. It is probably impossible to prove, yet tempting to speculate that Allan's painting may also have played a role in the invitation Moshe Elḥanan received to move to the Russian capital.

In 1818, Moshe Elḥanan left Tulczyn and the aristocratic world of the Potockis, and "reunited" with the "tree," Alexander I and his court. The sight of an elderly rabbi mingling with Russian dignitaries clearly caused a stir in the capital. A few years after Moshe Elḥanan's passing, the Russian poet

Fedor Glinka (1786–1880) recalled hearing about "a famous Tulczyn rabbi who used to go play chess with [Mikhail] Miloradovich [the governor of St. Petersburg]."[65] In this sense, Moshe Elḥanan's panegyric was exceptionally effective in employing an image of hierarchical intimacy to strengthen the bond between author and ruler. Eventually, Moshe Elḥanan was able to relocate to St. Petersburg, realizing the wish expressed in his poem to live in proximity to the Russian court under the tutelage of the Tsar. This success can be attributed not only to the strength and ingenuity of the Hebrew text but also, and perhaps primarily, to the extensive social and political networks that Tulczyn facilitated: the sophisticated translation and cultural mediation by a French aristocrat, the publication of the poem in a sumptuous bilingual edition in Munich, and its strategic circulation as a gift from Tulczyn to European nobles and Russian officials, ultimately reaching the Tsar himself.

Moshe Elḥanan's Tulczyn period represents the "road not taken" in Eastern European Jewish history: a prosperous, multiethnic cultural center that flourished under the patronage of a Polish noble family within the framework of Russian imperial rule. In the case of the Potocki court, the idea of the peaceful coexistence of Polish noble estates under Russian rule would come crashing down after the Polish uprising of 1830–1831 (the so-called November Uprising). "Everyone has heard of the magnificent gardens of Sofijówka," wrote Jean-Henry Schnitzler in 1847. "Unfortunately, the fidelity of Count Alexander, the brother of Count Felix [Potocki], to the cause of the Poles entailed the confiscation of the Sofijówka, which is now the Tsar-itsyne-Sad [the Tsarina's orchard], or the 'emperor's garden.'"[66] At the same time, Moshe Elḥanan's disdain of the enlightenment notwithstanding, a new generation of Russian Jewish maskilim aspired to follow the same path he trod, sometimes literally. In 1812, shortly after Moshe Elḥanan's departure, Yitzḥak Ber Levinsohn (RIBAL, 1788–1860), later known as the father of the Russian Haskalah, settled in Tulczyn. During his residence in this town, Levinsohn maintained a close relationship with Prince Wittgenstein, who had served as Moshe Elḥanan's patron only a few years earlier, and later supported Levinsohn's scholarly efforts.[67] This phenomenon extended to Galicia as well, where Joseph Perl benefited from the patronage of the Polish noble Franciszek Korytowski (1763–1833), as I discuss in chapter 4. In this sense, the enduring local prominence of the Polish nobility continued to shape the emergence of the Russian and Galician maskilic literature for decades after the partitions.

TWO

Arresting Stories

The Rise of State Law in Partitioned Poland and the Beginning of Haskalah Literature, 1811–1820

As soon as a law has been properly published, no one can excuse himself that he had no cognizance of it.

[GENERAL CIVIL CODE OF AUSTRIA, (1816) 1866][1]

THE FIRST CHAPTER FOCUSED ON panegyric poetry as a gateway into the Jewish experience of the partitions. Although, as a genre, Hebrew poetry devoted to rulers never assumed a central place in nineteenth-century Jewish literature, it nonetheless exerted a lasting influence on the emergence of maskilic literature in Eastern Europe. Several early figures of the Haskalah launched their literary careers with panegyric poetry. In 1812, a year after Moshe Elḥanan's poem was published, the young Russian maskil Yitzḥak Ber Levinsohn (RIBAL, 1788–1860) composed *Kol ʿanot gevura* (The Voice of Victory), celebrating Alexander I's triumph over Napoléon. The poem earned him his first government post as a translator.[2] Levinsohn later included another panegyric to Nicholas I in the preface to *Teʿuda be-yisrael* (Testimony in Israel; 1828), the programmatic work of the Russian Haskalah. Shlomo Yehuda Rapoport, Meir Letteris, and Yaʿakov Shmuel Bick each composed panegyric eulogies for the governor of Galicia.[3] In this respect, it may be the case that panegyric poetry was one of the contributing factors to the association between literary and political expression in the maskilic mind.

These examples notwithstanding, panegyric poetry had limited overlap with Eastern European Haskalah literature. Many panegyrics were composed by traditional Jews outside maskilic circles, and some of the most prominent maskilim never engaged in this genre. At the same time, one can discern a panegyric impulse in maskilic prose. The emerging genre of Maskilic fiction, this chapter shows, conjured a world that is governed harmoniously by Habsburg state law and by the principles of maskilic ideology. In so doing, it expanded the praise of monarchs found in panegyric poetry into an idealized vision of the imperial state and reframed the panegyrists' wish for symbolic union with the ruler as a desire for voluntary integration into the imperial bureaucracy.

ARRESTING STORIES, PART I: WRITING LAW AND WRITING STORIES IN THE HABSBURG LANDS

This chapter aims to straddle two seemingly disconnected phenomena in Jewish history: the encounter between Jews and the concept of state law in partitioned Poland, and Jewish enlighteners' turn to writing fiction in prose. I illuminate why these two are connected and explain how I will explore one in relation to the other.

The rise of modern Jewish literature in Eastern Europe is usually studied as a primarily Jewish story, as part of an internal scramble for dominance in the Jewish community. Scholars have conventionally interpreted the rise of modern Jewish literature in Eastern Europe as a Jewish response to Hasidism, and, more specifically, to the 1815 publication of two collections of Hasidic stories: *In Praise of the Besht* (Shivḥei ha-besht), the hagiography of the Ba'al Shem Tov, and the *Tales* of Rabbi Naḥman of Bratslav (Sipurei ma'asiyot).[4] This argument contends that the fact that Hasidic doctrines were delivered not only in sermons or homilies, but also in stories, was seen by Galician maskilim as a threat. For this reason, according to Dan Miron and others, maskilim themselves turned to stories, which enabled them "to fight Hasidism . . . and fend off its widespread literary influence."[5] Narrative, in other words, allowed for disarming the Jewish reader and introducing anti-Hasidic ideology in an attractive way. This scholarly interpretation of the turn among maskilim to literature aligns with reigning views of Galician Haskalah, Enlightenment, whose raison d'être was, according to Emmanuel Etkes, "the struggle against Hasidism."[6] Fittingly, the scholarly interest in the body of literature produced by maskilim was devoted almost exclusively to the exploration of how these texts parodied Hasidic practices.[7]

This chapter revisits this argument by placing the events surrounding the rise of literary prose in Eastern Europe within the context of both the Austrian annexation of Galicia and the development of new types of relations between the Jewish population and the imperial authorities. Jewish enlighteners, I argue, attempted to partake in the Austrian project of creating a public legal culture, positioning themselves as mediators of legal know-how by translating newly articulated Galician laws into Jewish idiom. In Maskilic fiction, narrative functioned as a vehicle for naturalizing the concept of state law, disseminating the logic of the imperial state, and promoting the values of loyal subjecthood. Rather than an end in and of themselves, maskilic critiques of Hasidism were thus one component of a much larger project to legitimize the logic of the centralized state among the Jewish population.

In highlighting the interconnectedness of political and literary activity and particularly the nexus of literary and legal projects, I aim to place Galician Jewish Enlightenment in conversation with the late Austrian Enlightenment, and particularly with the concept of art as a vehicle for propagating civic values. The vision of law and literature as inherently interconnected loomed large in the Viennese intellectual sphere of the second half of the eighteenth century. It was identified primarily with Joseph von Sonnenfels (1732–1817), a jurist and novelist, who was central both to the reformation of the Austrian legal system and to the shaping of the Viennese literary and cultural scene.[8] Sonnenfels was, according to Jonathan Israel, the leading Enlightenment spokesman in Vienna, who shaped the development of "mainstream Enlightenment attitudes" in the Habsburg Empire.[9] The son of a rabbi from Nikolsburg, Moravia (today Mikulov, Czech Republic), Sonnenfels converted in his childhood to Catholicism, and his family was ennobled a short time later. His biography exemplifies some of the political and cultural possibilities open to converted Jews in the eighteenth century, a realm of possibilities that would not be available to other Jews, converted or not, in the following generation.

Sonnenfels, who specialized in law and was a practicing lawyer, became the first professor of political economy (Polizei und Cameral Wissenschaften) at the University of Vienna in 1763. Beginning in 1765, he was the editor of the most influential journal of the Austrian Enlightenment, *Der Mann ohne Vorurteil* (The Man without Prejudice). There, he expressed his ideas about politics, literature, and theater. Sonnenfels was one of the main drafters of the legal reforms under Maria Theresa and Joseph II. In this role, he led an effort to ban torture and capital punishment, advocated for the establishment of a public police force, and oversaw legislation concerning Jewish religion in the framework of the Edicts of Tolerance.[10]

Sonnenfels saw literature and law, and particularly theater and law, as co-constitutive, inseparable elements, shaping together public morals.[11] In his scholarship, he moves freely between one and the other, reflecting on legal theory in essays devoted to Viennese theater, and musing on literature and art in an academic treatise on law. Sonnenfels viewed literature as central to the dissemination of legal knowledge. In his most celebrated collection of teachings about political economy, *Grundsätze der Polizey, Handlung und Finanzwirtschaft* (1763–1767), he argued that lawmakers should be involved in the field of arts for the sake of educating the public. "The legislator," he wrote, "must know how to use popular entertainments as an effective means of moral education." Sonnenfels likened the practice of lawmaking to the work of a "gifted architect, who can place the decorative elements in his building in such a way that they contribute to the building's stability."[12] Theater and law, he argued, should work together to inculcate the same moral grounds and popularize the same body of knowledge about legality and ethics. The role of literature and theater, he further argued in *Briefe über die wienerische Schaubühne*, a series of essays about the Viennese theater, is to convince people to obey the law. In Sonnenfels's succinct expression, "An ignorant people obeys because it must, an educated people obeys because it wants to" (*Das dumme Volk gehorcht, weil es muß: das unterrichtete, weil es selbst will*).[13] Theater, he argued, was to function as a "school of morals" (*Schule der Sitten*),[14] propagating a set of moral ideas that are influenced by and work in tandem with state law.

This happy union of legal and literary activity, which was exemplified in Sonnenfels's career and intellectual inheritance, was not possible for Jews in the following generation, converted or not, who wished to gain influence in the Habsburg Empire. This chapter picks up these two threads, the legal and the literary, which were so perfectly interwoven in Sonnenfels's career, and shows how Jewish intellectuals in Galicia tried to bring them together in a religious, political, and cultural setting that differed dramatically from Vienna in the 1780s. Galician Jewish enlighteners were, by and large, removed from the real centers of power, and their road to the mobilization of the coercive power of the state was much more difficult. Moreover, they did not have a ready-made arena of public culture or literature they could shape: in the 1810s, there was no Jewish literature in Eastern Europe to speak of, nor any highly creative project in which a group of intellectuals imagined a new role for themselves and carved their Jewish theater, nor any concept of a Jewish writer. Writing prose was thus part of a niche within Jewish society and within imperial networks of power. This chapter connects legal reforms in Galicia and the emergence of the literary scene, revealing how these two seemingly separate phenomena functioned with respect to each other.

A Journey to the Land of Many Laws: Making State Law Matter in Austrian Galicia, 1772–1815

The centrality of imperial law in the transformation of Galician Jewry has already received a fair amount of scholarly attention.[15] The picture that emerges is as follows: In the wake of the first partition (1772), the Austrian policy toward the Jews of Galicia was guided mostly by Maria Theresa's wish to perpetuate the status of the Jewish population as a separate estate. Starting in the mid-1780s, the legal status of Jews was radically reformed in the light of Joseph II's enlightened absolutism, culminating in the 1789 Edict of Toleration (Toleranzpatent), which promised equality of rights of Jews and Christians. Finally, after 1792, under the rule of Francis II, most of the emancipatory policies and promises of reform were reversed, and the state delegated much of its governing and organizing functions to local Jewish elites.[16]

In this section, I aim to combine attention to the different state laws targeting the Jewish population of Galicia with an exploration of the reforms in the status of state law itself between 1772 and 1815. During this period, the societal role of state law, its applicability, its source of legitimation, its political function, and accessibility were all significantly transformed. When comparing the different laws targeting the Jewish population in the 1770s and the 1810s, one needs to factor in the dramatic changes the concept of law underwent in this period. The transformation of state law, I argue, complicates our understanding of the relations of Jews with the legal system and of the way in which the law was experienced by Jewish subjects. To further explore the changing relationship between Jewish subjects and state laws, I reflect on how Austrian policy toward Galician Jewry intersects with the reformation of the imperial legal system.

The creation of Galicia in 1772 coincided with a large legal project in the Austrian Empire intended to change some fundamental aspects of its legal culture. The so-called codification movement advanced the centralization of the Austrian Empire by monopolizing lawmaking and by trying to create legal unity and uniform administration of the law. The process of legal homogenization resulted, according to Werner Ogris, in a new perspective on law, which came to be viewed as "the only way in which the ruler should or could express and enforce his political aims."[17] It is during these years that Austria became a "'Rechtsstaat,' a 'state of law,' namely, a state whose legal order is based on law in its various forms and appearances."[18]

The majority of the Jewish population in Galicia was not directly governed by state laws before the first partition. For this group, the encounter under colonial rule with state law, both as a practice and a concept, was entirely novel. When Poland was partitioned, three-quarters of Polish Jews lived in private holdings, villages, and towns owned by Polish aristocrats in a political structure that retained many of the characteristics of a feudal system.[19] The Commonwealth of Poland, a decentralized state, was what Charles Tilly called an "intensely fragmented sovereignty."[20] Since the sixteenth century, the Polish nobility succeeded "in appropriating nearly all state functions, leaving their central governments with only meager capacities for direct rule."[21] It was also able to achieve full jurisdiction over the residents of their estates—the peasants and the burghers.[22] Residents of private holdings were "formally made subject to the jurisdiction of the landowners" and had no access to the royal court.[23] The legitimacy of law in the private estate did not derive from its resemblance to some order of a natural or universal law. The "concept of a state law," of an "objective legal order"—a product of the "conceptual separation of the 'state,'" to quote Weber—did not have much bearing on the legal reality in private estates.[24] Rather, the social function of law was grafted onto the structural hierarchy of ownership and abstracted from the daily interactions between residents and landowners.

Jewish privileges, one of the central sources of law in private estates, exemplify how legal contracts among Jews and landowners were spatialized. The documents that regulated almost all aspects of Jewish life: the relationship between Jews and non-Jews, as well as the "scope of the judicial jurisdiction exercised by the . . . landowner in relation to . . . the community organization,"[25] constructed a concept of legality that was inherently bound to the lived space of a specific community. The legitimacy of the law originated primarily from the authority of the Polish landowner. Polish magnates signed their names next to the official seal, and documents that were not personally sanctioned by the current landowner were often deemed void or obsolete in court. Not only was the general legitimacy of the law derived from the authority of the landowner; the entire legal autonomy of the different estates, the ruling of both the city court and the rabbinic court, was personally endorsed by the town's owner or by his bureaucrats.[26]

Within the context of the Austrian occupation of Galicia, the process of centralization resulted in a "move toward a . . . hierarchically structured legal order defined in part by the assertion . . . of imperial jurisdiction."[27] Under Austrian rule, estate residents could apply to imperial legal bodies for support. Serfs were granted the right to lodge a complaint about their landlord with the imperial authorities.[28] Disputes that were traditionally negotiated between landowners and the Jewish community could be submitted to the state authorities, a return to the political structure famously called by Yosef Haim Yerushalmi the "royal alliance," a model in which the state occupied the role of the final arbiter, the ultimate defender of rights in cases of local disputes.[29]

The reforms in the Austrian legal system not only ensured that every subject could access imperial law but also tried to communicate legal knowledge as widely as possible. The aforementioned Joseph von Sonnenfels, the great architect of this legal project under Maria Theresa's rule, called for the state to make its structure knowable to the public, to publish its laws, and to popularize information concerning its political structure. "Every citizen," he wrote, "had the right to know the powers and competence of each official and of each public authority . . . [and should] be informed concerning the power of each official and of each department of government," in order to "forestall arbitrary measures and oppression."[30]

The experience of the growing presence of law across the empire was documented in a number of contemporary Jewish sources. For example, Avraham Trebitsch (1759–1837), the secretary to the Moravian Land Rabbinate, described in his chronicle *Korot Ha'itim* (*Events of the Times*) the legal reformers under the rule of Joseph II in the following words:

> Day by day and year by year, / One decree succeeds another / One is no (longer) compelled to (submit to) Torah law / A court is erected in every city, every province / The law of the state is the binding law
>
> [*Ḥadashim li-vkarim mitḥadshim be-khol shana / Tsav le-tsav ze aḥar ze ba'a / 'eyn kofim le-din tora / Rak he'emid yustits be-khol 'ir u-medina / Dina de-malkhuta dina.*][31]

In Trebitsch's account, state law was introduced at a striking pace, changing the terms of the autonomy of Jewish halakhic law and transforming social reality.

For the residents of the Polish territories annexed by Austria in 1772, the concept of law as a publicly accessible body of knowledge was perhaps even more foreign and staggering than for Moravian Jews like Trebitsch. In eighteenth-century Poland, the state did not attempt to collect and publish laws, let alone print and circulate new legislation. Instead, a private initiative, the so-called *Volumina Legum*, collected the Sejm's legislation and circulated it among subscribers. The *Volumina Legum* lacked state support and proper continuity and, for this reason, never became a viable tool to access legal knowledge. The first six volumes appeared in 1732, followed fifty years later by the seventh volume. During this half-century gap, the only other sources documenting Sejm legislation were individual volumes of court books. Other legal documents—privileges granted by the nobility to cities, communities, or individuals—were available only in manuscript and in a low number of copies. By and large, residents were not expected to know the law and legal knowledge was a matter left to specialists.[32]

In Austria, the year 1787 saw the advent of an imperial project to publish laws on a regular basis and to make them publicly available.[33] The publication of new laws, so the government hoped, was to become part of the daily life of Austrian subjects. Bureaucrats in district offices copied and publicly posted laws as soon as they arrived from Vienna.[34] Subsequently, Austrian legislators continued to find new ways to make legal knowledge accessible to the public. A particularly ambitious law enacted in 1810, for example, required homeowners to circulate legal orders among their tenants and to collect signatures testifying that the laws were indeed read by them.[35]

In the wake of the partitions, in the context of a relatively sparse governing infrastructure, the Austrian government actively sought to communicate new laws, statutes and regulations to the Galician population. The communication of new laws was the way in which the imperial power intended to announce itself, legitimize itself, and make itself knowable and recognizable. In a time when the Austrian bureaucracy was rather meager, no more than 1,500 bureaucrats for a population of around 2.3 million during the first decade after the creation of Galicia, the publication of laws was oftentimes the most visible representation of the governing powers.[36]

After 1791, all new laws and statutes were to be published and hung on city gates and doors of religious institutions, "so they could reach everyone's awareness" (*damit dieselben zu Jedermanns Wissenschaft gelangen mögen*). In small towns, new laws were read out loud in the city hall every Sunday afternoon.[37] In other words, it was through the existing leadership (landowners, mayors, priests, rabbis) and in the most familiar public spaces (churches, synagogues, town halls) that knowledge about the imperial state and its laws was disseminated.

How, we may ask, did the local population experience this change in the accessibility, knowability and social function of law? Franciszek Karpiński (1741–1825), a Polish noble and poet, described the growing incursion of law into the public realm as shocking. He called Galicia "the Land of Many Laws" (*kraj pełen uniwersałów*), where, upon crossing the border, one is overwhelmed by "volumes of decrees, charters, statutes, warnings and regulations" (*wiecznych prawnych foliałów, / I kursoryj, instruktarzów, / Ostrzeżeń, cyrkularzów*), which "multiply a hundred an hour." This torrent of legal information, he concludes, is the reason one can't possibly remember all these new laws: there are simply too many! (*Któż je wszystkie nawspomina, / Gdy ich sto rodzi godzina!*).[38]

Legal knowledge was distributed unevenly among different ethnic and religious populations; Karpiński's complaint about being overwhelmed with new legal requirements, for example, was characteristic of his particular milieu of Polish-speaking nobles. Upon seizing the new Polish territories, the first priority of the new Austrian regime was to communicate knowledge about the new political order to the nobility, particularly to landowners. Nobles were personally invited to pledge an oath of alliance to the Austrian monarch as a way to announce their submission to the new legal order.[39] The first Austrian publications of laws in Galicia, beginning in 1772, included a translation to Latin, which still functioned as a lingua franca in this region. In 1774, Latin was superseded by Polish, which made these publications significantly more accessible.[40] It is clear, then, why, as a result of this project, new laws loomed so large in the political consciousness of nobles like Karpiński. This was not the case for the rest of the population of Galicia. In contrast, Ukrainian-speaking serfs, 40 percent of the population in 1828,[41] did not enjoy the same privilege of having access to laws in Ruthenian, their daily language. According to Jan Fellerer, Ruthenian serfs could rarely make sense of the highly technicalized Polish in which the law was conveyed; this was one reason legal knowledge among their ranks was generally low.[42]

In Russia, laws targeting the Jewish population were translated into Yiddish.[43] In Austria, there is some evidence of a short-lived project of disseminating legal knowledge in the much more exclusive Hebrew. The magnitude and impact of this project are unclear. The Bodleian Library preserves a manuscript of the 1776 Judensystem, the General Order for the Jews of Galicia, translated in its entirety into Hebrew; it is a lengthy legal document of around fifty pages. The first paragraph states overtly the motivation behind this translation project: the document "was translated into easy Hebrew [*be-lashon 'ivri raka*], so every reader would understand its content."[44] It also states that the document was "copied and brought to be printed in Hebrew" to make it accessible for the wider Jewish population. While the introduction to the manuscript reflects an intention to circulate the legal code in print, the surviving manuscript is handwritten. There is evidence, however, of at least one copy in print, which was lost during World War II.[45] Given the lack of additional information, it is hard to assess the extent to which this document was accessible to the Jewish population. The year 1776 also saw the publication of another administrative communication in Hebrew, addressed to the Jewish community in Brody. The translation of official documents into Hebrew was very much in line with Maria Theresa's policy toward the Jews, as she wished to keep the Jews as a socially, culturally, and linguistically separate element in society. The introduction of the Josephinian reforms, in contrast, which focused on "Germanizing" the Jewish population, ended this governmental campaign of providing legal knowledge in Hebrew.[46] Since the 1780s, it was only through the acquisition of German that the residents of Galicia could have access to legal texts.

The culminating point of the two projects I have traced here, the homogenization of the law system and the popularization of legal knowledge, can be located in the 1811 publication of the new Austrian Civil Code, the ABGB, *Das Allgemeine bürgerliche Gesetzbuch*, a document that structured the "establish[ment] [of] monarchic absolutism on a rule of civil law."[47] The ABGB sought to homogenize civil law across the empire, applying to the Austrian and Bohemian lands as well as to Galicia. It abolished all local regulations unless the state actively renewed them: "Only those statutes of single provinces and districts of the country have obligatory force," states paragraph 11, if they "have been expressly confirmed by the Sovereign."[48] Along the same line, the ABGB also sought to eliminate the legal autonomy of estates and corporations: cities, churches, universities and guilds, whose "privileges and immunities are to be judged of the same as other rights" (*keine besondere Bestimmung enthalten*).

The legalists who drafted the ABGB viewed legal pluralism with absolute horror. Franz von Zeiller, the principal architect of this new body of laws, cautioned against pluralism, warning that "contradicting statutes, customs, adjudications, doctrinal opinions, and prescriptions" which "endlessly accumulate," would lead judges to "refer to their own philosophical views in lieu of legal provisions."[49] A comprehensive, well-organized, and accessible legal code, he hoped, would solve this confusion, encouraging the legal administration to adjudicate according to state law rather than their personal judgment.

The ABGB also injected new meaning into the project of disseminating information about the law among all the residents of the empire. It linked unequivocally legal knowledge with legal responsibility. The ABGB introduced, for the first time in Austrian legal history, a concept of liability that presupposed a considerable degree of familiarity with state laws on the part of the empire's subjects: "As soon as a law has been properly published" (*Sobald ein Gesetz gehörig kund gemacht worden ist*), explained the lawmakers in the document, "no one can excuse himself that he had no cognizance of it" [*kann sich niemand damit entschuldigen, dass ihm dasselbe nicht bekannt geworden seyn*].[50] According to this particular formulation of the principle *ignorantia legis non excusat*, ignorance does not excuse, legal knowledge is imagined to be central to civil legal obedience.[51] Legal authorities were committed to publishing the law publicly, and the empire's inhabitants were responsible for educating themselves about the law.[52] To do otherwise was to proceed at their own peril. In short, the ABGB imagined a homogeneous state law, which was knowable, accessible, universalized, and abstract.

"Many of Them Don't Know That Their Ways Are Against the King's Will": Galician Maskilim and the Project of Disseminating Legal Knowledge

The new Austrian Civil Code came into effect in Galicia on January 1, 1812, formally establishing the concept of rule of law, furthering the homogenization of the legal system and curtailing the power of the estates. The publication of the Civil Code was followed in 1815 by the release of an expanded edition of the Austrian Criminal Code (*Gesetzbuch über Verbrechen und schwere Polizey- Übertretungen*).[53] The year after, 1816, the first maskilic literary piece, Joseph Perl's *Tales and Letters*, appeared.

Perl's *Tales and Letters* was traditionally interpreted by scholars as an anti-Hasidic text, "primarily a maskilic anti-thesis to Naḥman of Bratslav's tales," with "no substantial innovations in terms of the representation of Hasidism," to quote Chone Shmeruk.[54] This appreciation was later repeated by other researchers.[55] Yet the innovation in *Tales and Letters*, I argue, lies in the way it responds both to the Hasidic tales and to the centralization of the Austrian legal system. The first modern Jewish fiction in prose that came down to us is a highly imaginative effort to envision a maskilic utopia within a perfectly centralized empire. To further explore how the homogenization of the Austrian legal system and the publication of the ABGB prompted Joseph Perl to write *Tales and Letters*, I turn to a discussion of

Perl's intellectual and political career between the years 1809 and 1816, focusing on his relationship with the Austrian authorities and the way it informed his politics within the Jewish community.

The Annotated Judenpatent, 1819

The portrait of Joseph Perl (1773–1839), which hung at least until World War II in the administrative office of the Tarnopol German Jewish School that he founded, presents a powerful, resolute man in his fifties. The painting's most striking details are the two medals, one pinned to his chest and the other high at his neck, both attached to his clothing. One medal bears the image of the Habsburg Emperor, and the other that of the Russian Tsar. These medals echoed the authority and commanding presence of Perl's own visage. According to Arye Avnun-Broynshtayn's memoir, in the 1920s, schoolchildren, so impressed with these medals, were convinced that this was, in fact, a portrait of the (Austrian Emperor), Joseph II.[56]

Tsar Alexander I awarded Perl the first medal, a large silver badge, in 1816, for founding the German Jewish school in Tarnopol (today Ternopil, Ukraine) during the brief Russian rule of the city (1809–1815). The Emperor Francis I of Austria awarded Perl the second medal in 1820, when the state granted the school official recognition and gave it financial support. An official certificate, signed by Francis I, was sent to the administration of the school:

> I hereby decorate Joseph Perl, in view of the considerable sacrifices and the commendable eagerness he has shown, with the second rank golden medal of honor with loop and ribbon . . . (Emperor) Francis
>
> [*In Ansehung der gemachten ansehnlichen Aufopferungen und des bezeigten lobenswerthen Eifers verleihe Ich dem Joseph Perl die mittlere Goldene Ehrenmedaille mit Öhr und Band . . . Franz*][57]

Perl's self-presentation as a person who maintained close relations with the state held sway over the local Jewish population. Tarnopol Jews told stories about Emperor Joseph II visiting the city, walking hand in hand with Perl.[58] Another local legend claimed that when, in 1815, Russian forces retreated from Tarnopol, Alexander I, the Russian emperor, expressed dismay at the thought of leaving his friend Joseph Perl behind.[59] In his self-presentation,

Perl is revealed to us as a person so intimate with the authorities that the faces of monarchs appear to be an integral part of his body. Each of the two medals testifies to the success of his project to harness the logic of bureaucracy and master its language. It is through close collaboration with state authorities that Perl exerted his influence on the Jewish community in Tarnopol and on Galician Jewry as a whole. It is thus very clear why mastering legal knowledge is central to his career as a local activist.

How well did Joseph Perl know Austrian law? To what extent did he have access to legal publications? A list of Austrian laws in Perl's handwriting reflects his strategies in familiarizing himself with new laws and regulations. Perl titled the document "Judenpatent, May 7, 1789, with Accompanying Comments" (*nachfolgende[n] enleitungen*).[60] From this point, I refer to this document as *The Annotated Judenpatent* (fig. 4). The work is a handwritten copy of the 1789 Edict of Tolerance to the Jewish population of Galicia, which Perl adapted for his own use. The document follows the general outline of the edict: religion, education, community structure, supplementing each section and each subsection with the relevant laws and regulations that were issued on these matters after 1789. The last law referenced in this document is from September 1819.

The Annotated Judenpatent helps us appreciate what kind of legal knowledge was available to interested individuals like Perl. For example, one may wonder, how was the 1789 Edict of Tolerance accessible to Galician maskilim. In this case, it was copied, according to a note on the first page, from the so-called *Pillernia*, a Lemberg-based annual publication of Austrian laws targeting the Galician population.[61] Perl also mentions another legal publication, a collection of imperial laws dating to 1811, and an astonishingly great number of individual edicts.[62] Perl emerges as an intellectual who is very much invested in the collection of all kinds of legal publications and in producing systematic legal knowledge on the basis of these publications. *The Annotated Judenpatent* sheds light on the degree to which Perl was informed of Austrian law regarding the Jewish population in his communications with Austrian authorities.[63]

Reading the *Annotated Judenpatent* against the 1789 Edict of Tolerance also enables us to reconstruct the degree of awareness maskilim like Perl had of the gap between the emancipatory promises of the 1789 Edict

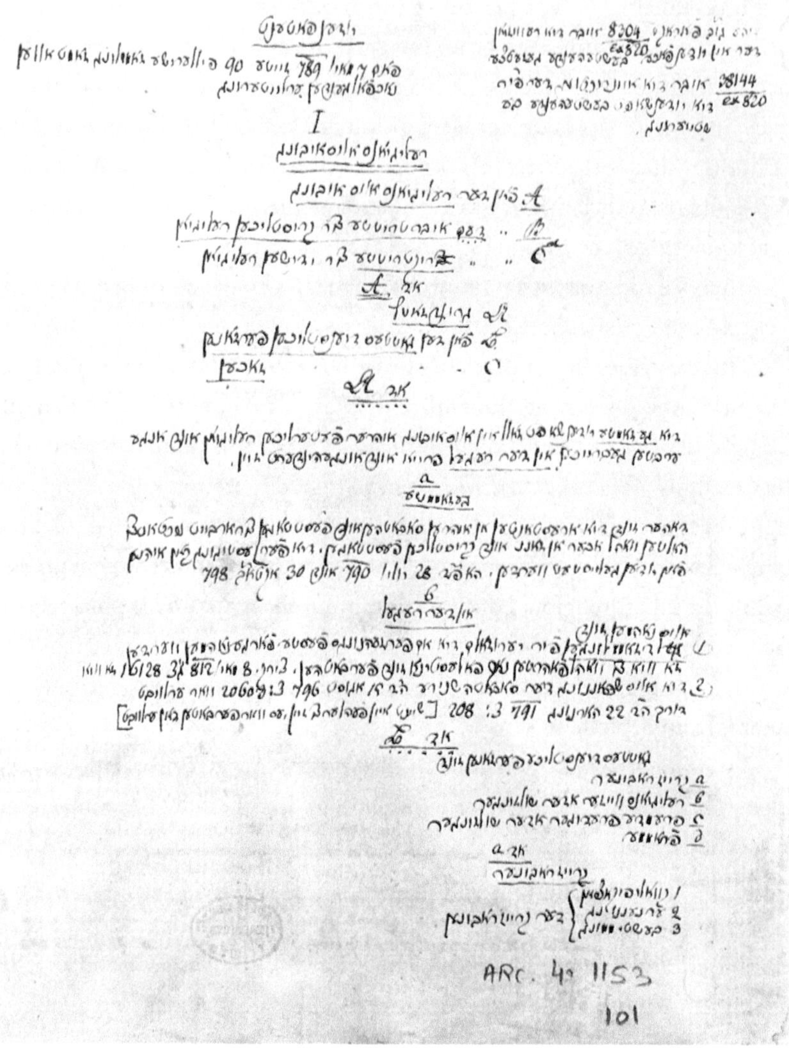

FIGURE 4 Joseph Perl, *Annotated Judenpatent*, 1819 or later. From Joseph Perl, "Takanot ve-hamlatsot bi-dvar ha-pulḥan ha-dati shel yehudei galitsya, 1789," National Library of Israel, Joseph Perl's Archive, ARC. 4* 1153 / 101.

of Tolerance and the edict's partial implementation under the reign of Francis II.[64] The Edict of Tolerance, for example, famously promised to establish a German Jewish school in every community to promote "better education" for the Jewish population.[65] The "updated" version comments dryly that these Josephinian schools were closed by the state in June 1806, putting an end to the promise of state-sponsored Jewish education in German.[66]

Finally, the *Annotated Judenpatent* tells us something about the position of its composer vis-à-vis the state. This is a legal document, a continuation of the state-sponsored project of disseminating legal knowledge and, at the same time, a private document, reflecting its author's individual, communal, and ideological interests. The content of the document is analogous to Perl's position and, more generally, to the position of maskilim in relation to both the Jewish community and the Austrian authorities. The overwhelming majority of the maskilim, Perl included, sought to engage with the state and its bureaucracy. Joseph Perl and Yehuda Leib Mieses, for example, both sent denunciation letters in order to outlaw Hasidic activity, and Shlomo Yehuda Rapapport maintained close relations with the Austrian administration in Lemberg and Tarnopol.[67] None of them, however, had any formalized relations with the authorities. In the 1810s there were already a number of Jews working for the Austrian provincial government, mediating between colonial policies and the local Jewish population: Jewish police supervisors, state rabbis, and later on censors of Hebrew books.[68] In contrast, maskilim did not hold similar positions. The lack of a legitimized societal function and stable relations vis-à-vis the regime, on the one hand, and vis-à-vis the Jewish community, on the other hand, may explain some of the fluidity between paperwork and letters of denunciation, between poems and short stories and communication with the authorities.

In the first part of the chapter, I discussed two opposing processes that shaped the relations between Jews and the imperial state: the slow retreat of the state from its project to revolutionize and reform Jewish life and the concurrent increase in the state's visibility alongside the rise of law as a knowable entity. The Annotated Judenpatent exemplifies one way these two vectors intersect: as the state became more knowable and law more accessible, contradictions between the promise of enlightened reforms and the disinterest of the state in implementing them became increasingly evident. It was this contradiction, I argue, that shaped the emergence of Galician Haskalah, which was not only a fulfillment of the Austrian Emancipation project or a response to its retreat, but a negotiation of both, an attempt to fill in a void, to take upon itself the role of mediating between the state and the Jewish population.

One might ask, What drove maskilim to nurture hope to be part, in one way or another, of the state-building project in Galicia? At least in Joseph Perl's case, there was a brief period in which he was able to fulfill this coveted role of mediator between the state and the local Jewish population. Notably, this occurred under Russian rather than Austrian rule. Between 1809 and 1815, in accordance with the Treaty of Schönbrunn, the Russian Empire annexed Perl's hometown, Tarnopol.[69] Eager to secure local support, the government relaxed certain Austrian laws, allowing Jews, for example, to buy houses from Christians, transactions strictly forbidden when Tarnopol was ruled by Austria.[70] After the Austrian retreat from the city, many governmental and public institutions were shut down, and for this reason, the Russian authorities looked favorably on local initiatives to normalize civil life. It is during this period that Perl was able to open a Jewish school, the only operating school in Tarnopol while the province was under Russian rule.[71] The financial support for the founding of the school came primarily from a local Polish magnate, Franciszek Korytowski (1763–1833).[72] In appreciation of Perl's educational initiative, the Russian governor of Tarnopol, Ignaz Theyls, sent him a letter, thanking him for his efforts to create "a new generation of productive, loyal and patriotic Russian subjects."[73] The Russian authorities were so pleased with Perl's educational initiative that it was decided he would receive a medal for the project, the same medal that was depicted in his portrait.[74] When Tarnopol returned to the Habsburg Empire, in early 1816, Joseph Perl was able to make this school, which was built with Polish money under Russian rule, his entry ticket into the Austrian circles of local bureaucracy.[75]

Later that year, the new governor of Galicia, Franz von Hauer, made an official visit to Perl's school. Von Hauer was impressed both with the school and with Perl.[76] For his part, Perl saw this personal connection with the Galician governor as a springboard to embark on a new career, as a mediator of knowledge about the Jewish population to the Austrian authorities. He sent the governor a manuscript he authored, entitled *Über das Wesen der Sekte Chasidim Aus Ihren Schriften gezogen Im Jahre 1816* (On the Essence of the Hasidic Sect Drawn from Their Writings, in the Year 1816.). The manuscript was an anthology of Hasidic texts with which Perl intended to show the threat inherent to this religious movement. It is worthwhile to emphasize the timeline: this manuscript was written during Perl's first year as a new Austrian subject, after six years under Russian rule, in a time in which the residents of Tarnopol were required to take symbolic acts to show their loyalty to the Austrians.[77]

Perl was not only fighting Hasidism; he was also positioning himself as a loyal subject. For example, the opening of one paragraph, titled "Der Staat" (The State), reads:

> The primary duties of a resident of a state toward the latter are: Obedience to the authorities, loyalty and devotion to the sovereign and to the fatherland. Obedience stems either from good principles or from fear of punishment. This sect [of the Hasidim], however, has no motive to be obedient to the state, since commands that do not emanate from the *tzaddik* [the Hasidic leader] carry no authority, and the latter [the *tzaddik*] considers himself or at least pretends to be a king, who teaches even God how to rule.
>
> [*Die Hauptpflichten der Einwohner eines Staates gegen denselben sind: Gehorsam gegen die Obrigkeit, Treue und Anhänglichkeit an Fürst und Vaterland. Der Gehorsam fliesst entweder aus guten Grundsätzen oder aus Furcht vor Strafen. Da nun bey dieser Sekte alles dasjenige, was nicht ihr Zadik befiehlt, gar kein Gewicht hat, und dieser sich selbst als König, der selbst Gott das Regieren lehrt, betrachtet oder wenigstens sich dafür ausgiebt, so hat sie keinen Beweggrund, dem Staate Gehorsam zu leisten.*][78]

The association of Hasidism with antigovernmental activities was almost as old as the history of Hasidism as a movement.[79] Here, however, Perl offered a full-fledged project of positioning Hasidism as an inherently antinomian movement, as the opposite of good subjecthood. In addition, "The State" reproduced knowledge that is supposedly obvious, foregrounding the duties of subjects toward the state, an overt statement of where the author's political loyalty lies. This double move—self-aligning with the government and questioning Hasidism's compliance with the law—eventually became naturalized by Perl and other maskilim in their prose. Moreover, writing a manuscript on Hasidism for the use of the local authorities served another cause. Perl was trying to gain a role within the new division of power, as a voluntary expert on Jewish subjects, as a person able to produce knowledge on his coreligionists, to make them more governable. In this respect, Perl's communication with Austrian officials, in German, and his literary texts in Hebrew and Yiddish served similar roles. In his German essays, Perl was mediating knowledge about the Jewish population to the authorities. In his literary texts in Hebrew and Yiddish, he was mediating knowledge about the state to the Jewish population.

"A New Torah for Galicia"

While Perl was waiting for authorization from the Austrian censors to publish his German essay, he came across a new publication of Hasidic stories, a collection of tales of Naḥman of Bratslav (1772–1810), the founder and master of the Bratslav Hasidic sect. Naḥman of Bratslav's book of tales was unique in the landscape of Hasidic publications. Most Hasidic texts were either a hagiography of a Hasidic leader or a collection of his sayings. In contrast, this was a compilation of stories told by Naḥman of Bratslav himself. The content of the stories was also unusual; rather than overtly discussing Jewish spiritual life, the stories dealt with "bewitched princesses, kings and heroes, wood spirits and wizards, mysterious beggars and the like."[80] Joseph Perl saw this new publication as "both a horror and an opportunity," to quote Jeremy Dauber—horror because of the apparent appeal of the tales, and opportunity because of the potentiality of hijacking the legend-like narrative for his own purposes.[81] This was his chance to create his own maskilic version of the Hasidic tales, a chance to imbue obscure, theologically ambiguous tales with an unequivocal meaning that reflected his own ideology. In an appendix to the 1815 collection of Naḥman of Bratslav's tales, *Siḥot ha-ran* (Conversations with Rabbi Naḥman), Perl found a curious piece of information: Naḥman of Bratslav traveled from Russia to Lemberg in 1807 in search of a treatment for his tuberculosis. He did so alone, without the company of his disciple and scribe, the person who documented all his tales, Natan Sternhartz.[82] This piece of information prompted Perl to create an elaborate "hoax," inventing the discovery of a new manuscript, which was a fake collection of "Habsburg" Hasidic tales, stories that were supposedly told by Naḥman of Bratslav while he was on his own in Galicia. Like the vast majority of maskilic writing dating to this period, Perl's collection of pseudo-Hasidic tales was never published, and we know nothing of its final form, dissemination, or reception. The 1969 publication of *Tales and Letters* is a scholarly reconstruction of three fragments which contains a fictional letter exchange between two Hasidic followers, one in Russia and the other in Galicia, "trading" stories of Rabbi Naḥman of Bratslav (Hebrew), and the "completion" of "The Loss of the Princess" (Hebrew); and "The Loss of the Prince," a Hasidic-like original tale (Hebrew and Yiddish).

Since Naḥman of Bratslav's collection of tales was bilingual, it is evident that Perl sought to emulate this format by producing a bilingual edition of his own Hasidic parody. The surviving Hebrew and Yiddish drafts, however, are not identical. The Yiddish version is more fully developed, representing a later stage of composition. In my analysis, I draw on both versions to trace the development of Perl's political thought.

Tales and Letters opens with a letter from a Russian Hasid, Avreml Chmelniker, addressed to Moshe Baraz, a Hasid residing in Lemberg. In it, Chmelniker expresses his desire to collect the Hasidic stories that Rabbi Naḥman of Bratslav told during his stay in Galicia in 1807:

> I heard from our fellow [Hasidim] who spent time in your community that you were close to our Rabbi when he had visited Lwów . . . and had the privilege of hearing his sweet words . . . we had heard some of the Rabbi's tales without their endings, while other are missing altogether . . . This is why we all agreed to contact you . . . Perhaps the Rabbi did not wish to tell the end of the story in our state, and perhaps he shared its conclusion while being in your state.
>
> [*Shamaʿti mi-ʾanshei shelomeinu ʾasher hayu be-kehilatkhem, sheʾatem hayitem mi-ha-mekoravim shel rabbeinu . . . be-ʿet ʾasher haya bi-Lvov . . . ve-haya la-hem zekhiya lishmoʿa devarav ha-metukim . . . ʾetsel kama maʿasiyot lo zakhinu lishmoʿa ha-sof u kama maʿasiyot ḥaserot . . . al ken hiskamnu . . . likhtov lakhem . . . ki ʾefshar lo haya rotze rabbeinu lesaper ha-sof be-maʿase be-medinatenu, ve-ʾefshar be-medinatkhem haya mesaper ʿad gmirah.*][83]

Chmelniker's letter portrays the international border between Russia and the Habsburg Empire as an obstacle in the act of narration itself. The first tale told by Rabbi Naḥman of Bratslav, "The Loss of the Princess" (Maʿase mi-ʾavedat bat melekh), is presented here as an ostensibly unfinished narrative, its ending remained incomplete while the rabbi was in Galicia. The search for the Hasidic tales from the other side of the border is a radical exaggeration of the power of control of the state and of the potential of laws to shape social and political reality. Perl's text imagines a hyperpoliticized map of Eastern Europe, in which borders are rigid and states are impenetrable. This was, in many ways, the very opposite of Perl's own immediate experience. Not only were the borders relatively penetrable; they were also constantly changing: between 1772 and 1816, the year *Tales and Letters* was written, the border between Austria and Russia was redrawn time and again, first because of the ongoing partitions of Poland and later as a result of the Napoleonic Wars. As I discussed earlier in this chapter, Perl himself experienced this fluidity intensively as a resident of Tarnopol, an enclave that exchanged hands between Austria and Russia. It is not only people and ideas that were constantly exchanged across borders; the borders themselves were also moving, and states frequently exchanged populations. In preaching the ideology of the centralized state, *Tales and Letters* goes even further. In response to the demand to supply the Galician tales, the Hasid from Lemberg, Moshe Baraz, confides in his Russian friends that the Hasidic tales from Galicia are not just broadening the canon of Hasidic tales but also contain a new, secret doctrine, a new Torah (*torah ḥadasha*). According to Rabbi Naḥman of Bratslav, they were to be revealed only in Habsburg Galicia:

> He explicitly stated that he could not tell some of the tales in your state for reasons known only to him.
>
> [*ʾAmar be-ferush she kama me-ha-maʿasiyot lo haya yakhol lesaper be-medinatkhem mi-ḥamat teʿamim ha-yeduʿim lo.*][84]

Naḥman of Bratslav, so we learn from this correspondence, has supposedly revised his entire theology after his stay in Galicia. The reader is thus encouraged to glean the content of the "Torah revealed in Galicia" (*Torah sheʾamar be-kurdan*) from the appended pseudo-Hasidic stories, the completion of "Loss of the Princess" and the "Loss of the Prince." To state the obvious, there is no indication in any of the sources that Naḥman of Bratslav became an apostle of the Austrian Empire during his visit to Lemberg.

Joseph Perl's political reading of the tales emphasizes their contemporary political dimensions while largely ignoring their kabbalistic content. Yet this interpretation should not be dismissed as irrelevant; on the contrary, I argue that Perl was highly attuned to the text, no less than modern scholars of Hasidism. The main target of Joseph Perl's parody is Naḥman of Bratslav's "The Loss of the Princess" (Maʿase mi-ʾavedat bat melekh), the first story in the 1815 collection of Hasidic Tales.[85] In order to explore Perl's critique of the text, I will offer a brief descriptive presentation of the original Hasidic story, followed by an exercise in a "Habsburg" reading of the text, an experiment which uses Perl's parody in order to reconstruct his political critique. Naḥman of Bratslav's "The Loss of the Princess" opens as follows:

> Once there was a king. The King had six sons and one daughter. . . . On a certain day when he [the King] was with her, [the princess], he became enraged at her and from his mouth slipped the sentence: "May the Not-Good take you away." That night she went to her room, and in the morning, no one knew where she was.[86]
>
> [*Maʿase be-melekh ʾeḥad she-hayu lo shisha banim u-vat ʾaḥat . . . paʿam ʾaḥat haya mitvaʿed ʿima . . . ve-naʿasa berogez ʿaleha ve-nizreka mi-fiv dibur she-ha=loʾ-tov yikakh ʾotakh . . . ba-layla halkha le-ḥadrah. U-va-boker lo yadeʿu heykhan hi.*][87]

Following the loss of the princess, the viceroy (*sheyni la-malchut*) decides to rescue her: "he traveled for a long time . . . [until] he saw a castle with many soldiers," where he managed to locate the princess but failed to liberate her. After a series of attempts to rescue the princess, the tale ends abruptly with an editorial note. Rabbi Naḥman, we learn from this final comment, revealed that the princess was, eventually, set free, but refused to reveal the circumstances of her release.

Joseph Perl's parody of "The Loss of the Princess," entitled "The Loss of the Prince," opened with a plot similar to those in conventional Hassidic legendary landscape:

> There was once a great, great king, who ruled over many states, possessed many slaves and was wealthier than any other man in the world, but he did not enjoy all this, because he had no sons.

> [*Paʿam ʾaḥat haya melekh gadol meʾod meʾod ve-hayu lo harbe medinot gedolot ve-harbe ʿavadim ve-ʾashirut gedola she-ʿein kamoha ba-ʿolam kulo. ʾAkh lo haya lo taʿanug mi-kol ha-nal miḥamat she-lo hayu lo banim.*][88]

As in the Hasidic story, the plot takes place in an unspecified kingdom. As with Naḥman of Bratslav's tale, the entire complexity of the state apparatus is reduced to an individualized, personally motivated set of interactions. The difference between "The Loss of the Princess" and "The Loss of the Prince," however, lies in the representation of the political makeup of the state.

Perl, a resident of Tarnopol, a private town, which was ruled both by Polish nobles and by Austrian imperial bureaucrats, was acutely sensitive to the representation of power in Naḥman of Bratslav's tales and its possible political implications. Naḥman of Bratslav's "The Loss of the Princess" takes place in a world in which nobles live in proximity to one another and speak the same language, where the boundaries between their jurisdictions are blurred, and where subjects can move freely from one region to the other. In short, they live in a political unit very much akin to the decentralized Commonwealth of Poland. The entire theological allegory in the Hasidic tale, the tension between good and evil sharing the same space, rests on a decentralized political structure, a cohabitation of equal powers. Perl's challenge was thus to tell the same story within the context of a fictionalized imperial state in which there is only one source of power, a polity where, in contrast to the political reality he faced as a resident of Galicia, centralization has already been fully achieved.

If in the original Hasidic story "The Loss of the Princess" good and evil share the same territorial unit, then in Perl's "The Loss of the Prince," this idea of two sources of power within one state is presented as intolerable. The unfolding political conflict in Perl's tale translates the rivalry of equal powers in the Hasidic tale into a succession dispute within one royal dynasty.[89]

Is "The Loss of the Prince" a pro-imperial manifesto that was converted into an anti-Hasidic text, or the opposite, a parody of Hasidism that was later injected with imperial ideology? The Yiddish manuscript preserved at YIVO suggests the second, a move from an anti-Hasidic text to a text advocating imperial ideology. It reflects how Perl gradually introduced imperial markers into the anti-Hasidic parody.[90] The Hebrew version emphasizes that the king "ruled over many states." In other words, this is not just a king, but an emperor. The Yiddish text makes the imperial ideology even more explicit; it reads, "The king had many states under his control" (*der meylekh hot gehat zeyr fil medines unter zikh*), underlying the centralized political structure of the empire. The last editorial stage, the comments on the margins of the Yiddish version, pushes the project of disseminating knowledge about empires even further. Perl adds in the margins of the page an additional line, expanding his description of the king's imperial rule: "And he loves the states he possessed" (*un hot zayne medines zeyr lib gehat*), presenting the relations of the centralist regime to the disparate territories under his control as homogeneous and equal. Other additions stress the imperial context: the linguistic and ethnic diversity of the empire, for example, commenting on the need of the King's messengers to master different languages as they move across the different imperial regions.

Later in the text, the reader discovers that the evil sorcerer is the founder of Hasidism himself, according to the Hasidic tradition, the Ba'al Shem Tov, Israel Ben Eliezer (c. 1700–1760). Hasidism, within the imagined political structure of the state, is thus a danger not only to the Jewish community but also to the empire as a whole: it is an illegal movement that seeks to harm the state. The parody of Hasidism is thus subsumed under a general concern of propagating a concept of adherence to the laws of the state.

The resolution of the narrative's conflict, the king's infertility, which is caused by the sorcerer's curse, is achieved through a violent intervention of the state's armed forces and the imprisonment of the sorcerer.[91] Perl's narrative is structured around the concept of a single, unified state law that draws its legitimacy from the emperor. On the background of a reality of multiple sources of law, the narrative positions one law as its normative ethical landscape. The entire structure of the plot is organized around that law: the conflict between characters is a conflict against the state, the maskilic deus ex machina is that of the intervention of the state, and the resolution of the narrative's conflict is achieved by a reimplementation of the state's laws.

The story "The Loss of the Prince," the original Hasidic story, is framed by a saying of Naḥman of Bratslav, which proclaims the story has a power of encouraging its listeners to repent: "Rav Naḥman answered and said: On the way, I told a tale (of such power) that whoever heard it had thoughts of repentance."[92] The act of repentance, in Perl's version of the tale, is the process of return not to some sort of primordial faith, but to civil obedience, to an alliance with the imperial state. The text concludes with a manifesto-like definition of the mission of maskilim:

> One should send tzaddikim to preach to the people and to show them that according to the King's laws and customs, they are all acting against the King's will, for many of them don't know that their ways are against the King's will, and if the King's officials will clearly show them that they are acting against the King's will, they will improve their ways and repent.
>
> [*Yesh li shlo'aḥ 'anashim tsadikim le-hoḥiakh et ha-'am ve-ledaber 'al libam, ve-le hare'ot la-hem she-'al pi nimusei ve-ḥukei ha-melekh kulam 'osim neged ha-tsiva' shel ha-melekh, ki rov me-hem 'eynam yode'im she-darkeyhem hu* [*sic*] *neged ratson ha-melekh, ve-be-'im she-'anshei ha-melekh yare'u la-hem be-re'ayot berurot she-'osim ne-ged tsivat ha-melekh yaḥzeru be-teshuva ve-yitḥartu 'al 'avonoteyhem.*][93]

This passage reflects an internalization of the nexus of legal knowledge and liability as it was articulated in the 1811 Austrian Civil Code, the ABGB. The mission of maskilim, this text asserts, is to join forces with state officials and disseminate legal knowledge. The new "Torah" from Galicia that Perl's text announces is the Torah of the Austrian imperial law, the Torah of subjectification, of civil obedience, the Torah of the ABGB, which has just been "revealed" in Galicia.

Finally, Perl's "The Loss of the Princess" concludes with the publication of an imperial edict, which uncovers the evildoing of the Hasidim and publicly denounces this religious movement: "[The king] ordered that the entire description [of the evil that lies in Hasidism] would be printed and published across the state" (*hot er geheysen me zol di gantse bashryaben darfn opdruken. Un me zol zi in gantsn land publikirn*).[94] As Perl's *Annotated Judenpatent* testifies, he was well aware that this was an unfounded expectation. As he noted in his personal records, the Austrian Empire had, in fact, tolerated Hasidism since 1788.[95] The parody concludes with an imaginary edict that reverses this decision, rendering Hasidism illegal.

The choice to end the anti-Hasidic parody with the publication of a state law is very telling. One of Naḥman of Bratslav's tales, "The King Who

Decreed Conversion" (Ma'ase mi-melekh shegazar shemed), centers on a publication of law regarding the Jewish population, which calls for the conversion of the entire population:

> Once there was a king who decreed for his country exile or conversion. Whoever wanted to stay in the country would have to convert, and if not, they would be exiled from the country.[96]

The tale portrays the publication of state law as a bad omen, as a threat to the mere existence of the Jewish community within the political borders of the state. Perl's story, in contrast, positions the publication of state laws as a favorable event, a form of protection of the Jewish population.

ARRESTING STORIES, PART II: THE 1816 LEMBERG EXCOMMUNICATION AND THE FIRST MODERN YIDDISH PLAY IN EASTERN EUROPE

Joseph Perl's *Tales and Letters* offered a fictional vision of the Austrian Empire as a place where the project of legal centralization has already happened. In Perl's fictional world, the state exists as a fully homogenized legal polity, perfectly governed according to the principle of the rule of law. By emphasizing the connection between legal knowledge and liability, *Tales and Letters* imagines a secure place for Galician maskilim as a voluntary extension of the empire's bureaucratic infrastructure, propagating knowledge about the state and its laws to the Jewish population, presumably in Hebrew and Yiddish. Similar political aspirations were attractive not only to Jewish enlighteners but also to other intellectual elites of different ethnic groups. The partial, intermittent centralization of power in Galicia and the continual need of Austrian authorities for local elites to oversee and implement state control created an opportunity for different intellectual groups to fill in the bureaucratic void and position themselves as mediators between the state and their own religious or ethnic group to propagate knowledge of the imperial state and its laws in accordance with their respective ideologies. For example, Konstanty Słotwiński, a Polish noble and a lawyer by profession, published in 1832 a catechist book for Galician serfs, entitled *Katechizm poddanych galicyjskich: O prawach i powinnościach ich względem Rządu, Dworu i samych siebie* (Catechism for

Galician Serfs: On Laws and Duties toward the Government, the Estate and Themselves).[97] Słotwiński's book is a continuation of the state-sponsored project of disseminating legal knowledge. It provides a clear exposition in Polish of numerous Austrian laws governing the obligations of serfs to the state while also addressing their duties toward Polish landlords. Słotwiński's *Katechizm* thus encourages compliance with both state legislation and the authority of estate owners. In doing so, it embodies the ideology and interests of the Polish nobility, who sought to align themselves with the Austrian administration. Galician Jewish enlighteners, one might expect, would be engaged in a similar project, creating their own fusion of state law and personal ideology in Hebrew, taking on the role of preachers of knowledge about the state, the way it is envisioned in Joseph Perl's *Tales and Letters*. Only they were not allowed to do so, at least not in a Jewish language. A letter from Shimshon Bloch to Joseph Perl, written in 1823, recounts an appeal of a local Galician maskil who wanted to publish a collection of imperial laws in Hebrew translation. The Viennese censor denied the maskil's appeal, reasoning that "the will of the king is that Jews will learn living languages, the languages of the land" (*ki ratson ha-melekh hu ʾasher yilmedu leshonot ha-ḥayot ʾasher tehalekhna ba-ʾarets*), and, for this reason, Jews should refer to legal publications in German.[98] This may be one reason maskilim turned to writing fiction in Hebrew and Yiddish that dramatize the rule of law, mediating legal knowledge and, at the same time, preaching their own ideology.

To further examine the relationship between the circulation of legal knowledge and the emergence of literary production, I focus on the following case study: the 1816 Lemberg excommunication and the subsequent appearance of the first modern Yiddish play, *Di genarte velt* (The Deceived World). On May 10, 1816, an anonymous letter was posted on the doors of the Lemberg synagogue calling for a ban on two young local men, Shlomo Yehudah Leib Rapoport (1790–1867) and Binyamin (Hirsh) Natkes. Rapoport and Natkes had purportedly introduced Western education and popularized the use of the German language. Natkes and Rapoport, the victims of the ban, appealed to the Lemberg authorities, who, in turn, called for a police investigation to locate the person behind the letter and, at the same time, force the rabbi of Lemberg to publicly annul the ban.[99]

In maskilic historiography, the events surrounding the annulment of the ban were considered, to cite Shmuel Feiner, "a pivotal experience in the evolution of the Galician Haskalah movement . . . described again and again . . . nurtur[ing] their hope that this example would typify cultural and social progress everywhere until they achieved a complete victory."[100] For later waves of Galician maskilim, argues Rachel Manekin, the 1816 excommunication became an origin story, an archetypal struggle that "gestured towards the enemy and portrayed the heroic figures."[101] These retrospective interpretations of the nullification of the ban as a public gesture of governmental support overshadow the immediate reception of the events surrounding the ban: maskilim interpreted the intervention of the state as a public demonstration of a successful mobilization of legal knowledge. *Ḥerem*, excommunication, constituted, as Jacob Katz noted, one of the *kehila*'s most significant disciplinary tools: the exclusion of an individual from the community, which barred their participation in the social and symbolic interactions of communal life. This mechanism functioned as a means of ensuring that the views of either the rabbinic authorities or the lay leadership were upheld among the broader public.[102] While in France and Prussia the ban was decreed illegal in the late eighteenth century, in Austrian Galicia it was fully embraced by the authorities as part of the subjection of communal authority to imperial interests. An 1808 law proclaimed that bans were legal, as long as they were approved by the state.[103] An additional 1823 law provided further details concerning the legal recognition of bans.[104] It seems that direct knowledge of Austrian legislation concerning the ban was not available to most contemporary maskilim. What we see, rather, is the acquisition of what Mary Gallagher calls "strategic knowledge through legal mobilization," namely, the deduction of knowledge from public displays of legal enforcement—in this case, the public annulment of the ban by Ya'kov Orenstein.[105]

A letter recounting the events of the ban, preserved in Joseph Perl's personal archive, shows how "strategic knowledge" about legal procedures became popularized among maskilic circles. The letter is a copy, presumably produced by Joseph Perl himself or someone from his circle, of an anonymous account authored by a maskil who had arrived in Lemberg. It reports on the ban, copying a public letter authored by yet another maskil from Tarnopol about the ban.[106] In short, it is a copy of a copy of a copy. Rachel Manekin has questioned the reliability of the letter, pointing to the discrepancy with the archival records. To that we can add that the person who wrote the letter describes simultaneous events taking place in three different synagogues, which calls into question what he could personally have witnessed. If the letter appears to be a rather unreliable source for the reconstruction of the historical events, then it is, for the very same reasons, an excellent source for popular legal knowledge, "knowledge (and misinformation) that laypeople (and lawyers) possess about legal rules."[107] Following is a translation of a fragment from this letter:

> Concerning this summer's letters of excommunication that were flying back and forth, targeting the learned in science and non-Jewish languages, and specifically the four people, indicating their names. Not only did the [person who issued these letters] transgress the edicts of the emperor, [but] they also disobeyed one of the state's laws: a state law prohibiting the casting of a ban. Once the identities of the offenders are revealed, they will be punished as criminals and rebels who have transgressed the emperor's laws.
>
> [*Bi-dvar megilot ḥaramot 'asher 'afu ba-kayits ze 'al dorshei ha-ḥokhmot ve-leshonot ha-goyim u-vifrat 'al 'arba'a 'anashim ha-nekuvim bi-shmotam . . . lo' dai ki ḥalfu ḥukot hakeysar yerum hodo heferu brit dat medina 'asher aḥat mehina hi livli yifares mikhmarot ha-ḥerem 'al mits'adei gever. Ve-lakhen im gam ba-yamim yavo'u yivade'u 'osey ha-nevala ha-zot yinaku ve-taḥat shevet ha-musar ya'avru ke'aḥad mi-ha-posh'im ve-ha-mordim 'asher datei ha-keysar 'eynam 'osim.*][108]

The letter described how the law functions in practice and how it is enforced. In effect, it served as a source of legal knowledge, as an imaginary participation in the state's project to announce itself, its ideology, and its laws. The fact that, as it happens, the law that the letter discusses does not exist points to the gap between the concept of legality, on the one hand, and actual legal knowledge, on the other hand. The reader learns of the content of the law in action within a narrative in which it is successfully enforced.

Compact narratives concerning the rule of law are embedded in other maskilic letters. Naḥman Krochmal (1785–1840), a maskil based in Żółkiew (Today, Zhovkva, Ukraine), writes to Abraham Goldberg of Rawa Ruska (today, Rava Ruska, Ukraine), who sought his advice concerning an impending ban. In this letter, Krochhmal imparted his own experience with legal action. Instead of referring to a specific law, Krochmal referred to a specific case in which denunciation to the authorities was proved effective when the police intervened and incarcerated the Hasidic leader Hersch of Żydaczów (today Zhydachiv, Ukraine).[109] The letter concludes with guidelines on how to write a petition to the authorities in case of a ban:

> If you have been threatened with ostracism and excommunication, and were forced to burn many of your books, you must seek vengeance, especially against the head village master, striking him with the axe of the emperor's laws . . . all you need to do is to send me a signed letter of consent [*koa'ḥ harsha'a*] and a letter specifying the time and place of the event, and I guarantee that he will be incarcerated and punished in proportion to his crime.
>
> [*Ki 'iymu 'alekha be-ḥerem ve-niduy shimkha, ve-hetsikukha li-msor rabim mi-sfareykha li-srefa, ra'uy le-hinakem me-hem, u-be-yiḥud mi-ha-rosh moreh kfar ha-nal ve-la'alot 'alav be-kardomot datei ha-moshel yerum hodo . . . eyn lekha . . . li-shlo'aḥ elay ḥatimat yadkha le-koa'ḥ harsha', ve-'im ha'igeret kolelet zman u-makom u-firtey ha-ma'asa. Va-ni ha-'arev ba-davar ki yusar ve-ye'anesh kfi ḥet'ato 'asher ḥata'*]

Krochmal evokes the power of imperial law, imparting very specific know-how of how to make an appeal effective: a clear indication of the time and the place of the offense and a detailed description of the legal transgression, showing the less experienced maskil which information would enable an effective activation of the power of the state's laws.

The letter to Krochmal offers insight into the manner in which maskilim were able to disseminate this type of legal knowledge among their ranks—in this case, a young, inexperienced maskilim turning to an established, influential figure. The anonymous letter from Perl's archive represents another model of dissemination of knowledge: a chain letter. The highly convoluted history of the transmission of the above-mentioned letter concerning the excommunication in Lemberg—a copy of a copy of a copy—demonstrates the difficulty of publication in the absence of maskilic journals. The copied letter was effectively one of a few "public spaces" available to people without rabbinic posts.

This letter was both an extension and an alternative to the public space of the synagogue, which, as I previously mentioned, was the designated space for the dissemination of legal information by the local authorities since 1791: an extension of the public space, since it further disseminated information originating from the regime, and an alternative thereof, since the Lemberg synagogue itself was a monopoly of the state rabbi and his circle, and maskilim had to look for another safe place where they could discuss the law freely.

The first modern Yiddish play, *Di genarte velt*, emerged from a time in which this lack of public space for the dissemination of legal information persisted.[110] The play is in a sense an elaboration of the narratives on the rule of law in maskilic letters.[111] It comments directly on the events surrounding the 1816 excommunication.

Much of the early history of *Di genarte velt* is shrouded in mystery: it was published anonymously, and no external evidence has yet surfaced to establish the identity of its author. The one clue the play provides concerning the identity of the author, the assertion that the author is a woman, seems questionable, even if this possibility cannot be entirely excluded. Further obscuring this work's provenance is the fact that the first documented edition of this play, dating to the 1820s, has not been preserved. Finally, modern scholars have access to only two editions, dating from 1863 and 1865, which differ from each other significantly.

Within the scope of this study, I focus on a single aspect of the play: its dramatization of state laws. To begin, a brief summary of the plot is as follows: a merchant hires a melamed (religious instructor) for his son, only to discover that the teacher is a hypocrite. Married, the teacher openly pursues the merchant's niece, a poor orphan. When the merchant learns that the melamed intends to divorce his wife to coerce the orphan into marriage, he expels him from the household. In the play's final scene, the melamed is chased from his home after being caught making sexual advances toward the housemaid.

> Merchant (furiously, to the melamed): A Sinful Jew! Get out of my house!
>
> [*Soykher (mit ka'as tsum melamed): Poyshe'a yisroel! Aroys fun mayn shtub!*]

The merchant's last words foreground the play's moral in halakhic language: the immoral behavior of the melamed, his infidelity to his wife, is publicly denounced as a transgression of religious laws, thus fulfilling the play's introductory promise to "reveal the shame of false people, who disguise themselves as . . . pious people."[112] This, by itself, is a rather cautious move on part of the playwright: the melamed is displayed as transgressing some of the most fundamental halakhic prohibitions and the merchant merely articulates what has already become an established fact and pronounced as such by other characters. *Di genarte velt*, however, contains one last stage direction, which exceeds the initial promise of shaming:

> The day after, the melamed is expelled from the city by a policeman. End.
>
> [*Dem andern tog shikt men dem melamed mit a shupos oys der shtot aroys. Ende.*][113]

As suggested by this final line, between the merchant's last words and the expulsion of the melamed, someone contacted the police. Later in this chapter, I reconstruct how the melamed's misconduct could have been perceived as an offense under Austrian law and how the text maneuvered between the two legal systems. At this point, however, I stress the mechanism of the appeal to the police itself. To mobilize the police, the same person who contacted the authorities must have translated the moral offense, which was hitherto conveyed in halakhic, religious terms, into legal language. Why, one wonders, was it necessary to call the police?

One possible answer is that bringing in the police was merely a literary convention. At the outset, *Di genarte velt* draws inspiration from a seventeenth-century play by Molière (Jean-Baptiste Poquelin), *Tartuffe, or the Impostor*. Indeed, the earliest documented reception of *Di genarte velt*, dating to around 1825, describes it as a Jewish adaptation of Molière's work.[114] In *Tartuffe*, the eponymous hypocritical religious teacher strives to gain control of the household where he teaches until the police eventually arrest him. Police apprehend him, however, after Tartuffe has already succeeded in taking legal possession of the house in which he resided and worked. As a matter of fact, in the French version, it is Tartuffe himself who calls the police, intending to force the family for whom he worked out of their house! By the time the police arrive, there is no longer a possibility for a viable solution without an intervention from the outside. The conclusion of *Tartuffe* is, according to literary scholar Sheryl Kroen, the "classic deus ex machina, perfectly suited to its context at Versailles under Louis XIV, with the all-seeing, all-knowing king acting to save the day."[115] The political logic of the play highlights the difference between legal and moral justice. The police, summoned by the king, are necessary because Tartuffe's immediate actions are immoral but not necessarily illegal. *Di genarte velt* adopts the structure of *Tartuffe*; however, it assigns a different role to the police, which here function as an instrument of the law.

Another possible model for *Di genarte velt*, it has been argued, is the Yiddish play *Silliness and Sanctimony* (Laykhtzin un Fremelay), authored around 1796 by the Prussian maskil Aaron Wolfson-Halle (1754–1835). In the play, Reb Yosefkhe, a cynical and corrupt melamed from Poland, is hired by a Prussian merchant, Reb Henokh. Reb Yosefkhe spends the money he earns from teaching Torah on prostitutes and gambling. He is finally caught in a brothel, and the play ends as follows:

> Reb Henokh: You hear, brother-in-law? He pawned his tefillin! That enemy of Israel! I must say, I never would have dreamed such a thing in all my days. Such a heretic and an apostate! And now what he was doing with the maid comes back to me!
>
> Legmin: Look how the rascal stands there, rooted to the spot! Ha ha ha! You see, Jew—that's what happens to all rogues! But if you think I am keeping you in my house overnight, you've got another thing coming. You'll have to sleep in the woodshed tonight. It's plenty cold there, but you're full of hot air. March, march, get a move on
>
> [She drags him out of the door].
>
> Curtain.[116]

The literary resemblance between the Galician and the Prussian plays is very clear: Once the melamed is deemed "an enemy of Israel" (*poshe'a yisroel*), he is punished for his misdeeds. In the Prussian play, the resolution of the conflict is limited to the private sphere: in Wolfson-Halle's moral world, a police intervention is even less desirable than an appropriate punishment for the villain. There is no call for intervention by the authorities, and Jewish legal autonomy is fully maintained. Unlike its French and Prussian counterparts, *Di genarte velt* concludes with two gestures of order making: a reaffirmation of the vitality of an internal, familial "Jewish" order, the merchant chasing the immoral melamed out of his house, and that of the legal order, the police arresting him and chasing him out of town and, implicitly, outside the state's jurisdiction.

Despite its apparent novelty, the conclusion of *Di genarte velt* has not received much scholarly attention: the first scholar to compile an academic edition of the play, Meir Viner, doubted the authenticity of the last lines of the play. The curt stage direction, he argues, was too curt, too condensed, to be an integral part of the text. Perhaps, he suggested, this was a belated addition of a compiler who sketched the end from memory.[117] When Chone Shmeruk analyzed the play, he readily adopted Viner's mistrust of the conclusion and similarly doubted the significance of its ending. Shmeruk reads the play as a continuation, rather than a break, with the political agenda of *Sanctimony and Silliness*. The turn to narrative, he argued, was part of a larger cultural program to use the "weapon of satire" (*neshek ha-satira*) as an alternative to direct political intervention.[118]

The year Chone Shmeruk's study appeared in print, 1978, a longer version of the play was located at the Frankfurt Municipal Library.[119] This edition, originally published in Lemberg in 1865, featured a somewhat extended and more complete ending. While the differences between the two endings are significant, the one element that persists in both versions is the concluding appeal to civil authorities. In the edition preserved in Frankfurt, calling the police is not a stage direction, but part of the merchant's final lines. Thus, no matter how one interprets the complex textual history of the play and the relations between the two versions, it is clear that the turn to the authorities was not an auxiliary addition to the play, but an integral part of the plot and, in a sense, the raison d'être of the entire play. As Viner has shown, the play contains direct comments on the 1816 Lemberg excommunication.[120] Viner concludes his summary of the plot in the following words:

> The melamed instigates all sorts of intrigues, followed by counter-intrigues on part of the accountant . . . [until] the merchant puts an end to the intrigues, marries his son to the orphan and the sanctimonious Hasidic melamed is finally exposed.[121]

The intrigues and counterintrigues downplayed by both Viner and Shmeruk, are, in fact, the centerpiece of the play, the key to our understanding of the bewildering, harsh ending. The motivation behind summoning the police stems from a threat of excommunication.

The first scene, a dispute between the melamed and the family's enlightened accountant, sets the stage for the ideological tension that permeates the plot, dramatizing several familiar tropes of the maskilic-Hasidic debate in maskilic literature: the accountant praises the study of science, which he associates with rationality, while the religious teacher advocates a theology that preserves a distinction between the natural and the supernatural. The accountant presents himself as the "defender of Jewish law," a stance identified by Jeremy Dauber as "maskilic traditionalism."[122] Meanwhile, the melamed insists on the value of custom, minhag, practices not codified as part of the orthodox halakha. The entire debate concludes when the provoked melamed calls the accountant an "apikoyres," a heretic. Upon leaving the scene, the melamed mysteriously refers to a "great trouble" he is about to cause the accountant. The discussion about obedience to the law, which, until the very last paragraph, refers unequivocally to Jewish law, and the accusation of heresy frame the constant reference to the threat of a ban. The term "apikoyres," I argue, was understood to be a cue for discourse that relates to the ban. The German translation of the excommunication documents, preserved in the imperial Austrian archives, replaces the traditional ritual curses with a curt note: "profanities," namely "curses."[123] One can reconstruct the missing "curses" by turning to other Hebrew sources concerning the excommunication. For example, in Joseph Perl's *A Test for the Righteous* (Boḥen tsadik), the act of casting the 1816 ban is described as follows: "For they are heretics [apikorsim] and evildoers" (*ki hem 'apikorsim 'osim ma'ase resha'*).[124]

Later in the play, the melamed openly threatens the merchant's son:

> You learn [Western] wisdoms, foreign languages, crafts. Well, you yourself will probably be excommunicated.
>
> [*Du lernst dikh oykh epes khokhmes, leshoynes, shoyn vi ikh ze kenstu di melokhes oykh. Nu shoyn ligt du dokh mistome oykh in der khet*].[125]

Finally, the 1865 version includes a penultimate scene in which the melamed, intoxicated, calls the family "apikorsim," in the plural, which reveals a plan to use his connection to excommunicate the entire household. The interaction between the melamed and his employers is not the only site where threats of excommunication take place. As the merchant announces earlier on, the recent *ḥerem* in Lemberg ended with an intervention of the local authorities: "Those who [initiated the ban] already regret it, as they were forced to annul it in public" (*zey hobn gor kharote, vos zey hobn ongehoybn, vorn me hot publitshne gemuzt di khet* [*kheyrem*] *farnisht makhn*).[126] Armed with this legal knowledge, the merchant turns to the police, who hurry to take legal action against the melamed.

Di genarte velt offers a structure of a narrative embedded within a narrative: as the characters watch how the events surrounding the Lemberg *ḥerem* pan out, they conclude that *ḥerem* is deemed illegal in the eyes of the authorities and later apply this strategic legal knowledge in order to solicit state intervention. Clearly, the play invites the readers to take this course of action as an example they can apply in their daily lives.

To conclude my discussion of this play, I draw attention to the figure of the *shrayber*, the accountant, the person who represents the maskilic agenda. In the play, the *shrayber* is an accountant in a family business. The term *shrayber*, or the Polish equivalent, *pisarz*, has other connotations: this was one of the very few bureaucratic professions Jews were able to hold in the Polish latifundia administration.[127] At the same time, *shrayber* also means "writer," alluding to the position of the anonymous maskil who wrote this play.

In light of the accusation against the accountant, the merchant recalls older times, when Jewish intellectuals were praised and had a clear societal function—as intercessors:

> I remember that in my day only a handful of people knew anything at all. [These rare individuals] were appointed as intercessors . . . People would nearly wash their feet in reverence and drink the water . . . and today, these great men are branded apikorsim.[128]
>
> [*Ikh gedenk in mayne tsaytn az es iz geven eyner in a shtot oder tsvey a gantse mishpokhe vos hobn epes nor gekont . . . Hot men im far a shtadlen gemacht . . . kimat hot men zey di fis gevashn un dos waser getrunken . . . haynt ruft men di greste briyes apikorsim.*]

At the same time, *shrayber* also alludes to a professional writer, and in this respect, it associates the figure of the accountant with the anonymous playwright. In the historiography of Jewish literature, the figure of Mendele the Book Peddler, Mendele Moykher Sforim, created by Shalom Ya'akov Abramovitsh (1835–1917), has represented a genealogy of professional writing in the profession of bookselling.[129] This passage from *Di genarte velt* associates literary writing with accounting, with intercession, with legal knowledge, and with communication with the state authorities. This genealogy is metonymic to the plot of the play and to the larger function of Galician maskilic literature, which brought together the act of narrating and the mobilization of the law. I opened this chapter with the figure of Sonnenfels, who was both a writer and a jurist. The maskilim could not be identified as writers: in the 1810s there were no Jewish writers in Eastern Europe. They could not be identified as official intercessors for their communities either: this practice fell out of use after the abolition of the kahal. *Di genarte velt* is an expression of both the frustration and the creativity of a group that operated without the support of the state, without the endorsement of a larger Jewish population, and had to imagine its own role, and fictionalize its own success.

CONCLUSION

The year 1820 saw the publication of the first Habsburg maskilic journal, an annual entitled *Bikurei ha-'itim* (First Fruits of the Times).[130] Beginning in the second volume (1821), the journal concluded with a section in German in Hebrew letters, entitled: "Habsburg patents and decrees . . . the way they were printed in the *Wiener Zeitung*, (organized) according to their content, the time of their publication, and the page number" (*k.k. Patente und Circulare vom Jahre . . . noch ihrem Inhalt, der Zeitfolge ihrer Erlassung und mit einzigen der Seitenzahlen, wie selbe ihm Amtsblatt der Wiener Zeitung bekannt gemacht worden*).[131]

This was a list of imperial laws published in the previous year and a key to find them in official publications. The major literary works of Galician Haskalah—for example, Yitzḥak Erter's early prose, "Ha-tsofe le-vet yisrael" (A Watcher unto the House of Israel), "Mozney mishkal" (Scale), or Meir Letteris's poems—were all printed alongside detailed descriptions of imperial laws, decrees, and regulations. In this respect, the vision of literature and legal knowledge as inherently connected has found its ultimate expression in the maskilic Habsburg press, which became a source for new literary works as well as imperial laws.

Pointing toward the centrality of law in maskilic publications throughout the nineteenth century is one way to conclude the narrative of this chapter. An alternative way would be to reflect on stories about the law that were not represented in maskilic writing—dark stories about the exploitation of law, about law as a vehicle to perpetuate injustice, rather than justice. Publicly, maskilim sang the praises of the imperial law, but what, we wonder, did they think in their heart of hearts? These parallel histories of the entanglement of state law, colonization, and the transformation of Jewish society, which were amply recorded in archival documents, have left very little traces in maskilic literature, and as such, they are much more difficult to recover from an internal Jewish perspective.

The personal notebook of the Brody-based maskil Ya'akov Shmuel Bick contains one highly curious poem in Yiddish and Hebrew translation, titled "Ha-tsadik ha-'amiti" (The Real Pious Man).[132] It recounts the story of a Lemberg merchant named Naftali Rapaport who took advantage of an 1814 law that deemed void legal documents in Hebrew letters: personal checks, contracts, and promissory notes.[133] Rapaport was able to convince the Lemberg community to accept his personal checks in Hebrew. Later on, he took advantage of the fact that the notes were legally void to avoid paying back his creditors, using the imperial law for his own personal gain, at the expense of the Lemberg Jewish community. The scam was of such magnitude that it affected many Jewish merchants across Galicia, including maskilim like Naḥman Krochmal.[134]

The poem addresses Naftali Rapaport, wryly saluting him for his clever exploitation of Austrian law at the expense of his coreligionists:

> You, Naftali Rapaport, have succeeded! The Lwów community
> took notice of you
> and accepted your promissory notes written in Hebrew script.
> For Naphtali, good and deceit are one and the same,
> And he'll never repay his debts, despite the notes' claim.

[*Hetslaḥta! ve-kehal lvov 'aleykha samu 'eyneyhem.*
U-vikhtav yehudit mi-yadkha lakḥu shitreyhem . . .
Naftali 'eḥad darko be-tov u-ve-ma'arumim
Ve-noshav katuv yehudit lo yashiv le-'olamim.]

In Bick's masterful rendition, the text offers an ironic comment on state law, which is supposedly meant to protect from evildoing but, in fact, is only a tool for the powerful to take advantage of the weak. Bick employs maskilic discourse only to subvert it, highlighting the apparent gap between legal rhetoric and the actual functioning of the law:

We keep the King's laws in order to multiply peace in the land
Without laws, men would swallow one another alive
[There are laws] so that wickedness may not transgress them

[*Ḥukei ha-melekh yishmor le-harbot shalom ba-'aretz*
Hen bli ḥukim ḥayim yivla ish et re'ehu
U-leval yavo ha-resha' lifrots bam perets]

The poem concludes with an ironic blessing addressed to Naftali Rapaport:

Happy is the pious man who hides behind the letter of the law
In his mercy, his promissory notes are forever void

[*'Ashreikha tsadik mistofef be-tsav ha-ḥukim*
Shitrei ḥovatkha la-'ad be-raḥamim nimtakim]

The poem from Bick's personal notebook betrays the tensions and ambivalence in the maskilic community's vision of state law—an ambivalence often glossed over in their fiction. It reveals both the high hopes that maskilim placed in state law and the profound disappointment that followed when those hopes were dashed.

THREE

Naḥman in Bratslav

The End of the World and Beginning of Hasidic Literature, 1802–1810[1]

I heard a witticism in the name of the Rebbe. Ever since the Russian Tsar conquered the country, the money has become dross and the drink, punch. "Your silver has become dross, your wine mixed with water." (Isaiah 1:22)

[NATHAN STERNHARTZ, *ḤAYEI MOHARAN* §428][2]

WRITING LITERATURE, THE PRECEDING CHAPTER argued, was one of the strategies Jewish enlighteners adopted in order to partake in the new political order in the Polish territories. Taking their cue from the Austrian Enlightenment, I argued, the Galician maskilim considered literary texts an effective tool to propagate legal knowledge. In their fiction, they crafted utopian narratives in which Jewish religious law, Austrian state law, and maskilic ideology coalesce. This chapter complements this argument by showing that Naḥman of Bratslav's 1806 turn to storytelling was also motivated by a response to the new political reality in the Polish lands and shaped by his experience as a resident of Bratslav. In his allegorical tales, I contend, Naḥman crystalized his theological-political vision, which located the beginning of redemption in the contemporary events of his time. This sui generis genre structured both contemporary political and future eschatological events within a homogeneous, continuous, and compact narrative frame. In so doing, this chapter demonstrates, Naḥman sought to encourage his believers to interpret the political transformation they witnessed as a framework for understanding the way in which God rules the world, envisioning the imminent messianic era as a direct and immediate continuation of contemporary politics. Whereas the maskilim saw fiction as a vehicle to prepare the Jews for the advent of a new political era, the rise of the imperial state, Naḥman's tales urged his audience to reject the state and its promises and to prepare for what he considered the end of the world.

KABBALAH AND FOLKLORE

The claim that Naḥman's canonical tales thematize political events appears self-explanatory. Even a cursory look at their titles reveals the extent to which Naḥman was fascinated with state politics. "The Loss of the Princess," the first story he told, in the summer of 1806, revolved around a king, a lost princess, and a viceroy. Naḥman continued to tell stories about kings—"King Who Decreed Conversion," "King and an Emperor," and "King Who Had No Children." In "The King's Son and the Maidservant's Son Who Were Switched" and "The Humble King," he talked about states— a "stupid state," a "smart state," and "the essence of the state." Yet this pronounced interest in politics has received little attention because the political dimension of the tales has been subsumed under the category of folklore.[3]

Before telling his first tale, Naḥman shared with his followers his source of inspiration: folktales, which, according to him, held "lofty and hidden matters."[4] Inspired by this comment, modern scholars have interpreted Naḥman's tales as adaptations of folktales that he imbued with esoteric meaning, kabbalistic allegories void of any mimetic value. "The materials borrowed from folktales are only the cover in the tale," argues Yosef Dan, while "the essential materials . . . were taken from the world of Kabbalah."[5] Along the same lines, Arnold Band argues that the essence of the tales was "the elaborate system of the *sefirot*" (divine emanations).[6]

The reference to state apparatuses and governmental systems was thus lumped together with other folkloric motifs. For example, according to Ora Wiskind-Elper, the protagonists of the tales, the "beautiful princess, clever son, evil king, [and] loyal servant," are all symbolic representations of theological concepts: "the Shekhinah, . . . the Messiah, the true *tzaddik*, or the

King of Kings."[7] In Naḥman's tales, Arthur Green concludes succinctly, "the king is always God."[8] As a result, interest in the nontheological aspects of the tales was confined almost exclusively to an examination of their relationship to folklore. Simkha Petrushka, Avinadav Lipsker, Martin Mantel, Chone Shmeruk, and Chana Hendler, among others, sought to locate a specific "original" folktale, or a folkloric motif that, according to them, inspired Naḥman.[9]

These general theories aside, the rapidly burgeoning scholarship dedicated to Bratslav literature has revealed that, in the case of "The King Who Decreed Conversion," the interpretive model does not fully align with the allegorical structure of the tale. Scholars generally agree that in this tale one cannot apply the aforementioned formula that "the king is always God." The tale centers on a royal dynasty: a king who issued a harsh decree for the Jewish population to convert or leave the country and his three successors. Throughout the tale, it is clear from the way the king who decreed conversion operates that this is a reference to a flesh-and-blood monarchic ruler. Wiskind-Elper associates the kings with biblical monarchs, while Aryeh Kaplan links them with European absolutist monarchs.[10] David Roskies and Yitzhak Lewis, in turn, place the political events in the tale in the context of the early nineteenth-century Russian Empire.[11] Be that as it may, there is scholarly consensus that the king who decreed conversion is a king and not God, and that the folktale-like narrative allegorizes political events rather than kabbalistic notions.[12] The idea that there is a political dimension to the production of meaning in "The King Who Decreed Conversion," I argue, is not an exception, but the rule. The interpretive model I offer extends to most of Naḥman's canonical tales and accounts for the borrowing from folklore, politics, and theology.

FOLKLORE, KABBALAH, AND POLITICS

While much scholarship has explored the affinities between Naḥman's tales and folklore, less consideration has been given to the function these borrowings serve in the tales. My intervention asks: Which folkloric themes did Naḥman adopt, and to what end? Is there a selective process that is shared among all of Naḥman's canonical tales, on the one hand, and unique to these tales alone, on the other hand?

There is one conspicuous theme that is characteristic of Naḥman's borrowing from folktales: the representation of state politics. Of the thirteen canonical tales, twelve, the overwhelming majority, incorporate the folktale trope of simplified state apparatuses and governmental systems: kingdoms, kings, queens, ministers, princes, and princesses.[13] While monarchs and kings occasionally feature in folktales, their prevalence in Naḥman's tales is striking.[14] When Naḥman heard folktales about royal families, princesses, and kings, he was probably thinking of the symbolic language of the *sefirot*, the Shekhinah, and the king of kings. These were the "lofty and hidden matters" he had in mind. To be sure, Naḥman's choice to portray God as a king is not unusual in and of itself.[15] On the contrary, it is a highly conventional symbol in the Hebrew Bible, in midrash, and in Jewish mysticism. It is not, however, the only way kabbalists allegorized their mystical visions. Other symbolic relationships were available to Naḥman in kabbalistic literature—husband and wife, father and son—and these feature in his sermons and conversations—but not in the tales.[16] This is not to say that there are no fathers and sons or lovers in the tales. Kinship relations are prevalent, but they are almost always subsumed under the organizing metaphorical language of political hierarchy. For example, in "The Loss of the Princess," the father is a king, the daughter is a princess, and her lover is a viceroy.

Moreover, these royal attributes in the tales are not contingent but essential to the plot. Unlike the "king parables" in midrash, which, to cite David Stern, "have nothing intrinsically royal about them," the royal aspect is central to the plot in all of Naḥman's tales. Whereas, according to Stern, the "king could easily be replaced by an anonymous man" in midrash, replacing the king with an everyman in the tales would radically change their meaning. For example, one cannot substitute the figure of the king in Naḥman's "The Fly and the Spider" with the figure of an anonymous man. The entire plot rests on the specifics of the political relations between monarchs and minority groups. Thus, to make sense of the tales, we should ask not only which folktales inspired Naḥman, but also which political forms excited his imagination.

THE LITERAL AND THE FIGURATIVE

When Dan, Wiskind-Elper, and Band portray the literal dimension of the tales as a "cover," "façade," or "garb," respectively, they share a widely accepted literary theory that conceptualizes allegory as a form that "says one thing and means another."[17] Is the political discourse just a cover? Or does it carry over to the production of meaning in the tale?

The interpretation of allegories, argues Maureen Quilligan, is not vertical but horizontal. Their meaning accumulates as the audience gradually deciphers the text. Following Quilligan, I argue that the political, literal dimension of the tales is central to the creation of their meaning, even when it is absolutely clear that they are theological allegories.[18] Naḥman himself thematized the importance of the political dimension of the tales for making sense of their theological meaning. In "The Clever Man and the Ordinary Man" (1809), the clever man draws on his political experience as he tries to make sense of God's rule in this world. Upon being summoned to the royal court, the clever man refuses to believe that he is important enough to meet the king. Since the invitation to visit the royal court does not come from the king directly, the clever man concludes that the king does not exist:

> "Do you know what I think? . . . that there is no king in the world at all . . . the whole world is misled by this nonsense . . . that there is a king." When asked who rules the country, the clever man answers: "This I can tell you . . . because I am an expert . . . I have traveled in many countries, and I was in Italy [Italia]. In Italy the custom is that there are seventy councillors . . . and the authority is shared by all the country's people in turn."[19]

The encounter with Italian politics, argues the clever man, is helpful to him in his attempts to understand how the state—and, by extension, the world—operates.[20] Building on his encounter with the Italian political system, he concludes that there is no one king and, analogously, no one God. However, the clever man is proved wrong. Despite his worldly experience and rational methods, the analogy he draws is false. There is, in fact, a king ruling this kingdom and, analogically, a God. The distribution of power in the world, we learn, is very much like an absolutist monarchy.[21]

This survey of different contemporary political models as potential analogies for the manner in which the world operates de-automatizes the formulaic interpretation according to which a king stands for God. Perhaps, one wonders, the divine power is like a council, a multiplicity of voices, the way the clever man has it. Thus, the tale trains the reader to dwell on the political form in all its specificity and reflect on what it tells us about divine governance.

NAḤMAN'S POLITICS: CONTEMPORARY EVIDENCE

An interpretation of Naḥman's tales in their political context poses a considerable challenge. The contemporary Bratslav sources are relatively poor in providing information concerning Naḥman's response to politics, with two notable exceptions. *Ḥayei moharan*, Nathan Sternhartz's biography of Naḥman, famously opens with Naḥman's response to the statute of 1804 targeting the Jews. Fittingly, there is a robust literature dedicated to locating Naḥman's response to the statute, which extends from the earliest maskilic writings.[22] This is also true of another event Sternhartz documented, the Napoleonic Wars.[23] Other political events Naḥman witnessed—for example, the political transformation of the Polish lands in the wake of the partitions, the decline of Polish noble estates, and the rise of centralized forms of rule—became utterly opaque for later generations and therefore have not registered either in the Bratslav interpretive tradition or in scholarly interpretations of the tales.

Naḥman was born a resident of the Polish-Lithuanian Commonwealth and came to be a resident of the Russian Empire in 1793, at the age of twenty-one. During the thirty-nine years of his life, he lived in a private town, Międzybóż (currently Medzybizh, Ukraine), owned by the Polish nobles the Czartoryskis; in Zlatopol, (Polish: Złotopol, currently Zlatopil, Ukraine), on the premises of a private estate that was transferred to Russian nobles the Potemkins; in a royal town, Bratslav (Polish: Bracław, currently in Ukraine); and finally, in Uman (Polish: Humań, currently in Ukraine), a private town owned by the Potockis.[24] In addition, Naḥman spent time in Ottoman Palestine, passing through Odessa (currently Odesa, Ukraine), Istanbul, Rhodes, and Galatz (currently Galați, Romania), as well as in the Austrian Empire, in Lemberg (currently Lviv, Ukraine). Private noble estates, royal towns, capital cities, decentralized states, and centralized empires—these constituted the political concepts he employed when crafting his stories. To what extent were Naḥman's contemporaries sensitive to the political dimension of his tales? The Bratslav sources did not preserve any information on how Naḥman's followers interpreted his tales during his lifetime.[25] We do have evidence, however, from maskilic circles.

In the preceding chapter, I demonstrated how Joseph Perl's 1816 *Tales and Letters* drew on the Bratslav tales as a way to articulate a maskilic utopia of imperial centralization.[26] This chapter returns to the same source to show what this early maskilic interpretation of a Bratslav tale reveals about Naḥman's political world. Perl's parody of "Loss of the Prince" directs the reader's attention to a fact that has escaped the notice of Hasidism scholars. As I have shown, Perl relocates the Bratslav tale to a new political context: a centralized imperial state. The parody centers on a king who did not rule over one kingdom but "over many states," and "adored all his states." Perl continues to highlight several distinct characteristics of an empire: its multilingualism, the subjugation of the provinces to a centralized form of rule (the emperor summons provincial subordinates to the capital city), and the role of the emperor.

In so doing, Perl sensitized the readers to the political dimension of Naḥman's "Loss of the Princess." Reading Naḥman's tale through Perl's eyes, we can see what bothered the Galician maskil. Naḥman places his narrative within a fragmented and heterogeneous political entity. The inhabitants are dispersed across legally autonomous jurisdictions that lack clear borders and share a common language. In essence, this imagined polity evokes the political landscape of the former Polish-Lithuanian Commonwealth. A monarchy composed of semisovereign political units governed by a king who has limited direct control over his subjects—this is the political reality the viceroy encounters as he searches for the lost princess.

What motivated Naḥman to draw on the political system of the Polish-Lithuanian Commonwealth as a way to reflect on messianic redemption? The political landscape of the Polish-Lithuanian Commonwealth that Naḥman encountered in his youth, I argue, proved a suitable political model to express a specific theological message: the dualism of good and evil. As Yoav Elstein points out, "The Loss of the Princess" narrativizes a theory of evil that draws on a dualistic tendency within kabbalistic sources.[27] This is the Zoharic doctrine, which draws "precise parallels . . . between the powers of uncleanness and the power of holiness" and imagines the world as a "space both the Shekhinah and the evil forces share," one always striving to defeat the other.[28] In "The Loss of the Princess," the model of a decentralized state, the coexistence of autonomous power in the same political unit—the same state—explains how it is possible for the demonic force of *sitra aḥra* (other side) to have a "quasi-independent" power, to borrow Elliot Wolfson's term, and for good and evil to exist side by side.[29]

Drawing on the decentralized model for the allegorization of the dualistic doctrine may also have served another purpose. Following Quilligan's theory of allegory, we can speculate how the representation of the political system in the tale colored its theological message. In the tale, the political reality is marked by a sense of security and stability. There are no evil decrees, no corrupt rulers, no political agents seeking to overpower each other.[30] It may be the case that Naḥman's restorative messianism, as it is narrated in "The Loss of the Princess," was associated with a sense of nostalgia for a bygone Polish era. In this sense "The Loss of the Princess" echoes Naḥman's conversations with his followers, in which he painted the Russian annexation of the Polish lands as the root of all evil. "Ever since the Russian Tsar conquered the country the money has become dross and the drink, punch," Naḥman told his students. This witticism, wordplay, drew on Isaiah's prophecy, portraying the fate of the Polish lands that had fallen under Russian rule as a realm that, following the partition, "became a whore," mired in deceit and corruption, to quote the prophet's words.[31]

"The Loss of the Princess" is framed by Naḥman's call for *teshuva*, or repentance: "This is a tale he told along the way . . . everybody who listened to it began to think about repentance." *Teshuva* is related to the Hebrew root *shin-vav-bet*, "to return." The tale may thus associate repentance, a moral return to the path of righteousness, the return of the Shekhinah, and a political return to a previous state of political affairs. In this respect, Perl was at least partially right in his attempts to uncover politically subversive elements in the Bratslav literature. A close reading of the tale supports Perl's accusation, showing that, indeed, Naḥman held a nostalgic vision of Poland before the partitions, which the Galician maskil interpreted as resistance to the imperial political order.[32]

Most of the scholarship devoted to Naḥman's tales was published before 2006, the year his so-called secret scroll became publicly available. This scroll is of particular importance to our understanding of the tales. The two prophecies it contains, which date to 1806 and 1809, are coterminous with Naḥman's storytelling.[33] Strikingly, the scroll's secret messianic prophecy is grounded in the politics of the time.[34] For example, the 1806 scroll centers on how the Messiah will gradually extend his power over greater territories until he acquires the land of Israel from the Ottoman Empire, which resembles Napoléon's 1806 dissolution of the Holy Roman Empire, occupation of the western Polish territories, and call for the creation of a Jewish Sanhedrin.[35] The 1809 sermon adds another crucial detail. In Naḥman's messianic vision, he himself (or his descendants) will be involved in political activities on the world stage before the coming of the Messiah. The secret scroll and the tales signify, in a sense, the two faces of Naḥman's theology between the years 1806 and 1809: the secret message and the public message. When read together, the stories and the scroll demonstrate the extent to which the political and the theological, the historical present and the messianic future, were inseparable in Naḥman's mind.

"THE HUMBLE KING"

To demonstrate my interpretive model, I turn to a close reading of one of Naḥman's tales, "The Humble King," showing how it offers a narrative that contrasts a corrupt bureaucratic order with a vision of divine justice. My analysis is guided by a set of questions that, I argue, should be incorporated in the analysis of all of Naḥman's tales: Which political markers appear in the tale? Where did Naḥman encounter these political forms and how did he perceive them? Building on both of those, how do the political and theological dimensions of the tale inform each other?

"The Humble King" follows the journey of a wise man who is tasked with exploring an unknown land and producing a portrait of its king. The tale has received a considerable amount of scholarly attention.[36] Zvi Mark interprets the journey of the protagonist to provide a portrait of the king as an expression of the desire to know God.[37] Similarly, Arthur Green reads the tale as parallel searches of God and man to see the face of the other.[38] Following the interpretive model I offer here, my suggestion is to suspend the presupposition that this is a tale with a theological message and focus instead on its political dimension.

Together with the protagonist, the reader first encounters an unknown state from the outside. It is "surrounded by a sea, and a fleet of ships with cannons [is] . . . keeping people from drawing near. And at the edge of this sea, there is a swampy bog . . . and the only way to walk through the mire is on a narrow path, wide enough for only one person."[39] This highly fortified border zone suggests that this unknown political entity is markedly different from the other fictionalized polities that populate Naḥman's tales. It is nothing like the decentralized state of "The Loss of the Princess," in which the borders are porous and nobles roam freely from one estate to the other. This is also not the state featured in "The King and the Emperor," in which two rulers, a king and an emperor, find themselves touring the same land without knowing about the presence of the other. The territory under the rule of the humble king, in contrast, is geographically defined, closely monitored, and surrounded by rigid, impenetrable borders.[40]

The opening paragraphs of "The Humble King" speak of a king who hides behind physical obstacles that only the true believer can cross; it is a story that was probably familiar to Naḥman's audience as another iteration of the "Parable of the Walls" of the Ba'al Shem Tov (Israel Ben Eliezer, 1700–60). A comparison between the two allows us to appreciate how "The Humble King" draws on older Hasidic literary traditions and locate its innovation. The Ba'al Shem Tov's "Parable of the Walls" reads as follows:

> A great wise king made walls and towers and gates by means of illusion . . . [and] commanded that persons will come to him. . . . And there was one person who went until the first gate . . . and returned. And there was another . . . until his son, the beloved one, made a great effort to go to his father the king . . . (and) he saw that . . . it was all an illusion.[41]

In many respects, "The Humble King" follows the general contours of this compact narrative: the protagonist crosses a seemingly insurmountable series of obstacles until he meets the king, a metaphor for the unification of the believer with God. The difference, however, is striking. In "The Humble King," the apolitical walls are transformed into political barriers: a highly fortified international border and, later in the tale, the hierarchy of the state's court system.

The comparison between the Ba'al Shem Tov's tale and Naḥman's tale further substantiates the argument that Naḥman's interest in folktales was motivated by his political interests. Both "The Parable of the Wall" and "The Humble King" borrow from folklore as a way to allegorize the relationship between God and the believer.[42] Naḥman's innovation thus lies elsewhere, in drawing on the folklore motive for its political potential, shifting the focus from the king to the kingdom—its army, courts, and economic system. As the opening of the tale demonstrates, Naḥman's keen interest in politics allowed him to reenergize the use of conventionalized metaphors of God as a king and endow them with all the specificities of concrete political meaning.

The description of the state from outside is followed by an exploration of the "essence [*mahut*] of the state," a curious Hebrew term glossed in Yiddish as "the way the state operates" (*vi azoy di medine firt zikh*). According to the wise man, the "essence of the state" is the following:

> Now there is a state that contains within it all states. And in that state, there is a city that contains all the cities of that state that contains all states. And in that city, there is a house that contains all houses of that city that contains all the cities of that state that contains all states. And in that house is a man who bears within him all of this. There is one there who is laughing; he clowns and pulls all the pranks of that land.[43]

What is the meaning of this passage? A belated Bratslav tradition, preserved by Naḥman Goldstein (Naḥman of Tcherin, 1825–1894), interpreted this as a reference to the temple in Jerusalem:

> "There is a land that includes all of the lands." That is the aspect of the totality of the holiness of the community of the land of Israel. "And in that land, there is a city that includes all of the cities in that land." That is the aspect of Zion and Jerusalem. "And in that city is a house that includes all of the houses in that city." That is the aspect of the Temple and the *heikhal*.[44]

To my mind, the association of the unknown land with the historical land of Israel is difficult to substantiate. The state the tale portrays is deeply and irredeemably corrupt. No matter how misguided the service of the priests in the Temple in Jerusalem, Naḥman certainly did not consider it irredeemably immoral, intentionally deceptive, or irreparably corrupt. Goldstein's interpretation reflects, I argue, a historical moment when the original political context in which "The Humble King" had been told lost its relevance.[45] When Naḥman's students heard a story about two kings, they may have linked this unusual political situation to their own political experience as Polish Jews in partitioned Poland who often had to navigate the rule of more than one king. When talking with his students, Naḥman shared his own experience of double subjectship, Russian and Austrian, the way it appeared in his dreams.[46]

Along the same lines, when the students heard the passage about the "state that includes all of the states," this was probably a reminder of a much more immediate political experience, that of a centralized empire. This is the principle of political centralization: an empire is divided into provinces ("a state that contains within it all states") and governed from the capital city, which presides over all the capitals of the provinces ("a city that contains all the cities of that state that contains all states"); in the capital city are the central authorities and a ruler ("And in that house is a man who bears within him all of this"). The meaning of the Hebrew phrasing is clarified in the Yiddish. The phrase "a state that contains within it all states" is glossed as "that is to say, the state is the principle and the representative of all the states" (*kloymer di medine iz der iker un der klal fun ale medines*).[47] This interpretation gains further support in Naḥman's "hints" (*remazim*) appended to the tale, in which he discusses a "landmark [*tsiyun*] of each state where everyone congregates," perhaps a flag or a governmental building, and "the city of our assemblies" (*kiryat mo'adenu*), a city that serves as a center, two expressions that thematize the idea of political centralization.[48] According to the first hypothesis of the wise man, this essence of the state is its centralization. The states are governed from the center, where a clown-like ruler, an emperor or a tsar, "is laughing; he clowns and pulls all the pranks of that land."

The following passage, which depicts the wise man's encounter with the state's legal system, further supports the association between the unknown land and the audience's immediate political reality: "The wise man . . . saw that . . . the state was shot through with lies . . . When one comes to plead with the magistrate, it is full of lies, and they take bribes. One goes to a higher court [*sond*], and there, it is also all lies . . . until one comes to the Senate."[49]

According to this passage, the state has three courts: a district court (magistrate), a higher court, and a supreme court (Senate). This important piece of information, which points to a specific historical and political context, has been overlooked by all modern scholars of the tale. The tripartite legal system described in this passage reflects the reforms of the legal system in partitioned Poland. In Russia, Catherine the Great's legal reform of the administration of the provinces, promulgated on November 7, 1775, homogenized the state's legal system. According to this statute, townsmen were subject to a hierarchical legal system that included a district magistrate, a gubernia (provincial) magistrate, and the Senate, a superior land court. In the wake of Poland's second partition in 1793, this system was gradually implemented in the annexed Polish territories.[50] This context is important for how we read the story. If, for example, Naḥman had told this story before the Polish town of Międzybóż fell under Russian rule (1793), it would have fallen flat, since this legal procedure would have been completely foreign to his listeners, who, as residents of private estates, had no access to higher courts.[51]

In principle, the centralization of the legal system in the Polish lands harbored the promise of greater justice. Following the centralization of the imperial legal system, Jews residing in noble estates across the Polish lands took advantage of this new access, appealing their cases in higher courts. For example, in 1802, the year Naḥman moved to Bratslav, some of the wealthiest families in the district, including the Nusimovich family from Nemirov (Polish: Niemirów; currently Nemyriv, Ukraine), took advantage of these new legal provisions, appealing in the district and provincial court against their town's owner, the Potocki family.[52] According to "The Humble King," this was a false hope. The state is inherently immoral, governed by an unjust ruler who "pulls all the pranks of that land." From the district court up to the Supreme Court, they are all corrupt.

FROM POLITICS TO THEOLOGY

Once the wise man deduced the essence of the state, he proceeded to meet with "the king himself." Unlike the ruler, who operates from the center of the capital city, the humble king hides behind a curtain, far from the kingdom whose lies he "cannot stand." As Green and Mark have substantiated, there is ample evidence to suggest that the humble king is God: the image of a king revealing or hiding his face is a recognizable marker of God's concealment or revelation of himself in kabbalistic imagery; the shrinking of the king is a dramatization of *tsimtsum*, the kabbalistic concept of God's contraction; and the description of the seal of the humble king relies on the description of God at the beginning of the Amidah prayer.[53] At this point, the possibility of suspending the theological interpretation collapses. This king is the King of Kings.

Most scholarly attention to this tale has focused on this final episode. For this reason, I limit myself to commenting on only one aspect of the conclusion, namely, the way it comments on contemporaneous Russian political tropes. The conclusion reveals a crucial piece of information: the humble king is nothing like the state he governs. If the state is corrupt, the humble king is a "man of truth." In making a distinction between the bureaucracy and the king, the tale rehearses a widely documented trope in the popular Russian political discourse: popular monarchism.[54]

According to historian Maureen Perrie, Russian folktales imagined the benevolent Tsar as completely removed from the rampant corruption among state officials. For example, folktales about Ivan the Terrible portrayed the Tsar as the only protector of the people, operating alone in a deeply corrupt state. These tales, writes Perrie, pit the honest, noble Tsar against "the villains . . . the boyars and voyevody—they are acquisitive, take bribes, and cheat the treasury."[55] There is evidence of a similar political vision among some of Naḥman's contemporary Hasidic leaders, for example, in the correspondence of Shneur Zalman of Liady.[56] "The Humble King" subverts this idea. The flesh-and-blood ruler, the king, is shown to be as corrupt as the state's judges and bureaucrats. Only the humble king, God, is just.

The final paragraph of "The Humble King" contains no linguistic indication of a shift to future events. Similar to all the canonical tales, it appears to be part of the same temporal continuum that is narrated in the past tense. There is evidence that Naḥman's students, when hearing him recount his tales, had a difficult time discerning between stories that took place in the past and the mystical use of the past tense as a reference to the messianic future.[57] In a private letter, Nathan Sternhartz instructed to interpret the conclusion of "The Loss of the Princess" as a future event, narrated in the past tense: "Even though it was told [as if] it were a tale that had already happened . . . [it] is referring to the future."[58] One has a sense that this is the case with the conclusion of "The Humble King" as well.

A secretive Bratslav tradition of Naḥman's 1806 messianic prophecy, recorded in Avraham Ḥazan's 1935 *'Avaneha barzel*, further supports this reading: "During our Rebbe's journey from Ładyżyn to Bratslav, some Cossacks passed us, and our Rebbe began to tell us of Russia and what would transpire until the coming of our redeemer and from then until the resurrection of the dead."[59] According to this source, Naḥman gave a speech that opened with the political situation in Russia in 1806 and ended with the resurrection of the dead, connecting contemporary politics with redemption. This relationship between political and eschatological events, I argue, is the key for interpreting "The Humble King," which also opens with "Russia," a political entity, and extends to the "coming of our redeemer," only in a coded manner.[60] In his tales, I argue, Naḥman structured contemporary politics and future eschatological events within a homogeneous narrative frame. In so doing, Naḥman sought to encourage his believers to interpret familiar political forms as a key to understanding the divine rule of the world and to envision the messianic era as a seamless succession of the prevailing order.

NAḤMAN IN BRATSLAV

"The Humble King," this chapter has argued so far, defamiliarizes the political reality in the Polish lands under Russian rule, offering a narrative that defers the promise of justice to the world to come. The rest of the chapter shows that the tale may have gestured not only toward Russia but more specifically toward the town of Bratslav, where Naḥman resided between 1802 and 1807. As I demonstrate, the tale offers several clues that point to Bratslav and its surroundings while engaging with the town's special status both in Naḥman's theology and within the Russian administrative hierarchy.

Bratslav occupies a special place in Naḥman's theology. After moving there, in the summer of 1802, he declared, "Today we have planted Bratslav Hasidim! This name will never disappear, for our people will ever be named after the town of Bratslav," ensuring that the community of followers would forever bear the town's name. "In the future," he prophesied, "the entire world will become Bratslav Ḥasidim" (*vet di gantse velt zayn braslaver khsidim*), and Bratslav would become "the [most prominent] manufactory of

Jewishness (*di fabrik fun yidishkayt*)."[61] "The Humble King" was told in early 1807, a short while before he relocated from Bratslav, and offers, as I show, one of his final reflections on this chapter in his theological biography.

The tale contains at least two clusters of textual clues that, I argue, gesture toward Bratslav: the physical landscape and the juridical system. The wise man accesses the foreign land through a "big swamp [with] only one narrow path and on the path only one man can walk at a time."[62] According to the 1806 cartographical survey of Bratslav, to enter the town from the north or from the east—from Haisyn or Ladyzhyn (both currently in Ukraine), Naḥman's preferred route—one had to cross the swampy Bug River through a narrow bridge (figs. 5 and 6).[63] In winter, parties of people had to use a ferry, a practice that continued well into the twentieth century.[64] The passage, according to "The Humble King," is protected by cannon. In the first decade of the nineteenth century, the Russian army stationed cannon in Bratslav.[65]

FIGURE 5 Napoleon Orda (1807–1883), *Bracław rzeka Boh* [Bratslav, the Bug River], 1871–73. The town of Bratslav is visible on the right side of the image. From *Napoleon Orda, III-r.a. 2938 (teka Podolia), National Museum of Poland.* Image courtesy of the National Museum of Poland, Kraków.

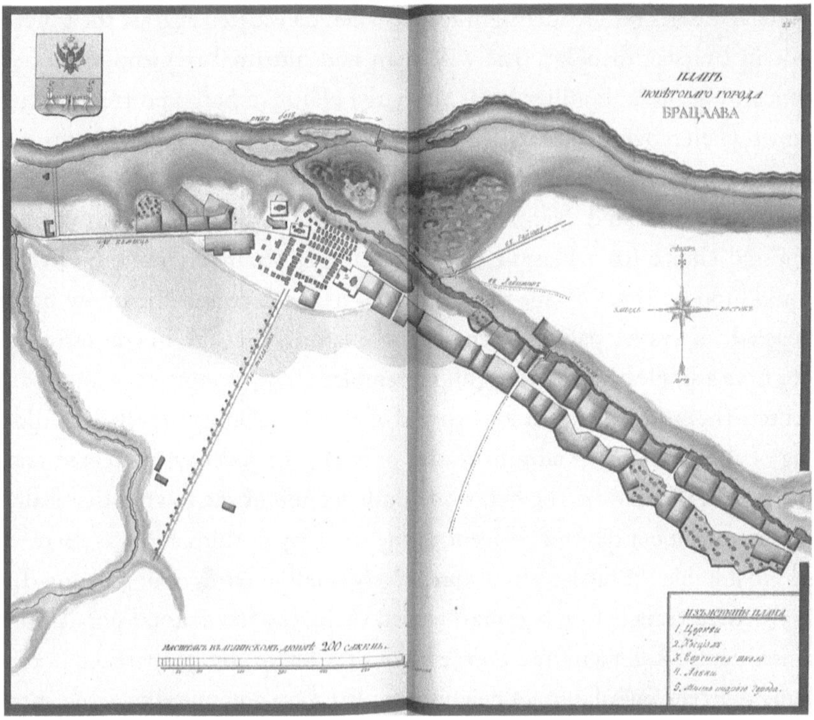

FIGURE 6 Bratslav, c. 1799. From *Podolia 1806 Land Survey*, OP F.IV.605, Russian National Library Archives, St. Petersburg.

The second set of clues relates to the status of Bratslav in the Russian imperial geography. Once the wise man ventures into the foreign kingdom, he finds himself in an administrative center, a town with a magistrate, which suggests that this is a royal town (district courts were erected on state-owned property), as well as a district capital (district courts were located in the district capital).[66] Bratslav was both a royal town and the capital of the Bratslav district, "a town that contains all towns," the only district capital and the only royal town in which Naḥman ever resided.

The immediate effect of this rhetorical move, connecting the tale to Bratslav and its surrounding, is easy to recover. Telling a legend about a distant land that is an allegory not just of Russia, but also of Bratslav, the location of Naḥman's court, surely intensified the tale's defamiliarization conceit and heightened the audience's surprise upon realizing how familiar, are, in fact, these supposedly foreign landscapes. However, I argue, the tale's allusion to

Bratslav carries far broader significance when considered against the town's role in Bratslav theology. The wise man had nurtured tremendous hopes concerning the unfamiliar land. Similarly, Naḥman harbored tremendous hopes when moving to Bratslav.[67] The question, then, is, What did Naḥman encounter when he relocated to this town?

On the one hand, Naḥman's choice to move to Bratslav in 1802 was an unusual choice for a Hasidic leader looking to secure a community that could support him.[68] While the nearest towns, Tulczyn and Niemirów, both boasted impressive palaces of the Potocki family, Bratslav, in contrast, did not have a single brick building and resembled a village more than an urban center. The entire town was constructed of wood, including the official building of the *starosta* (the administrative official), the government center, and the seat of the mayor. The old, stone-built section of the town, historically the more opulent quarter adjacent to the river, lay in ruins and was deemed uninhabitable.[69] Bratslav was also relatively small in terms of population. In 1799, three years before Naḥman settled there, the town's total population amounted to 846 men (494 non-Jews and 352 Jews). For comparison, in the same year, the population of neighboring Vinnitsa amounted to 3,460 men (2,197 non-Jews and 1,263 Jews).[70] The Jewish community of Bratslav was also relatively poor, which surely limited Naḥman's financial means while he resided there.[71] This is the Bratslav Naḥman encountered: a poor, sparsely populated, and desolate town whose glory days were behind it. However, he also found something else: a useful source of political imagination for his newly formed court, which would enable him to elevate Bratslav above all rival Hasidic centers. This small, underpopulated, half-ruined town was endowed with a particular significance in the Russian imperial administration. Catherine's Provincial Reorganization (1775) and Charter to the Towns (1785) had created district towns in each gubernia "as the first point of contact between the Russian government and its subjects," to cite Curtis Murphy. As Murphy showed, the state struggled to locate suitable district capitals, and as a result, it was often the case that new official district centers were actually significantly poorer, less developed, and less populated than adjacent private towns.[72] Bratslav represented a radical example of such discrepancy between an imperial role and lack of urban development. During 1795–1797, this tiny town of roughly eight hundred people was designated the capital of the vast

Bratslav viceroyalty (Russian: *namestnichestvo*). It thus presided over a population a thousandfold greater than itself—more than eight hundred thousand persons.[73] Since the town was hardly fit to fulfill such an exceptionally prominent role—not possessing, as previously mentioned, a single brick building suitable for an administrative center—some of its bureaucratic services were transferred to nearby Vinnitsa. In 1797 the Bratslav viceroyalty was abolished, and Bratslav was annexed to Podolia. Nonetheless, Bratslav continued to hold significant status as the district capital (Russian: *uyezdnyi gorod*) of the Bratslav district (*uyezd*). In parallel to these developments, in April 1795, Bratslav was designated the symbolic capital of the Orthodox diocese of Bratslav and Podolia, subsequently renamed in 1799 the Eparchy of Podolia and Bratslav. Due to Bratslav's limited size, however, the eparchial cathedral was actually located in Kamenets Podol'skii (now Kamianets-Podilskyi in Ukraine).[74]

By the time Naḥman settled in Bratslav in 1802, then, the town had gained a certain renown for its role as the administrative center of the Bratslav district, as well as its recent history as the capital of the entire Bratslav viceroyalty, a tiny head presiding over a gigantic body, so to speak. Bratslav may have been significantly poorer and smaller than the two adjacent private towns, Tulczyn and Niemirów, but it nonetheless took precedence over both on the imperial administrative ladder. Furthermore, Bratslav retained authority, albeit symbolic, over all Orthodox churches in Podolia. This circumstance no doubt furnished an attractive image to the newly established Bratslav Hasidic court, a small group that aspired to assume leadership of the entire Jewish world. According to Green, "Bratslav is depicted in Naḥman's teachings from this period as a new Holy Land, or a new Jerusalem . . . the new capital of the Hasidic universe, and thus, by extension, the new center of the world."[75] In this respect, the idea of a district capital and eparchy's capital dovetails with the notion of Bratslav as a Hasidic capital. If the Russian state could bestow upon the poor, unassuming town of Bratslav the lofty status of an administrative capital, Naḥman was able to sanctify Bratslav, rending it into a new land, or, in Naḥman's own words, a "world built anew" (*nivna 'olam meḥadash*).[76] These qualities of Bratslav, a town that was both poor and underpopulated, and at the same time endowed with tremendous symbolic meaning and proximity to the Russian state, I argue, were some of the "awesome secrets and deeper meanings" to this choice of Bratslav as a place to live that Nathan Sternhartz alluded to.[77]

"The Humble King" thus preserved some aspects of Naḥman's initial encounter with the town of Bratslav, for example, the idea that Bratslav was a new territory. When Naḥman transferred his court to Bratslav in 1802, he ventured outside of the familiar world of Jewish life under noble rule to a district town administered directly by the Russian state. While Naḥman had been a subject of Russia since 1793, the move to Bratslav occasioned an encounter with the Russian Empire, its symbols, and its bureaucracy on a much greater scale. "Until now," he reflected on his move to Bratslav, "I have dwelt alone, outside of the camp" (*miḥuts la-maḥane*).[78] In this respect, this was a move to an uncharted territory, a foreign land, an opportunity to learn something new about the essence of the state. At the same time, "The Humble King" subverts the vision of the state found in the theology Naḥman developed around the time he settled in Bratslav, which linked physical proximity to the Russian authorities with a spiritual capacity to alter the Russian policy toward the Jews. Before settling in Bratslav, Naḥman delivered a teaching addressing the link between symbolic and concrete proximity to Russian imperial authority. Speaking to his students, Naḥman compared the need to know where to direct one's prayers to the importance of bringing a legal case before the proper divine tribunal, emphasizing the significance of the provincial capitals:

> It is like when a person is being sued in the Kiev gubernia, but he hires an advocate (*to'en*) called piliptent [i.e., Polish and Russian for "plenipotentiary"] in Kamenets [Podol'skii]. Similarly, one cannot appeal for redemption [*pidyon*] without knowing in which [heavenly] court the case will be heard.[79]

This rare example in which Naḥman openly discusses the nature of the Russian administration reflects an awareness of the imperial governmental structure. If one is sued in Kiev gubernia, the province governing Naḥman's then residence of Zlatopol, it would be inappropriate and of no avail to hire a lawyer in Kamenets Podol'skii, the capital of Podolia. It is the same logic, I argue, that inspired Naḥman to view his move to Bratslav as a gateway to greater spiritual influence on Russian politics. Some of the sermons Naḥman gave immediately after his relocation to Bratslav betray a sense of privileged proximity to the Russian state. Naḥman spoke of a symbolic pact with Russia, compared himself to Mordechai and Esther serving in the Persian court, discussed the importance of gaining information concerning Russian legislation, and spoke about his ability to influence the budding conscription law.[80] Taken together, these teachings reflect both the degree of Naḥman's awareness of the Russian bureaucratic and legal systems and, I propose, his mindset when appealing Russian policies through prayer while in Bratslav. It is worth noting that the association between residency in an administrative capital and the ability to influence Russian politics was anchored in governmental policies. Jewish leaders residing in Russian administrative centers enjoyed privileged access to information about governmental regulations affecting Jews.[81] In other words, Naḥman's decision to reside in Bratslav had, alongside its symbolic and theological significance, tangible implications for his access to Russian politics.

Naḥman's enthusiasm for Bratslav as a new capital of Hasidism eventually waned. In the spring of 1807, he announced in a letter to his students that he had "wearied of living in Bratslav due to the many troubles and misadventures that had befallen [him]."[82] It was around the same time that Naḥman recounted "The Humble King," the last story he told during his Bratslav period. Thus, the tale may reflect Naḥman's attitude toward Bratslav as he was preparing to relocate elsewhere. According to the tale, the district capital, "the city that contains all the cities," may offer a connection to the capital city, to the heart of Russian politics. However, ultimately, this supposedly privileged position on the imperial map carries little significance, since, no matter where one is located, the entire state is corrupt, "shot through with lies," and its flesh-and-blood ruler is a vicious clown.

CONCLUSION: VIEW OF THE WORLD FROM THE BRATSLAV COURT

In this chapter, I have argued that Naḥman of Bratslav expanded the conventionalized metaphor of God as king in his tales, experimenting with novel political vocabulary and different modes of allegorization as a means to crystallize his theological message. Drawing on the folktale trope of simplified state apparatuses and governmental systems allowed Naḥman to convey his understanding of the divine governance of the world and the way it relates to human governance. Thus, to fully appreciate the tales' theological message, we need to recover their political dimension in its historical and experiential specificity. To conclude, I share one final reflection on how this insight contributes to our understanding of the entire canon of tales.

My analysis of "The Humble King," suggests that the tale may allude to Naḥman's project of establishing a court in Bratslav. In many respects, Naḥman's turn to storytelling is coterminous with his Bratslav period, a matter that requires additional scholarly attention.[83] It was during his final year of residence in Bratslav (1806–1807) that Naḥman told his first tale, "The Loss of the Princess," once on his way from Bratslav and a second time in the town itself.[84] During his Bratslav period, Naḥman told seven of his thirteen canonical tales, concluding with "The Humble King."[85] The Bratslav context is, therefore, central not only for the interpretation of "The Humble King" but also for Naḥman's storytelling project as a whole. Studying the group of Bratslav tales elucidates the rationale behind Naḥman's choice to focus on specific political forms at different junctures. It may explain why in his "The Loss of the Princess" Naḥman chose to look nostalgically at the political past and what led him to reflect on the potentiality of Jewish intervention in state politics in "The King Who Decreed Conversion," and, finally, which events prompted him to reject this possibility in favor of retributive divine justice in "The Humble King."

Finally, I argue that in reconstructing Naḥman's pan-European political experience as it was refracted through his residence in Bratslav, we should also consider Bratslav's proximity to Tulczyn. As the map of Bratslav shows (see fig. 6), Tulczyn was the next town over, and the distance between the Hasidic court in Bratslav and the Potocki court was a matter of sixteen versts (ten miles), three hours on foot, less than two hours in a carriage (fig. 7).[86] After departing Zlatopol in 1802, Naḥman settled first in Tulczyn. From there, with the help of his uncle Barukh of Międzybórz, he established his court in Bratslav.[87] Tulczyn, with its opulent palaces, vibrant Polish court, and the physical remnants of the old Polish-Lithuanian Commonwealth, may have symbolized for Naḥman the world that existed before the partitions and the Napoleonic Wars. In "The King's Son and the Maidservant's Son Who Were Switched," Naḥman portrayed a sculpture of "a man standing by the garden," and above which was a "tablet, and on it was inscribed that this man had been king several hundred years ago. And in the days of this king there had been peace."[88] This image of a sculpture of a king, serving as a vestige of a bygone era, is reminiscent of a well-known local attraction in Tulczyn. Along the road leading to the Potocki palace garden, La Roche, there once stood a dilapidated statue of Stanisław August, the last Polish king, bearing a plaque. By the 1840s, only two words of the original inscription would have remained: "Stanisław, Szczęśliwie" (Stanisław, happily).[89] Thus, the road connecting Tulczyn and Bratslav also functioned, symbolically, as a route connecting between the ever-receding past associated with the Polish-Lithuanian Commonwealth and the present and future rule of the Russian Empire.

Finally, Naḥman's residence in Bratslav afforded him direct visual observation of nobles from across Europe who had fled the French Revolution and the Napoleonic campaigns. Bratslav and Tulczyn were both located on the main postal road connecting Radziwiłłów (now Radyvyliv in Ukraine) in the northwest to Odessa in the southeast. All passengers traveling to

FIGURE 7 Pre–World War I photograph showing the road connecting Tulczyn and Bratslav. From *Tulczyn, Podole, Droga do Bracławia.* Photochemigraficzny B. Wierzbicki i S-ka, Warsaw, 1907(?).

Tulczyn from the north had to cross through Bratslav before reaching the Potocki palace.[90] From the outskirts of his town, Naḥman could view European rulers, princes, and princesses, all traveling to the Potocki court and passing through Bratslav with their luxurious chariots. During his residence in Bratslav, this parochial town in the easternmost region of Europe, Podolia, had a front seat to the most recent upheavals in European politics. When in 1806 Naḥman told his followers a tale about "The Loss of the Princess"—featuring a princess kidnapped by evil forces and the viceroy who traveled far and wide to save her—he was not merely spinning imaginative plots about far-off kingdoms but also alluding to political events unfolding along the road that connected the Potocki court in Tulczyn with his own Hasidic court in Bratslav.

FOUR

Discipline and Publish

The Hebrew Epistolary Novel and Other Intelligence Technologies, 1815–1845

For truth now came to be seen as something that will not reveal itself unless it is pursued through the clandestine methods of the secret police . . . Truth cannot be seen directly, it must be spied out.[1]

[ANDREAS GLAESER, *POLITICAL EPISTEMICS*, 2011]

Be advised that you are being prepared to make public matters that are of the utmost secrecy.[2]

[JOSEPH PERL, *REVEALER OF SECRETS*, 1815]

THE PRECEDING TWO CHAPTERS INVESTIGATED how Jews negotiated the centralization of the legal system across the Polish lands, and responded to the claims advanced by the new regimes, which identified law with justice. This final chapter traces the transformation of the maskilic conception of the centralized state in the aftermath of the Napoleonic Wars. As a new policing system was gradually taking shape, I contend, maskilim actively sought to participate in the state's surveillance apparatus, collaborating with the secret police and rendering in-group information about the Jewish community accessible to the authorities. Maskilic prose, I further argue, also sought to partake in this project, reproducing the gaze of the secret police for the Jewish readership therby training its audience to internalize and reproduce a mode of reading modeled on state surveillance.

FROM SURVEY TO SURVEILLANCE

The introduction to this book explored how, in the wake of the partitions of Poland, the local populations encountered a new kind of polity, the information state. In order to strengthen their control of the new Polish territories, the partitioning empires employed new technologies of information production, of measurement, survey, and counting, to produce knowledge about the local populations. The Napoleonic Wars (1803–1815) occasioned a new "information order," to adopt Christopher Bayly's term, a further expansion of the states' project to collect information on their subjects.[3] The Austrian and the Russian authorities, worried about an imminent revolution, started spying on their own residents, rather than on their enemies, moving from survey to surveillance, from mapping out lands to mapping out people's minds.

One way to demonstrate this shift is to follow the meaning of the term "police," *Polizei*, itself. When, in the wake of Poland's first partition, Joseph II asserted that "good governance must be based on knowledge of facts," these facts were quantitative, numerable.[4] The reigning political doctrine, cameralism, associated stabilization and optimization of governance with the maximization of state revenues, and, accordingly, the new administration of the Polish territories was tasked with providing statistical information to create an inventory of the newly acquired wealth of the imperial state: how many people live in such and such township, how many acres of land, how much livestock, how many acres of forest.[5] The collection of this information and its regulation was called, in the eighteenth-century political vocabulary, "policing." The "police" was not a law enforcement institution, but rather a much larger state project of regulating social and economic activities. This approach to governance was in vogue not only in Austria. Russia was also, to adopt Marc Raeff's formulation, a "well ordered Police State." Catherine the Great, a Prussian princess, was invested in importing cameralist state regulation, making Russia a state of "good police," or good order. In a series of reforms, she implemented cameralist and mercantilist views, reforming her domestic economic policy accordingly.[6]

The last two decades of the eighteenth century saw the emergence of a new meaning of "police," not only as a general project of the state but also as a concrete imperial institution responsible for the state's internal security.[7] In 1780, Catherine the Great, inspired by a meeting with Joseph II, published a memorandum for the creation of a centralized imperial police, whose role was to enforce "good order": to superintend trade and street commerce, to enforce the separation of sexes in public baths, and also to inspect the arrival and departure of foreigners.[8] In Austria, in 1789, Joseph II inaugurated an imperial police ministry. The concept of state policing, which was formerly a matter of political theorists, was translated into a formal state institution. This new form of policing on the imperial level entailed new forms of production of knowledge and new concepts of political optics.[9]

The imperial interest in political surveillance intensified during the Napoleonic Wars, when the Austrian and the Russian authorities, worried about an imminent revolution, started spying on their own residents. Within a few years, both Austria and Russia developed new and intrusive policing practices, which involved collecting information about their residents' private conversations, personal communications, and letter exchange. In the Habsburg Monarchy, the state was interested in knowing "what the general public is saying about the Emperor and his government."[10] Meanwhile, across the border, in 1807 the Russian Empire established a Committee of Public Safety, collecting information about "rumors concerning the restoration of Poland" and "insults to the Tsar."[11] In times of political instability, the residents of partitioned Poland came to be of particular interest to both the Russian and the Austrian police.

RECASTING SUSPICION: POLICING POLISH JEWS BETWEEN CRIMINALITY AND POLITICAL LOYALTY

Whereas the emergence of the political police during the Napoleonic Wars is the subject of robust scholarship, relatively little attention has been paid to the brief yet significant moment when Galician Jews became a target of its surveillance. This section demonstrates how Polish Jews, alongside Poles, were increasingly associated with pro-Napoleonic sympathies and, as a result, came to be perceived as potential threats to the state.

The surveillance of the Polish nobility dates back to the dissolution of the commonwealth. Following the Second Partition, Polish nobles were actively involved in organizing military campaigns, hoping to regain political independence. In March 1794, Tadeusz Kościuszko (1746–1817) announced in Kraków a general uprising. In 1797, twenty thousand Poles joined the Polish legions, which were formed in Italy under the aegis of the French. Some of the political aspirations of these Polish soldiers were captured in the song of the Polish legions in Italy, "Pieśń Legionów Polskich we Włoszech," which is today Poland's national anthem (with slight modifications):

> Poland is not dead yet
> So long as we live
> What the alien power has seized
> We will recapture with a sword . . .
> Bonaparte has given us the example
> Of how we should prevail.
>
> [*Jeszcze Polska nie umarła / Kiedy my żyjemy / Co nam obca moc wydarła / Szablą odbijemy . . . Dał nam przykład Bonaparte / Jak zwyciężać mamy*][12]

In light of the Kościuszko uprising, the formation of the Polish legions and the spread of slogans such as "Poland is not dead," it is easy to understand why the Russian police suspected Polish nobles residing in Russia of circulating rumors about the restoration of Poland's independence. Similarly, the governor of Galicia, Count Joseph Brigido (1733–1817), warned that the "Poles would revolt against the Habsburg dynasty and seek to reestablish an independent Poland."[13] In contrast, Polish Jews were not regarded as requiring systematic surveillance. In the aftermath of Poland's partition, the Austrian police were interested in Polish Jews not because they were suspected of any antigovernmental activity, but because they were perceived as predisposed to criminal activity. The head of the Galician Police, Daniel von Halama, deemed the entire Jewish population of Galicia dangerous, as they were prone, according to him, to be involved in "usury, fraud, mendicancy and secret theft" (*Wucher, Betrug, Betteln und heimlicher Dieberei*) and, for this reason, were closely monitored by the police.[14] At the same time, the Austrian police did not associate Jews with any form of political motivation.

For example, in another report, Von Halama complained that Galician Jews were so numerous "there seems to be a wish to make Galicia a Jewish kingdom."[15] In this context, the notion of a Jewish aspiration to political autonomy was regarded as absurdity, a laughing matter. This would change very quickly. Within less than a decade, during the Napoleonic Wars, Austrian bureaucrats would consider the prospects of Jewish political autonomy under Napoléon's aegis as a very serious concern.

On May 22, 1799, in the course of Napoléon's campaign in Palestine and Egypt, *Le Moniteur Universel* in Paris reported that Bonaparte had issued a proclamation calling upon the Jews of Asia and Africa to gather under his flag with the aim of reestablishing ancient Jerusalem.[16] This communiqué has never been found—some suspect it never existed—and is usually considered French propaganda. Be that as it may, news about Napoléon's plan to "reestablish ancient Jerusalem" circulated throughout the Jewish world, raising messianic expectations. The Jews of Lemberg, so it was claimed by a Hungarian newspaper, were so excited about the promised annexation of Palestine to the French Empire that they held meetings in cafés, planning their travel to Jerusalem.[17] The communications between Austrian officials reveal the extent to which this promise of a new Jewish state was taken seriously.[18]

In 1806, Napoléon's victorious campaign against Prussia brought the French army for the first time to the Polish lands. Upon entering Prussian Poland, Napoléon authorized the creation of the local Polish administration, which was interpreted by the local population as a first step toward Polish autonomy. The Poles as well as the Jews were also celebrating the entrance of the Polish-Napoleonic army. In Poznan, Jews were dancing and singing in the streets.[19] In neighboring Swarzędz, the local community welcomed Napoléon dressed in no less than Turkish military attire, expressing their willingness to join the forces of the new ruler, as François Guesnet argued.[20]

The same year, 1806, saw Napoléon's creation of a pan-European Jewish assembly, the Sanhedrin. As a result, in addition to the Poles, Jews were suddenly seen as a potentially subversive element, a people waiting to regain political liberation. In Italy, Napoléon was moving from city to city, opening the gates of Jewish ghettos, and allowing the Jewish population free access to all parts of the town. In Ancona, Jewish soldiers from the French army rushed to the Jewish Ghetto, crying, "Oh brother Israelites . . . we came to save you!" (*Nikhnesu ba'ir ha-tsarfatim . . . ve-nikhnesu ba-geto ve'amru le-ha-yehudim, 'aḥeynu bnei yisrael . . . hine 'anaḥnu b'anu lehoshi'a 'etkhem*).[21] These "dramatically staged liberations," argued Ronald Schechter, "publicized Napoleon's role as liberator [of the Jews]," and, analogously, propagated across Europe the image of Jews actively supporting the Napoleonic campaign.[22]

In Austria, Napoléon's call for European Jews to participate in the European Sanhedrin was interpreted as a revival of his 1799 promises regarding Jewish autonomy. The governor of Linz sent to Vienna information he had received about a French plan to occupy Jerusalem and to settle Jews in the city, where they will live freely according to the rules of the Talmud.[23] Klemens von Metternich (1773–1859), who was, at the time, the Austrian ambassador to France, warned that the establishment of the Sanhedrin was Napoléon's way of destabilizing European politics. Polish Jews, he argued, would see France as their homeland, pledging allegiance to Napoléon:

> The recent maneuvers with the Jews are worth considering, one wonders whether the [French] Emperor didn't conceive of the notion of a Jewish Sanhedrin to coincide with a military campaign, and he will surely present himself as a liberator of the Christians in Poland, a Messiah to the masses of Polish Jewry.[24]

Strikingly, Napoléon's pan-European policy pushed Austrian officials to position both the Poles and the Jews in the same political category, as a potential threat. The head of the Police Ministry, Thaddeus von Sumerau, likened Napoléon's tactics to enlisting the support of European Jewry to his support of the Freemasonry movement, which, Sumerau argued, Napoléon was planning to use as international secret police.

Napoléon's 1806 call for European Jews to participate in the Sanhedrin was a transformative moment in the Habsburg policy toward the Jews. For the first time, Jews across the empire were suspected of collaboration with the French. Secret police agents throughout the empire were tasked to estimate "what influence the news [about the Sanhedrin] had on the local Jewish community, specifically on the local teachers and Rabbis" (*welche Wirkung die diesfällige Nachricht im Allgemeinen auf die hierl[andige] Judenschaft vorzüglich aber auf die Rabbiner und Lehrer hervorgebracht*).[25] In addition, the communication between the empire's Jewish residents with Paris was intercepted, translated, and analyzed to detect possible relations between Habsburg Jews and the Napoleonic government. The same year, the Viennese authorities inquired of the governor of Galicia, Joseph Urmenyi, whether he believed the Jews in his crownland supported the French Sanhedrin. Urmenyi ruled out this option categorically. Galician Jews, he argued, were uneducated, provincial, and too conservative to grasp what was going on at the western front: "They are all, both Hasidic and Orthodox Jews, absolutely stupid, attached to their Torah and the Talmud" (*aussi bien les orthodoxes que les Hassidim sont absolument stupides et attachés à la Tora et au Talmud*).[26] According to Urmenyi, the only Jews who might pose a threat were those living in Brody, where, he pointed out, there was already a small community of educated Jews who were worldly enough to be in touch with their coreligionists in Paris. In 1806 it was acculturated Jews who were imagined posing a threat to the regime, not the Hasidim.

In 1809, Galicia was taken over by a Polish army, supported by Napoléon. Unlike the rest of Poland, Galician Jews faced a choice not between the existing government and an unfamiliar, western power, but rather between the Austrian government and the familiar Polish nobility. The meaning of political changes was not emancipation or reforms, but the possibility of returning to live exclusively under the rule of Polish landowners. In April, Napoléon's Polish army marched into Lemberg. Alexander Fredro, the Polish writer, was among the Polish forces, registering the popular support of both the local Polish nobility, as well as of the local Jewish residents:

> As I was going, I saw the Polish nobility, everywhere, ablaze with patriotic enthusiasm. Jews shouting: "Hurrah!" . . . The peasants were indifferent . . . And everywhere Germans, greeting us in Polish, bidding farewell in Polish.
>
> [*Jechałem, wszędzie szlachta patriotyzmem rozgorzała. Żydzi: "Wiwat!" krzyczący . . . , Chłopstwo obojętne . . . Wszędzie Niemcy . . . po polsku witali, po polsku żegnali.*][27]

"The political situation," noted the historian Markian Prokopovych, "was still uncertain, and the population rather tended to think that Napoleon would never be defeated . . . making a long-term investment in . . . a promising political outcome." Whether genuine or not, the Jewish support of the Napoleonic troops contributed to the Austrian view of Galician Jewry as politically suspect.[28]

When the Polish army entered Lemberg, the soldiers were warmly welcomed by the local Polish nobility and by the Jews. They were not alone: Austrian bureaucrats, who for the most part had remained behind, were also watching the scene. The very same bureaucrats returned to their offices only two months later, in June 1809, and reported that Jews had taken the "side of the Polish rebels."[29]

In 1811, two Lemberg Jews were investigated for offering lodging to the Polish general Jan Krukowiecki (1772–1850) during his stay in the city on a secret mission. The assumption behind this investigation was that the Jews were cognizant of the prominent identity of the general and collaborated with the Napoleonic Polish forces in hiding. These accusations were eventually dropped.[30] For Galician Jews, a decision to support a Polish general fighting for Napoléon in 1811 seems like a calculated risk. At this point, the Napoleonic Empire had reached the height of its expansion, encompassing territories from Spain in the west to the Duchy of Warsaw in the east, and governing a population of approximately forty-four million inhabitants.[31] The year 1812 also marked the failed Napoleonic campaign in Russia, a turning point that precipitated Napoléon's eventual downfall.

In Russia, in contrast, the 1812 Napoleonic campaign created a short-lived rapprochement between the imperial authorities and the Jewish population in the Polish territories. The wide support of the Russian army among the Jewish population during Napoléon's invasion changed the way Jews were viewed by the Russian bureaucracy. Whereas before the war, Jews had been seen as a suspicious, foreign element, in the wake of the war they came to be viewed as one of the more loyal ethnic groups in the Russian Polish territories and, as a result, won considerable governmental support. During the war, Jews were actively employed as spies for the Tsarist forces.[32] Paradoxically, the recruitment of Jews to the Russian secret police only further deepened Austrian suspicions of Galician Jews' involvement in subversive activities. In 1813, the Austrian authorities investigated the connections between Jewish merchants from Radzivilov, Russia (Polish: Radziwiłłów; today Radyvyliv, Ukraine) and the Jewish community of Brody, suspecting that the Jews of Radzivilov worked for the Russian intelligence services.[33] In April 1814, a Russian Jewish spy was caught and incarcerated in Lemberg, and several Galician Jews were interrogated on suspicions of collaborating with the Russian intelligence force.[34]

In March 1814, Napoléon abdicated the throne and was exiled to the island of Elba. The war was over, but the new political stereotype of Jews as politically suspect had a lasting effect. Publicly, at least, the Jewish community expressed its loyalty to the Austrian Crown. When, on June 29, 1814, cities across the Habsburg Empire, among them Lemberg, organized official festivities to mark the Paris armistice, the Jews played an integral part in the festivities. The celebrations embraced residents of the city of all stripes. Under the arch of triumph erected at the city center passed a long succession of representatives of the Ruthenian church, the Latin general seminary, the city's cloisters, the guilds, school students with their teachers, and municipal officials. In the synagogue, Ya'akov Ornstein, the *Kreis-Rabiner* (district rabbi), delivered a sermon, comparing Franz II's participation in the war to David's triumph over Goliath.[35] In the inner city, wealthy German residents hung large signs on their houses, wishing to express their loyalty to the emperor. Some of the very few Jewish house owners hurried to express their support as well: Menachem Schnayer attached to his wall two banners expressing communal Jewish support for the Austrian war effort: "Austria above all things, as it wills" (*Österreich über Alles, wenn es will*) and "Love—Jewish brothers" (*Liebe – israelitische Brüder*). A merchant named Gabriel Kaires likewise displayed a sign reading "Long live our much-beloved Emperor Francis I" (*Vivat! Es lebe unser vielgeliebter Kaiser Franz I*).[36] The ostensible gap between the suspicion of Jews as disloyal, on the one hand, and the Jewish participation in the celebrations, on the other hand, likely fueled distrust among the local population. As I show below, this tension also formed the historical backdrop for the emergence of the first modern literary text in Yiddish in Eastern Europe.

YIDDISH LITERATURE: A VIEW FROM THE GOVERNOR'S OFFICE

The year 1814 saw the publication of a curious work, a fictionalized Yiddish letter concerning the peace celebrations in Lemberg.[37] The work bears the lengthy German title *Schloime Klappzümbels treuherzige Beschreibung der von der Lemberger Judenschaft abgehalten wordenen letzten Friedensfeier – Seinem innig geliebten Freunde Hersch Schmeckpuedele als ein Denkmahl des dabei genossenen unvergesslichen Freudengefühls dargebracht* (Schloime Klapzümbels frank description of the peace celebrations of the Jewish community of Lemberg—given as a gift to his beloved friend Hersch Schmeckpüdle as a souvenir of his unforgettable happiness on that occasion).[38]

Schloime Klappzümbels is, for all intents and purposes, the first modern literary work in Yiddish to be published in Eastern Europe, and yet it has received very little scholarly attention. The one exception is a 1937 article by Filip Friedman.[39] In this article, Friedman speculates about the identity of the writer, Johann Eduard Sack, debating whether this is a Jewish enlightener assuming a Christian guise or—a hypothesis Friedman found more plausible—an Austrian who taught himself Yiddish. Friedman's intuitions were right. Sack (1776–1826), I have been able to ascertain, was indeed an Austrian, a bureaucrat working for Lemberg's *gubernium*, no less. According to governmental documents, Sack served as a kanzelist, a clerk, in the k.k. Gubernial-Expedits-Direkzion, the chancellery dealing with taxation.[40] Later in his life he became a *Gubernialrath* (councillor) in the town of Schmidt. Sack was a prolific author, a dramaturge, and a poet, yet he remained relatively obscure, and he is mentioned only in passing in German and Austrian literary lexicons.[41] Sack's professional identity as an Austrian writer, I show here, is central to the writing of this text.

How can we make sense of this text? Friedman himself was too cautious to provide any analysis or explanation. Dov Sadan, in turn, argued that the poem pertained to a genre he called *shpot lid*, or scorn poems, which were meant to ridicule Yiddish and, analogically, Yiddish speakers. At first blush, Sadan's argument is rather convincing. There is a long tradition both in German literature, as well as in Western Yiddish literature, in which linguistic expressions in idiomatic Yiddish are associated with pejorative qualities, with close-mindedness, for example, or with immoral behavior. The names of the characters, Klappzümbel and Schmeckpüdele, add to the sense that this is a parody, and what the author calls a "frank description of the peace celebrations" further strengthens the link between simplemindedness and folksy, colloquial Yiddish.

At first blush, Sack's poem can indeed appear as a joke at the expense of a simpleminded Jew and his limited perception of the political events in his town. Yet this interpretation remains ultimately unsatisfactory, as it fails to account for the text's political dimension—an exchange between two Galician Jews concerning Napoléon's defeat—and for the historical context in which it was written, a time of "state paranoia," to adopt Andreas Glaeser's term, which extended, as I have shown, to Galician Jews as well.[42] Recovering the political stakes of the poem hinges on two related questions: What were Polish Jews imagined to be writing about Napoléon in 1814, and in what ways does the fictionalized letter intervene in or challenge these expectations?[43]

Schloime Klappzümbels combines two texts—on the top of each page, the unrefined Yiddish of Schloime Klapzümbels, the narrator, describing "frankly," as the title of the piece promises, the succession of events since the news of the peace in Paris reached Lemberg. The bottom of each page, set apart in Gothic script, provides explanations of Yiddish for a German reader, focusing on words of Hebrew or Slavic origin and occasionally addressing local features for the "outside" reader, such as the topography or architecture of Lemberg.

Some contemporary Galician publications encountered significant challenges in addressing the Napoleonic Wars, carefully adapting their content to the prevailing censorship constraints. One conspicuous example is Shlomo Yehuda Rapoport 1814 essay intended to acquaint Hebrew readers with Napoléon's abdication and exile to Elba. Rapoport's book carried an exceptionally long title: *A description of the city of Paris its size, districts, the number of its inhabitants and their manners. Appended is a description of the island of Alba: its extent, its produce and climate, the number of its towns and fortresses, its population, its commerce . . .*[44] As the title suggests, the book offered only tangential information relevant to Napoléon's biography, without ever mentioning Bonaparte himself, let alone his defeat or abdication. This strange omission must have been a source of great frustration for the reader.

Schloime Klappzümbels, published the same year, navigated the same constraints far more successfully. Its most striking strategy lies in translating censorship limitations into a language of limited political awareness, a literary strategy that enabled Sack to engage fully and meaningfully with contemporary political tensions without ever addressing them overtly. For example, this is the opening paragraph, which aims to introduce to the reader the immediate historical context: Napoléon's abdication and the subsequent signing of the Paris armistice between France and the powers of the Sixth Coalition, including Austria:

> Just as David once loved Jonathan
> I love you my dear brother
> This is why, from this valley I pick up my pen
> And write to you what happened
> How the messenger came to us from Vienna
> In order [to announce] the peace [treaty]
> Following the governor's decree . . . in the [city main] square
> they set a [victory] arch
> high, up in the air
> to celebrate the return of our Emperor
> who brought peace home
>
> [*Wie Doowid Joonussen amohl / Lieb ech dich Brüder leiben, / Drüm thüt sec hooch oos diesem Thool / Haant mane Penne heiben / Und schraabt dir, woos sech hot gethün, / Wie die Stafett zü üns vün Wien Gekümmen weigen Scholem. / . . . es wird baam Platz /A grauisser, grauisser, Boigen . . . / Hoich in die Lüft gezoigen, / Noch dem Befaihl vüm Güverneer / Zü ünsers güten Kaiser Ehr' / Und Heim gebrachten Scholem*]

The Yiddish text foregrounds a simplified perception of the political context, reducing a historical event of international dimensions to the local geography of Lemberg and its surroundings. It refers to the physical topography of Lemberg, the valley in which it is situated, and to the triumphal arch in the town's main square. Absent, however, are the far more significant sites associated with the armistice: Fontainebleau, where Napoléon abdicated, and Paris, where the armistice was signed. The most distant place the letter writer is able to conjure is Vienna, the Habsburg capital. Similarly, the Yiddish text is also vague in respect to the political events it describes. The Napoleonic Wars are alluded to without explicit reference to Napoléon Bonaparte or to "war."[45] Klappzümbel's entire conceptual world is limited to Lemberg, Galicia, and the Austrian Empire. Politics, in this literary piece, is something that is never immediate but rather is always happening elsewhere, at a distance. Although Galicia was profoundly affected by the war and Lemberg came under Napoleonic rule, in *Schloime Klappzümbels* the conflict occurs elsewhere—in a distant place that has no direct impact on the lives of Lemberg's inhabitants.

In light of the widespread perception of Jews as supporters of Napoléon, one might expect the Yiddish text above to unfold as a drama of disloyalty. Since this was an internal communication between Jewish correspondents, one could plausibly have anticipated an expression of disappointment regarding Napoléon's downfall. This option, however, never materializes. As the reader gradually discovers, the Yiddish speaker possesses an unfaltering appreciation of the imperial ceremony. Not surprisingly, the manuscript that Filip Friedman discovered in the collections of the Austrian censor bore no marks or instructions for omissions.[46] Sack was thus able to compose a literary text that engages fully with the political discourse surrounding Jewish loyalty while simultaneously avoiding any expression that might provoke the censor.

The real drama lies in the German text, which introduces a higher register and a broader context. The German evolves from sporadic comments on the Yiddish into a full description of events in the celebrations, which illuminates the letter in light of the political context. For example, when the narrator describes the procession, he mentions in passing a portrait of the emperor with script in "High German." The Yiddish-speaking narrator is unable to decipher the text and, for this reason, is susceptible only to the visual elements of the celebrations. The footnotes in the German, which are, in this case, longer than the Yiddish, reveal the content of the script on the back of the portrait, making the reader privy to the concrete political message of the celebrations:

> The emperor's return, and the triumph of his banners,
> Brings great rejoicing to all his subjects;

Despite [differences in] clothing, morals, language, religion
One great people, only one nation.

[*Des Kaisers Rückkehr, und des Sieges seiner Fahnen,*
Erfreuen jubelnd sich, all' seine Untertanen;
Trotz Kleidung, Sitten, Sprache, Religion,
Ein Großes Volk, nur Eine Nazion.]

The German foregrounds in official language what the narrator performs as an obedient subject: a concept of political belonging that exceeds linguistic, religious, and ethnic differences. It is worth commenting that the use of the term *Nazion* in the Austrian context is rather unusual. According to the historian Arthur Haas, "the word nation could mean all sorts of things to the Austrian authorities of the Congress Era. It could refer to a large ethnic whole, or Kulturnation, such as the Italian, Polish or German 'nations,' or to a smaller organized ethnic or religious group such as the 'Serbian' or 'Illyrian nation.' However, it was generally considered as an anomaly to designate as a 'nation' a realm composed of several 'nations' such as the Ottoman or Habsburg."[47] Sack's unusual application of the term *Nazion* to refer to all residents of Lemberg alike goes hand in hand with the linguistic ideology of the text. As noted in chapter 2, 1814 saw Hebrew and Yiddish banned from court and public use, nullifying all documents in those languages. Jewish languages have a long history of being mistrusted in the Galician context: as early as 1781, Joseph II forbade the use of Hebrew or Yiddish in public and commercial communications, to "foster trust" among Jews and Christians.[48] In Bohemia, Austrian bureaucrats portrayed Yiddish as a "deckmantel," a cover for Jewish treachery and immoral practices.[49] In Germany, Gottfried Selig, a convert, published a study guide for Yiddish for bureaucrats, lawyers, courthouse and businessmen, since the use of Yiddish was imagined to allow deceitful practices both in business transactions and in court.[50]

In *Schloime Klappzümbels,* Sack is invested in presenting the local Yiddish dialect as perfectly legible for German speakers. While in the official discourse Yiddish was named the so-called Jewish language (*sogenannte jüdische Sprache*), Sack calls it specifically a "Galician-German-Jewish vernacular language" (*galizisch-deutsch-jüdische Volkssprache*), hierarchizing the Austrian-German and local Galician affinities of the "Jewish" component, presenting Yiddish as a German Galician dialect of an ethnic subgroup.

The most intriguing question—how an Austrian bureaucrat came to master Yiddish so well—is very difficult to establish. Joseph Errington, in his studies of colonial linguistics, has qualified imperial documentations of non-European languages as "opaque with respect to worlds of talk which they present in partial, written guises . . . offer[ing] few clear points of purchase for critical readings . . . back into the zones of colonial contact from which they emerged."[51] The colonial dictionaries of indigenous South Asian languages that Errington examined reflected an intensive and prolonged interaction between colonial linguists and the speakers of these languages. Unfortunately, one can only guess how, where, and when these interactions took place and what their content was. Similarly, Sack's poem is also "opaque with respect to the worlds of talk" that it represents, to adopt Errington's words. We don't know what the social setting of the interpersonal communication between Austrian bureaucrat and Jews was that led to the creation of this document. In this regard, Sack's knowledge of Yiddish indicates a direct connection with Yiddish speakers, just as Jan Potocki's familiarity with Ashkenazi Hebrew reflects his personal engagement with educated Eastern European Jews, as examined in the first chapter.

It is evident that Sack possessed sufficient fluency in Yiddish to render the local dialect in writing. But how did he acquire this proficiency? Did he eavesdrop on Yiddish conversations—and if so, whose? Was he able to speak Yiddish actively? Did he perhaps have access to documents written in Yiddish? The text provides a few clues concerning the degree of Sack's familiarity with the local Jewish community and, by extension, with its language. While Sack knew some of the surnames of the local economic elite (Rayces, Myses, Rosenthal, and Rapoport), he appears not to have known about the sermon in the Jewish synagogue and does not mention the name of Ya'akov Orenstein, the rabbi of Lemberg.[52] Similarly, while his Yiddish is fairly idiomatic, incorporating colloquial expressions such as "wie . . . der Saichel heist" (as logic [lit. the brain] dictates), he lacked knowledge of and correct terminology for religious matters. For example, Sack called the Jewish synagogue "synagog" instead of "shul," used the terms

"Jehova" and "Eloim [*sic*]" for God, a practice deemed religiously unacceptable among Jews, and, finally, referred to the rabbis who attended the synagogue "kimrim" (standard Yiddish: s. *koymer*, pl. *komrim*), a term that is reserved for Christian priests.

Building on this sparse information, we can safely exclude the possibility that Sack was a convert. Sack's interactions with Jews were most probably organized either around business or around governmental services. From the vocabulary used in the text, which relates to state procedures and local politics, it seems that Sack was drawing on his personal expertise in communicating with Jews on bureaucratic matters. It is tempting to place Sack's work in conversation with the Hebrew letters intercepted by the Austrians during the war; however, this does not seem to be the case. While the text is presented as a letter, the lack of formulaic opening and closure and other stylistic features of Yiddish or Hebrew letters suggest that Sack was familiar with Yiddish as a spoken language rather than in a written form. This impression of an oral rather than written knowledge of Yiddish is further reinforced by his accurate transliteration of the local dialect.

Schloime Klappzümbels could easily be dismissed as an anecdotal episode in the history of Jewish literature. Yiddish literature would not become a supranational project, and Austrian bureaucrats would continue to write reports, rather than poems, in Yiddish.[53] This work thus remains an exceptional instance in which a non-Jew attempted to write in Yiddish. Nevertheless, the episode of *Schloime Klappzümbels* offers important insights into the conditions under which Jewish literature was produced in the first half of the nineteenth century. In many respects, *Schloime Klappzümbels* continues some of the bureaucratic genres that were used to convey the political views of the local population, the so-called Stimmungsbericht, the reports on political "mood" of different ethnic groups. The Stimmungsbericht was part of a larger project of the state to "make sense" of its subjects, the so-called legibility project, an "attempt to make a society legible, to arrange the population in ways that simplified the classic state functions of taxation, conscription, and prevention of rebellion."[54] In this case, the fictionalized exchange between Jews was documented in full, as part of the efforts to render Galician Jewish internal communication subject to surveillance. Yet the information conveyed in the text itself suggests that such surveillance was, in fact, superfluous.

In his portrayal of Jewish political subjectship, Sack was not far removed from the governor of Galicia, Joseph Urmenyi's 1806 comment on traditional Jews as "too stupid" to follow Western politics. Yiddish, according to Sack, was only a vehicle to convey naive, unproblematic political concepts, and letter exchange among Jews was an occasion to express loyalty to the state. Sack published his book in 1814, the same year in which the first investigation into Galician Hasidism was already underway.[55] The community of maskilim, I now show, volunteered to provide insider knowledge, "affective knowledge," to borrow Christopher Bayly's term, to the imperial authorities. Jewish enlighteners projected wartime anxieties about Jewish disloyalty on internal differences within the Jewish community, and communication among Hasidism became the subject of suspicion, surveillance, and interception, both in secret police reports and in maskilic prose.[56]

REVEALING JEWISH SECRETS: JOSEPH PERL AND HIS *REVEALER OF SECRETS* (1819)

Sack's optimism in regard to the 1814 peace celebrations in Lemberg proved premature. A few months later, in February 1815, Napoléon escaped from his exile in Elba, returned to France, and took control of the government once again. Only in June 1815 was he finally defeated at Waterloo. Yet Napoléon's removal from Europe's political stage did not bring an end to imperial revolutionary anxieties. Rather, it marked the beginning of a new era of intensified surveillance and policing. After decades of war, European rulers were committed to reestablishing peace and stability and to restoring the old order. Fearing another revolution, they expanded their secret police networks. This "phantom terror," to borrow Adam Zamoyski's term, a fear of secret revolutionary movements, urged them to increase their spying on their own subjects.[57] Charles Sealsfield (pseud. Karl Anton Postl, 1793–1864) described in his 1828 memoir how Austria was contaminated with "aqua tofana," the most powerful poison: an oppressive government that suffocates the people's freedom of speech. The Austrian people, particularly the educated, are "dreading the crafty severity of their suspicious government." A new, pervasive surveillance system allowed the reigning emperor, Francis II, to monitor and police the empire's residents, suffocating any expression of intellectual and political freedom. "Every footman in a public house," this book claims, "is a salaried spy. There are spies paid to visit the taverns and hotels . . . Others will be seen in the Imperial library for the same purpose, or in the bookseller's shop, to inquire into the purchases made by the different persons." The surveillance system, the paragraph continues, is everywhere: "Thousands of secret spies are watching, not the foreigners, but the [emperor's] own subjects," in libraries, hotels, mass gatherings. Not only public spaces are constantly scrutinized, according to this book, but also personal letters, "if the least suspicious, are opened; and so little pains are taken to conceal this violation of public faith, that the seal of the post-office is not seldom added to that of the writer."[58] Sealsfield's account, while significantly exaggerated, captures the spirit of the time, a growing intrusion of the state into its residents' private lives, as well as public awareness of these repressive measures. In 1815, a local branch of the Secret Police Services was established in Galicia, whose duty was to "inspect the lands neighboring Galicia, the connections between the residents of these lands and the population of Galicia, and of people that pass through Galicia."[59] The historians Alan Sked and Peter Judson have questioned whether these new political measures had any significant effect on the general population, challenging the labeling of Austria as "a police state," given its modest number of employees, constant lack of financial resources, and very limited reach among most of the nonurban population.[60] If the Austrian secret police possessed only limited knowledge of the German-speaking rural population, their understanding of the Jewish population was even more restricted. How, then, could they have gained access to clandestine internal Jewish communication, and even if they had, how could they have interpreted it intelligibly?

The correspondence of high-ranking Austrian bureaucrats that I analyzed earlier—for example, the letters of the governor in Galicia, Joseph Urmenyi, or the head of the Galicia police, Daniel von Halama—reveals a markedly crude, simplistic, and ultimately misguided analysis of Galician Jewish society. In nineteenth-century colonial India, Christopher Bayly argued, the British power had a very limited knowledge of the Indian society. This changed with the creation of what he called "moral communities," communities of Indians acculturated into English culture, converts, offspring of mixed marriages, who aspired to serve as a bridge between the colonized community and the colonizers, not for financial profit, but for moral, ethical reasons, for what they believed was the betterment of Indian society. These moral communities provided insider information to the colonial authorities, deep knowledge that helped the British have a nuanced understanding of Indian society.

Similarly, in Austria, where, as Pieter Judson observed, the regime "could rarely match its ambitions with appropriate measures . . . when it came to policing," Jewish enlighteners stepped in to compensate for the administrative deficiencies.[61] The Galician maskilim constituted a "moral community" and provided insider information about the Jewish population to the Austrians.[62] Maskilim such as Joseph Perl (1773–1839), Yehuda Leib Mieses (1798–1831), and Shlomo Yehuda Rapoport (1786–1867) embraced a utopian political vision of a police state as the ultimate solution for the tensions within the Jewish community. They strove to take advantage of the increasing intrusion of the Austrian state into its residents' lives in order to shape the imperial policies in regard to the Jewish population according to their own ideology. To achieve this goal, they offered their services to the authorities as experts on Jewish matters, to provide insider knowledge to the Austrians. In so doing, they collaborated and competed with a larger network of Jewish "experts": Yiddish-speaking bureaucrats—like Johann Eduard Sack, censors of Jewish books, Jewish policemen, and Christian theologians, among others.[63]

In addition to his denunciation letters, Joseph Perl had another ambitious plan: to publicize his views on Hasidism among the wider German-reading audience in Europe. In 1816, Perl wrote an anti-Hasidic tract entitled *On the Essence of the Hasidic Sect according to its own writing, collected in 1816* (*Über das Wesen der Sekte Chasidim Aus Ihren Schriften gezogen Im Jahre 1816*). This anthology of Hasidic texts presented Hasidism as a revolutionary movement, drawing on the current political anxieties. These accusations apparently had some influence on Austrian bureaucrats, if briefly. For instance, in 1822, bureaucrats in Vienna went so far as to draw an explicit analogy between Hasidism and the secret revolutionary groups of Italian Carbonari.[64]

I have already introduced *On the Essence of the Hasidic Sect* in the second chapter. I return to it here, since it played a decisive role in the formation of Perl's first epistolary work, *The Revealer of Secrets* (Magele temirin). In December 1816, Perl sent the manuscript of *On the Essence of the Hasidic Sect* to be approved by the Austrian censorship. A few months later, the censor rejected its publication, arguing that it would not have any effect on the Jewish population, which did not read German, and would turn German enlighteners against the Jews.[65] In 1818, while still nurturing hopes to publish the German manuscript outside Austria, Perl sat down to write his own epistolary novel, the *Revealer of Secrets* in Hebrew. Perl had his own, innovative notion of epistolarity, to adopt Janet Altman's term, and what it could mean in times of increased state surveillance.[66] Much like Johann Eduard Sack four years earlier, Joseph Perl likewise engaged with the Habsburg regime of policing and surveillance. If, according to Sack, there was nothing to reveal, nothing secretive in private Jewish communication, then the *Revealer of Secrets,* by contrast, framed access to personal correspondence as an act of unveiling incriminating secrets. In so doing, this chapter argues, Perl aimed to train his readers to view Hasidism through the prism of the secret police, encouraging them to "spy out" the truths concealed in adherents' letters.

The Revealer of Secrets has already received ample scholarly attention.[67] The book, it was argued, was a parody of *Shivḥei ha-besht*—an "anti-*shivḥei ha-besht*" (*In Praise of the Ba'al Shem Tov*; 1811), a term that was coined by Jeremy Dauber and later developed by Yonatan Me'ir—an antihagiography that draws on an extensive library of Hasidic texts only to cast Hasidism in a murky light.[68] At the core of the book is a collection of letters exchanged among Hasidim from three Hasidic courts in Russia: "Dishpal" (a code name for Miedzybozh; today Medzhybizh, Ukraine), "Zolin" (Yiddish: Lozne; Polish: Łoźna, today Lyozna, Belarus), and "Aklo" (Yiddish: Olik; Polish: Ołyka, today Olyka, Ukraine). This sensational internal Hasidic correspondence reveals the misdeeds of the Hasidim as well as the increasing engagement of the state in the suppression of the movement.[69]

Strikingly, to date the work has not been analyzed within the context of the Napoleonic Wars or the broader European culture of policing and surveillance. Many scholars have taken note of the spying practices in the text but have interpreted them in a dehistoricized and decontextualized manner. This chapter aims to fill in this gap.

Although written only a few years after *Tales and Letters, The Revealer of Secrets* marks a sharp departure from the earlier work's central premise—the belief that legal knowledge would lead to its observance. "The Loss of the Prince" concludes with an appeal to inform the Jewish masses on the "laws and customs of the king," accompanied by a plea to the Austrian authorities to expel those Hasidim who, once they are made aware of the law, refuse to change their ways.[70] In the *Revealer of Secrets*, by contrast, the Hasidic followers are well versed in state laws and judicial institutions, fully aware that they are engaging in what they themselves call "criminal activity" (*ma'ase kriminal*), and yet they deliberately subvert the legal system.[71] As Dan Miron noted, the Hasidim "occasionally abide by state law when it works in their favor, for example, when they take advantage of Austrian extradition laws."[72] Thus, not only does legal knowledge fail to ensure compliance; the Hasidim in the book occasionally weaponize this knowledge as a means to advance their own objectives.

Thus, as the *Revealer of Secrets* testifies, by 1819 Joseph Perl had lost faith both in the reforming power of legal knowledge and in state law as a guarantor of justice. Instead, I argue, the work articulates Perl's growing belief in the necessity of a system of surveillance and policing directed at the Hasidic movement. This shift in perspective accounts for Perl's adoption of a different political framework in his depiction of the Hasidic movement in the *Revealer of Secrets*. Hasidism is no longer represented as a loosely organized group of fraudulent miracle workers, but as a conspiracy—a multiheaded clandestine movement that poses a threat to the very existence of the state. "The Loss of the Prince" focuses primarily on the political threat of a single powerful sorcerer. The Hasidic leader is depicted as a charismatic charlatan who associates with criminals and offers his magical powers in service of the opposition to the royal family. Appropriately, the remedy is both straightforward and individualized: once the sorcerer is imprisoned, the movement is effectively neutralized. In contrast, the *Revealer of Secrets* depicts the Hasidic movement as a network, a multitude of well-organized groups of conspirators. As Israel Davidson emphasized, the plot shifts focus away from the Hasidic leaders, the tsadikim, to their personal secretaries, reinforcing the impression of Hasidism not only as a charismatic religious movement but also as a shadowy secret society.[73] In this sense, the changes in the representation of the Hasidic movement from "The Loss of the Prince" to *The Revealer of Secrets* parallel the shift in Austria's policing culture, from targeting individual political threats to the royal family to monitoring the populace for ideologically suspect elements.[74]

Drawing on a Bratslav tradition, Perl suggestively calls the secretaries "the secret holder[s]" (*ba'al sod*), highlighting the lexical affinity between "secretary" and "secrets."[75] Fittingly, Hasidism is portrayed as a state-like organization, with its own shady bureaucratic network of secretaries, the holders of the secrets of the movement.[76] Within Perl's inverted vision of the relationship between Hasidism and the state, the Hasidim are the first to develop forms of surveillance and policing in order to ensure their political success. Very much like the contemporary German Freemasons, who "imagined Jesuits as their mirror image, but with far greater power and with malign intentions," to adopt Ritchie Robertson's analysis, Perl imagined Hasidism as a nefarious and immensely powerful secret police with a deep understanding of the Austrian political system.[77] For example, Zaynvl Verkhievker sends to Zelig Letitchiver, the secretary of the Liozno Hasidic court, a detailed report that informs him of changes in personnel in the local administration:

> All the noblemen tremble before our minister, since it's rumored soon, he'll be appointed vice-governor, because the current vice-governor will be governor. A few days ago, our minister got a letter from Petersburg from a friend of his [stating] that the Czar already signed his governorship.
>
> [*Ki kol ha-'adonim ro'adim lifnei ha-sar shelanu, miḥamat she-nishma she-bekarov yitmane le-vits-gubernator, ki ha-vits-gubernator she-hu ka'et yihiye gubernator, u-lifnei 'eizeh yamim kibel ha-sar shelanu 'igeret mi-peterburg me'ohev 'eḥad shelo, she-kvar ḥatam ha-'imperator et ha-vits-gubernatorstvo shelo.*] (§35 Hebrew 118, English [Taylor] 76)[78]

The Hebrew text of the letter incorporates several technical political terms in Russian, including *gubernater* (governor), *vitsgubernater* (vice-governor), and *vitsgubernaterstvi* (governorship), indicating an intimate familiarity with Russian political structures. According to the letter, Hasidic secretaries possessed exceptionally detailed knowledge of the organization and personnel of both local and imperial Russian bureaucracy, as well as of their appointment procedures. For instance, the secretary of the Liozno Hasidic court had access not only to rumors regarding prospective administrative changes but also to confidential communications among Russian officials:

> In God's great mercy and kindness . . . and by the merit of our holy rebbe, which stood us in good stead—a great miracle happened for us and a credit to our rebbe, by whose merit we got the letter from the post office! The same day the mail arrived here we sent the postmaster's agent, and he gave the postmaster a handsome gift, and he handed over to him the letter that arrived from your prince for the vice-governor.
>
> [*Ha-shem yitbarakh be-rov raḥamav u-verov ḥasadav u-bizkhut rabenu ha-kadosh na'asa lanu nes gadol, u-tehila le-rabenu she-bizkhuhto kibalnu et ha-'igeret me-ha-potsht. Be'oto yom 'asher ha-potsht ba'a 'etslenu shalaḥnu et ha-faktier me-potshtsmaynster, ve-natan leha-potshtmaynster matana haguna, u-masar lo ha-'igeret sheba mi-hasar shelkha leha-vits-gubernator*] (§8 Hebrew 57, English [Taylor] 32)

Russian Hasidim, the *Revealer of Secrets* claims, were able to gain access to letters and intercept entire correspondences, much like the Austrian secret police. In the topsy-turvy world of the novel, Hasidim have networks of spies, which they employ to collect information about state bureaucrats. One of the Russian state intermediaries describes how Hasidim are trying to mobilize him as a secret agent while collecting information about him from his household:

> They [want to] make me their friend, for they must know that I'm involved at the moment in an undertaking so as to be able to uproot them and send them to Siberia. They must know this because nothing is secret from them. If you do something against them in the most secret places, they find out about it, because they have spies in every house and corner. Even to my servants they must be giving money to inform them of what I do . . . everyone in my town—even if he doesn't side with them—is a spy for them.
>
> [*Hem rotsim . . . she-'ata ta'ase 'oti le-'ohev la-hem, ki bevadai hem yode'im she-ani ka'et 'osek be'esek 'eḥad, 'asher 'ukhal la'akor 'otam u-leshalkham 'otam le-sambir, hem bevadai yode'im zot, ki lifaneyhem lo' yesh sod, 'im ya'ase 'eḥad 'eyze davar negdehem be-ḥadrei ḥadarim yitvada la-hem*

> *ha-davar, ki yesh la-hem meraglim be-khol bayit u-fina, hem bevadai ʾafilu laʿavadim sheli notnim maʿot, lehodiʿa la-hem ma she-ʾani ʿose . . . ve-kol ʾeḥad me-haʿir sheli ʾaf ʾim hu lo maḥzik ʿimahem, hu meragel ʾet-slam*] [§106, Hebrew 261–62, English [Taylor], 182)]

In this regard, the *Revealer of Secrets* is highly reminiscent of the earlier-cited excerpt from Charles Sealsfield's *Austria as It Is.* Both Sealsfield and Perl depict "spies in every house and corner" and servants acting as informers. In the political imagination of *The Revealer of Secrets*, however, it is the Hasidim who oppress the state by their network of secret spies.

The plot of the *Revealer of Secrets* centers on the gradual collapse of the Hasidic political terror, as a result of a new publication, a German book, *bukh* in the language of Hasidim, which is making the rounds among nobles and state bureaucrats.[79] As a Hasid from the Liozno court explains to one of his fellows, the *bukh* is "a treyf travesty . . . that was recently published against our Faithful and . . . was sent from Galicia to the landowner of your community to read" (§[1], Hebrew 41, English [Taylor], 36).

Perl provides plenty of hints for the content of the *bukh*, which led scholars to conclude that it is, in fact, Perl's own German manuscript *On the Essence of the Hasidic Sect.*[80] As the plot progresses, a greater number of Russian state officials, Polish nobles, and Russian bureaucrats gain access to the *bukh*, learn about the secrets of Hasidism, and, as a result, join the battle against the Hasidic movement. According to Perl's reformist vision, the maskilic participation in the general economy of surveillance and policing, by way of providing insider Jewish knowledge, is the key to fighting against the spread of the Hasidic movement. The plot of *The Revealer of Secrets* fictionalizes how the state's growing knowledge of Hasidism transforms its policy toward this movement.[81] According to this fictionalized genealogy, historically, Hasidism was widely accepted, and Hasidic rabbis were able to attract the support of Jews and non-Jews alike. Zelig Letitchiver, the aforementioned secretary of the Liozno Hasidic court describes the effect the anti-Hasidic tract, the *bukh,* has on the same Polish nobleman:

> Your nobleman didn't use to be so very wicked . . . and now I see from your letter he is an enemy and a foe of all our Faithful . . . and it seems as this is all on account of the bukh.

> [*She-ha-sar shelkha lo haya mi-kodem rasha' kol kakh . . . ve-ka'et ani ra'iti mi-'igeret shelkha she-hu 'oyev ve-sone le-kol anshei shlomeynu u-lekhol ha-tsadikim, u-nir'e she-kol ze hu mi-ḥamat ha-bukh*] (§16, Hebrew 80, English [Taylor], 49)

How did this change come about? The *Revealer of Secrets* imagines that the reading of the *bukh* instructs its non-Jewish readership how to tell which Jew is a Hasid. In other words, the novel constructs Hasidic belonging similarly to a membership in a secret society—a matter that one strives to conceal. In reality, the identification of Hasidic followers was not immediately apparent, not because it was a matter of concealment, but since there was no clear-cut divide between Hasidic and non-Hasidic practices or between the communities of Hasidic and non-Hasidic believers.[82] In Perl's imagined world, Hasidim are a concrete, discernible, and identifiable group, and nobles and bureaucrats are able to successfully tell who is a Hasid once they gain access to the Hasidic secrets. For example, during a meeting between a Hasidic Jew and his Polish landlord, a "holy book *Seyfer Hamides* [The book of manners] . . . fell from the breast of the Hasid . . . Your book must be *Seyfer Hamides*," responded the local, gentile landlord. "You're a Hasid too!" In this scene, the gentile landlord is imagined as possessing enough knowledge about Jews to be able to decipher a Hebrew book's title and to know enough about Hasidism to determine that the book is an exclusively Hasidic publication. As soon as the nobleman realizes his business partner is a Hasid, he dissolves their collaboration: "In that case [of you being a Hasid]," continues the nobleman, "I will not lease you the mill because in that book it says you're allowed to cheat us."[83] In this respect, the *Revealer of Secrets* dramatizes the maskilic project of rendering Hasidism a visible entity in the eyes of the state. Baruch Kurzweil summarized the plot of *The Revealer of Secrets* as "The Battle of the Books" (Milḥemet ha-sfarim). According to Kurzweil, the motivation behind the *Revealer of Secrets* is that Haskalah will be able to win over Hasidism by writing maskilic books, which will make the general Jewish population immune to the destructive influence of Hasidic books. Kurzweil's argument is based on the supposition that the intended audience of the book was, for the most part, Hasidic. As Yonatan Me'ir points out, Perl did not create a book of an ambiguous message, which could, indeed, pass as a Hasidic book, but rather a highly sharp maskilic parody that could never pass, and never intended to pass, as a Hasidic book.[84] "The Battle of the Books," the way it was imagined by Perl was, thus, radically different. This was a battle to popularize incriminating knowledge against Hasidism among the state intermediaries. It offered a narrative that encouraged its intended readership, Eastern European maskilim, to render the internal Jewish knowledge about Hasidism accessible to the authorities by showing how it can positively affect the state policies toward the Hasidic movement.[85] Whereas "The Loss of the Prince" focuses primarily on the circulation of state laws among the Jewish population, *The Revealer of Secrets* reverses the direction of information dissemination, fictionalizing the effects of providing knowledge about the Jewish population to state officials and legal authorities.

Finally, *The Revealer of Secrets* imagines a shift in the traditional Eastern European economy of secrets, to adopt Daniel Jütte's terminology.[86] The author of the *bukh* is able to supersede the traditional trade of secretive Jewish knowledge and is ultimately to monopolize it on the expanse of the Hasidic leaders: Zelig Letitchiver, the aforementioned secretary of the Liozno Hasidic court, describes how, in the recent past, Polish nobles were "traveling through our community and asked about the [holy] *rebbe*." The goyim, the non-Jews, he continues, "were respecting us, especially our *rebbes*." Not only were the Hasidic leaders esteemed by the local non-Jewish population; they also were believed to possess secret knowledge of magic and extraordinary powers. "Some of the [non-Jewish dignitaries] sent money in the thousands and tens of thousands and some of them came and begged our *rebbes* to help them in their affairs" (*Ve-kama me-hem shalḥu pidyonot le'alafim u-lirevavot, ve-kamah me-hem ba'u ve-hitḥanenu le-raboteinu la'azor la-hem be-e'skeihem*) (§16, Hebrew 90, English [Taylor] 50).

In imagining the replacement of one form of secrecy (the alleged mystical powers of Hasidic Jews to aid in commerce) with another (the uncovering of the secrets of these very mystics), *The Revealer of Secrets* gestures toward yet another pathway through which esoteric Jewish knowledge was transmitted into broader epistemic frameworks. This dynamic resonates with what Daniel Jütte terms the "erosion of the economy of secrets," marking the decline of the privileged position in the early modern European "age of secrecy." Just as Jewish esoteric knowledge, as Jütte shows, found its way into university medical faculties, other learned Jews contributed similar forms of expertise to the operations of the state's secret police.[87]

THE SECRETS OF THE REVEALERS OF SECRETS.

I conclude my analysis of Perl's work by examining how the production and representation of secrecy in *The Revealer of Secrets* intersect with the personal secrets of its author, Joseph Perl. Recovering this relationship, I argue, ought to transform our reading of the novel itself and, more broadly, our understanding of the maskilic conception of the relationship between fiction and denunciation.

The *Revealer of Secrets* employs an extended metalepsis, a breakdown of the boundary between levels of narration. Instead of a conventional narrator, it features a fictional editor, the Hasid Ovadia ben Ptakhia, who features on all levels of narration: as a character, an associate of the Hasidic leaders, as the compiler and publisher of the Hasidic correspondence, and as an occasional commentator on their content. The employment of metalepsis, argued Elaine Freegood, "force[s] us to reflect on narrative construction and our suspensions of disbelief."[88]

In this instance, I show, this rupture prompts a reconsideration of the relationship between the status of the letters in the literary work and that of the Hasidic letters in the world of the author, Joseph Perl.

In the frame narrative, Ovadia recounts the circumstances that granted him access to his fellow Hasidim's writings and the reason for their publication. Walking at night, he stumbled upon a mysterious man:

> The watchman handed me that page and told me that by means of that manuscript I could be invisible, namely, when I hold it in my pocket . . . a cloud would take me and carry me wherever I wish.
>
> [*Ve-masar li ha-shomer 'et ha-niyar ha-nal, ve'amar li she'al yedei ha-ktav ha-nal 'ukhal lihiyot ro'e ve-'eyno nir'e, haynu keshe'aḥzik 'oto ba-kis sheli . . . yikaḥ 'oti 'anan ve-yisa 'oti la-makom she-'ertse.*] (Introduction, Hebrew 32, English [Taylor] 13)

Ovadia subsequently uses the power of invisibility to collect letters of Hasidic leaders:

> I resolved to go to all the Hasidic leaders in an invisible state, because when I was around them previously . . . I saw that many things they don't reveal . . . as a matter of fact the things they do in secret are probably more important to us, because from them their greatness and their thought is most recognizable. Thus, I went to the Hasidic leaders, and I heard what they say in secret, and I also took the letters that they or those who serve them sent to one another and they didn't see . . . I have reproduced some of their letters in this composition of mine in order to publicize them.
>
> [*Ve-gamarti be-da'ati li-lakh le-khol ha-tsadikim be-m'amad ro'e ve-'eyno nire'e, ki ka'asher hayiti 'etslam mikodem ra'iti . . . she-harbe devarim 'eynam megalim . . . ve-'adraba, ha-dvarim she-'osim be-hester yoter meḥuyavin lihiyot ḥasuv 'etslenu, ki me-hem nikar gdulatam u-maḥshavtam. Ve-halakhti kakh le-khol ha-tsadikim, ve-shama'ati ma she-medabrim ba-seter, ve-gam ha-'igrot 'asher hem 'o meshamsheyhem shalḥu 'eḥad le'eḥad lakaḥti ve-lo' hayu ro'im . . . ve-he'etakti kama 'igrot me-hem be-ḥiburi ze le-hotsi' 'otam la'or*] (Introduction, Hebrew 33, English [Taylor] 15)

How can we make sense of this fantastic device, the machine that enables the narrator to move across great distances and to invisibly watch the Hasidim and get hold of their letters? Scholars have usually interpreted the narrator's power to become invisible in the context of an anti-Hasidic critique. For example, Marc Caplan argued that Ovadia's magic power, his ability to travel without being seen, is a means to ridicule the miracles of Hasidic rebbes. "Perl," Marc argues, "presents through this device a conflict between competing notions of science. at one end Kabbalah . . . at the other extreme . . . the science of observable phenomenon."[89] While the ridiculing of the Hasidic magic and the hierarchization of science over magic is certainly at play, it doesn't fully explain why Perl chooses to associate the entire enterprise of this book, the practice of collecting Hasidic letters, with the powers of invisibility. Moreover, *The Revealer of Secrets* envisions a peculiarly limited form of invisibility. Although the narrator recounts that, once invisible, he "went to the Hasidic leaders and . . . heard what they say in secret," the text offers no account of what Ovadia actually overheard while exercising this power. Similarly, although Ovadia is described as *ro'e ve-'eyno nir'e*—the Hebrew term for "invisible," which, as Natkovich observed, denotes an active capacity to see while remaining unseen—he neither documents nor reports what he observes under the cloak of invisibility.[90] Curiously, Ovadia employs his extraordinary powers solely to intercept letters—an inexplicably constrained use of such formidable abilities.

The mystical power of Ovadia, I argue, is the power of the secret services to intercept letters. Perl himself was no stranger to these techniques of interception. As Chone Shmeruk has demonstrated, archival records indicate that in 1818, the year in which Perl was composing *The Revealer of Secrets*, he was solicited to translate Yiddish and Hebrew correspondence for the secret police office in Lemberg.[91]

Some of these letters, Shmeruk further argued, found their way into the novel. As Mahler has shown, Perl was solicited by the Habsburg authorities at least one more time for a similar task after the publication of *The Revealer of Secrets* in 1824.[92] In addition, Joseph Perl's personal archive contains the remnants of a collection of copies of letters exchanged by Hasidim, some authored a decade before and some years after the *Revealer of Secrets*.[93] It is under the impression of the state's interception technologies, I argue, that Perl turned to experiment with the epistolary genre, as a way to convey the experience of state omniscience.

The Revealer of Secrets thus offers a glimpse into a fictional "bag" of intercepted letters, raw material collected from Hasidic courts. In so doing, it helps the reader to imagine how Jewish society is seen under surveillance, from the point of view of the secret police office. As Yonatan Me'ir has suggested, Ovadia ben Petaḥia serves as a representation of Perl, a connection subtly indicated by the fact that the two names share the same gematria numeric value.[94]

Ultimately, as Olga Litvak demonstrated, Perl found the dramatic irony, the tension between Ovadia's ostensibly naive claim that the letters reveal the "greatness" of the Hasidic leaders and the letters' sensational, incriminating content frustratingly unsatisfying.[95] In the introduction to the Yiddish version of *The Revealer of Secrets*, Perl radically reshaped the figure of Ovadia, aligning him far more closely with his maskilic self in a gesture that verges on self-denunciation.

The introduction to the Yiddish translation dramatizes a scene set after the publication of *The Revealer of Secrets*. It recounts how Ovadia, overhearing two Jews discussing the *Revealer of Secrets*, joins their conversation and offers his own insights about the novel he compiled, without divulging his true identity:

> It seems to me that when the author copied the letters, more than once there were tears in his eyes and it was with a bitter heart that he copied them because he saw our dire condition—that one can't address people nowadays in a serious vein as one could in the past . . . The author of the *Revealer of Secrets* knows his brethren. He didn't intend just to write stories—he intended something different. He sees that we're critically ill and we won't take any medicine, so he mixed the medicine with sugar for us . . .[96]
>
> [*Mir dakht zikh, az der mekhaber hot di brif abgeshribn* [*sic*] *zenen im nisht eynmol di treren in di oygen geshtanen. Un mit a biter harts hot er zey abgeshriben voren er hot gezen unzer finstern maymed, az men ken mit unz nit shmuesen ernst azoy vi fartsayten izt geven . . . Der mekhaber fun dem megale temirin ken zayne brider, er hot nisht gevolt mayses shrayben, er meynt epes anders. Er zet mir zaynen mesuken krank, un mir veln keyn refues nemen, hot er unz di refues farmisht mit tsuker.*][97]

If in the Hebrew original introduction, Ovadia presents himself as an ardent follower of Hasidism who propagates their letters to show their greatness, the Yiddish reveals the true experience of Perl himself, the maskil, who considers his community "critically ill" and copies the letters "tears in his eyes." Notable is also the designation of Ovadia as an "author" (*mekhaber*), a point that Perl later emphasizes:

> "Dear Friend," the two cityfolk say to me, "how do you know all this?" "If one reads the *Revealer of Secrets* intelligently, one knows what I just said," I replied to them. "And furthermore, I must tell you that I know the author very well, as well as know myself."[98]

Invisibility, Svetlana Natkovich argued, was central to Haskalah literature because of its inherent ambiguity, serving both as a marker of "intellectual, physical, or symbolic prowess" and as a site of "weakness."[99] This doubleness operates in the Yiddish introduction to the *Revealer of Secrets*. Ovadia is, first and foremost, "invisible," in a negative sense. He is unseen, overlooked by the two interlocutors who first do not pay attention to him. Later, when he engages in a conversation with the two Jews, Ovadia articulates his sense of being both overlooked and misunderstood as a writer. While he pours out his heart "in tears," the readers of *The Revealer of Secrets* delight in its humor (the "sugar"), yet fail to absorb its moral message (the "medicine").[100] At the same time, Ovadia's social invisibility, the fact that he does not attract the attention of his fellow Jews, also allows him to function as a spy, to eavesdrop on their conversations and take notes. If Ovadia in the Hebrew frame story uses his magic powers to become invisible and copy the letters, the Yiddish version paints a picture which was much closer to the actual function of Perl as a maskil who copies letters, eavesdrops on conversations, and, in so doing, aims to contribute to the state's surveillance system.

Evidence indicates that, following the publication of *Megale temirin*, this literary-political ideal was embraced by a broader circle of Jewish intellectuals. These authors envisioned their social role not only as travelers disguised, to borrow Dan Miron's suggestive idiom, but also as spies in disguise, viewing narration and denunciation as fundamentally interconnected.[101] Shlomo Yehuda Rapoport (Shir, 1790–1867), who appears to have been at least partially aware of the connection between Perl's narrative techniques and his real-life practices of espionage (though seemingly unaware of Perl's involvement with intercepted Jewish correspondence), wrote the following in his review of Perl's 1838 novel *Boḥen tsadik* (*A Test for the Righteous*):

> It was made known to me that the author did not fictionalize [the conversations], but rather wrote down what he overheard.
>
> [*Venoda' li ki ha-meḥaber lo' bada 'otan me-libo, rak katav 'otan kefi 'asher hegi'u be'emet le'ozenav.*][102]

Rapoport's passing remark offers a glimpse into a wider culture of information collection among maskilim. Perl was not only inspired by his collaboration with the Austrian secret police; he also collected information on Hasidim on his own. Inspired by the Austrian and Russian secret police, maskilim themselves, it appears, created their own networks of information collection, surveillance, and spying. Two letters from Yitzḥak Ber Levinsohn

(RIBAL) to Perl, dating from 1821, lend further support to this interpretation, giving us a sense of how denunciation and narration were intimately connected in the maskilic mind.[103] In a letter from January 1821, for instance, Levinsohn expresses his enthusiasm upon reading Perl's *Revealer of Secrets* and outlines his own literary aspirations to write a satire about a certain Hasidic leader.[104]

Finally, Levinsohn turns to the other motivation for writing the letter. He switches to report of secret information, using a Yiddish phrase, "I will now start telling stories" (*ikh vel shoyn onheybn mayses dertseylen*). This is the well-known statement by Naḥman of Bratslav, announcing his turn to storytelling in 1806. In its parodic maskilic context, the phrase "I will now start telling stories" acquires another meaning. For Naḥman of Bratslav, this was the beginning of his project of turning storytelling into a means of conveying information about the coming redemption. In Levinsohn's mind, the turn to literature, was associated with spying on the Hasidim, and "stories," *mayses*, stood for reporting on their sensational crimes. In the rest of the report, Levinsohn reports to Perl on the information he was able to collect from his informant about legal transgression, corruption, and crime among the Hassidim, commenting on the credibility of his sources and on the accuracy of the information.[105] These two surviving letters are probably only a fraction of a much larger correspondence between a greater number of participants, testifying to the degree to which literature and surveillance were inextricably intertwined in the maskilic imagination. Some of this information, we can assume, eventually reached the Austrian and Russian authorities.

CODA: BREAKING THE CODE OF HEBREW LITERATURE

Finally, I suggest that in his prose, Perl also invites his readers to participate in the state-like practices of policing and interception. As I noted earlier, in the *Revealer of Secrets*, the real names of rabbis, Hasidic leaders, and places were given in an encrypted form, in gematria, numerical codes. If Perl's ambition was to incriminate Hasidim, why didn't he choose to provide real names and real places? When asked to provide a key to these ciphers, Perl stated that he could not reveal the numerological codes:

> Even if were we commanded to expose the deeds of evildoers and the teachers of wickedness, so as to warn our brethren lest they wander down crooked paths and forsake the ways of Torah and faith—are we not nonetheless forbidden to shame and publicly disgrace our fellow Jews?
>
> [*Legalot ha-ma'asim ha-ra'im ve-lomdei resha', le-ma'an le-haḥzir et bnei 'amenu le-val yelkhu derekh 'akalkalot, 'u-le-val yit'u mi-darkhei ha-tora ve-ha-'emuna ha-lo' ne'esar lanu levayesh u-lehalbin pnei ḥaverenu ba-rabim.*][106]

Perl's response is particularly revealing. On the one hand, he declines to disclose the specific names of the Hasidim, aiming to avoid "disgrac[ing] our fellow Jews." On the other hand, by providing decipherable numerical codes, he effectively transfers the work of disclosure and denunciation to the reader. Perl, I argue, was training his readers to break the codes in his prose, thus making his readership complicit with the practice of interception and policing.

The most radical example of the unique political-literary culture of Galician maskilim found its expression in the publication of "Let the Hasidim Exult in Glory" (Ya'alzu ḥasidim be-khavod), an intriguing poem that was published anonymously in a Hebrew maskilic journal, *Yerushalaim*, in 1845 (fig. 8). As a coda to this chapter, I uncover the story behind the publication of this poem and reflect on its meaning for our understanding of how Jewish literature intersected with the rise of the secret police.[107]

"Let the Hasidim Exult in Glory" stood out among all the other publications, for a few reasons. Not only was the name of its author not specified, but it was also substituted not with a pseudonym, but with the sign of three stars, drawing attention to its anonymity. The content of the poem was equally mysterious, unwavering praise of Hasidic piety, which hardly suited the general agenda of this maskilic journal.

Hasidism, the first sentence of the poem prophesied, "will exult," rejoice, prosper, and "will not be discouraged." The Hasidism, the second line continued, are "full of wisdom with no stubbornness or unfaithful heart" (*Ya'alzu ve-lo' yosifu 'etsev, mele'im ḥokhma belo 'ikshut ve lev tahapukhot*). The third

יעלזו חסידים בכבוד

יעלזו • יעלזו ולא יוסיפו עלב חסידים מלאים חכמה בלי עקשות או לב
תהפוכות, באהבה עובדים ה׳ ולא יטו עיניהם בהבלים בחסד
עני או רש יקרבו ולא יתרחקו להושיע לדלים, מיושבים המה בדעות ולא
ישכרו יין או שכר, בלבבם אמת ואין במפעלם רמיה, שלום ביניהם ואין
קנאה בקרבם בתפלותיהם גורמים לחולים שיהיו בריאים, בלב דאגה
יביאו שמחה לאיש, מהפכים גזרות אל ישועות בתחנתם, בעתירתם
מחליפים רעות אל טובות, צרות לצבור כשתהיינה משתתפים המה ואין
אומרים לנפשם שלום, נעלבים ואינם עולבים חרפתם שומעים ואינם משיבים
בזרוע מקרבים נדיבים משפחות ואין מקרבין בוז משפחות, חכמים וידי
נבונים יתמוכו לא ימעדו רגליהם עת תבא הרעה • —

FIGURE 8 Joseph Tarler, Hebrew palindrome titled "Let the Hasidim Exult in Glory." From Joseph Tarler, "Yaʿalzu ḥasidim be-khavod," *Yerushalaim* 2 (1845): 95.

line described how Hasidic believers "work God with love and do not pay attention to trifle matters" (*be'ahava 'ovdim et 'adonay, ve-lo' yatu 'eynehem ba-havalim*), and, among them "there is only peace, no jealousy" (*be-levavam 'emet ve'eyn kine'a be-kirbam*). The rest of the six stanzas provide more expressions of admiration, for example, depicting how Hasidic leaders help the poor or how strictly they keep the laws of the Shabbat.

Who was this anonymous supporter of Hasidism? Why would anyone bother writing this list of praises of the Hasidic movement? Why would a maskilic venue publish this text? A close reading of the poem reveals that there is more to it than meets the eye. The few opening phrases betray a number of unusual grammatical and syntactical characteristics. The syntax is cumbersome and awkward—a sequence of short sentences, connected with negative conjunctions, most often with *lo'* (not) or *ve-lo'* (and not). The word choice is also awkward and strained. Instead of phrasing the compliments in a straightforward, positive manner, the poem features an abundance of pejorative adjectives followed by a negation. Finally, the reason for the thematic connection between the sentences is unclear. The more one reads the poem, the more one has a sense that it was written under some form of formal constraint, suggesting that, in fact, something else is at stake.

The explanation for all these oddities was publicly revealed half a century after the publication of this poem. Meir Weissberg (1854–1930), himself a maskil of a much younger generation, who was privy to inside information about the publication of the poem, disclosed in a Polish-Jewish journal the key for its interpretation: One can read the text in two ways, from right to left and from left to right. When read in reverse, from left to right, the laudatory text turns into a condemnation. For example, the first sentence, "ya'alzu ve-lo' yosifu 'etsev" (They will rejoice and will not be discouraged) is read backward as "'etsev yosifu ve-lo' ya'alzu" (They will be discouraged and will not rejoice). The last two stanzas, if read in reverse, describe Hasidim as "lascivious as roosters" (*shtufei zima ka-tarnegolim*) and blame them for all sorts of halakhic transgressions and sexual offenses.

Before I move on, I would like to draw attention to the amount of labor the author of this poem dedicated to this ruse. "Let the Hasidim Exult in Glory" is a long text, six stanzas, roughly seventy sentences, and they all read in both ways. In comparison, the master of word games in the Hebrew literary tradition, Abraham Ibn Ezra (1089–1164), wrote much shorter palindromes, for example, "'avi 'el ḥay shimkha lama melekh mashiaḥ lo' yavo'" (My father is a living God why isn't the Messiah coming?). Reading the same text from both sides only reinforced its messianic message and its urgency. The person who wrote "Let the Hasidim Exult in Glory" had a different idea in mind. He wanted to create an extended, meaningful experience of reading an undertext that undermines the text, that positions the text as false and the undertext as true.[108]

The literary conceit, the need to know a special key for the reading of the poem, associates the anti-Hasidic text with secretiveness, as if this were a hidden knowledge in need of protection. Secrecy "magnifies reality," to cite Michael Taussig, "creating a world split between a visible exterior and an invisible depth that determines the exterior."[109] In other words, a secret is not only a distinct form of knowledge, but also a structure that leads to a hierarchization of knowledge. In this poem, the effect of creating an alternative form of reading that "unmasks" Hasidism is a form not only of "revelation" but also of labeling the "revealed" knowledge as secretive. The author of this poem offered a textual structure that produced two competing readings and, analogously, two competing and mutually exclusive views of the Hasidic movement. One could have easily written a text that presents Hasidim as corrupt without resorting to a division of secrecy and revelation. In fact, by 1845, the year in which the poem was published, there was already an entire library of both misnagdic and maskilic texts that did exactly that: offered a lengthy social and political criticism of the Hasidic movement. Instead, the choice was made to conceal this message. The reader thus moved from an "open" text, the praises of Hasidism, which, in its cumbersomeness and syntactic strangeness felt "off," suggesting that there is something "off" about its agenda, to a secret text, whose grammar and flow felt much more idiomatic, and "right." By deciphering the hidden, secretive text, the readership was recruited into the world of the writer and into the project of unmasking Hasidism. If secrecy is "an intentional process of differentiating . . . building solidarity among secret-sharers," to quote Gilbert Herdt, this poem offers to substitute the allure of Hasidic secrecy, of kabalistic secrecy, with sharing a different kind of secrecy, the secrecy of exposing Hasidism, of debunking its lies.[110]

When the poem was published, only a small group of readers shared the knowledge of the identity of its author. The secret was publicly revealed only posthumously. The author, we now know, was "Herr Peter Tarler, Hebräischer Bucher Revisor, zugleich Censor," the inspector and censor of Hebrew books in Lemberg. Peter Tarler, born Joseph Tarler, was a Jew who converted to Catholicism, and a short time after, he was nominated the official translator, inspector, and censor of Hebrew manuscripts. Tarler maintained close relations with the maskilim, before and after his conversion, most notably with his student, Yitzḥak Erter (1792–1851). For the few maskilim who knew that Tarler was behind this poem, sharing this knowledge meant also sharing the secret of the origin of the incriminating information about the Hasidim. This was not just accusations made by fellow Jews; this was supposedly knowledge Tarler had gained as the Austrian censor, the person who was privy to internal governmental correspondence concerning the Hasidim, which he now shared with a happy few. Maskilim may have lost the joy of participating in the secrecy of a Jewish religious group, but in return, they imagined themselves sharing the secrets of the state.[111]

Introducing the state into the equation helps us clarify another theme in the poem: biblical allusions. The title "Let the Hasidim Exult in Glory" is taken from Psalm 149, in which the word "Hasidim" simply stands for faithful, that is, for the faithful people of Israel.[112] The psalm itself, to be sure, has only positive things to say about the Israelites who were faithful to God. Knowing the identity of the author pushes us to interpret the psalm in a different, subversive manner. Following are verses 5–9:

> Let the faithful exult in glory
> Let them shout for joy upon their couches, with paeans to God in their throats
> and double-edged swords in their hand
> to impose retribution upon the nations
> punishment upon the peoples
> binding their kings with shackles
> their nobles with chains of iron.
>
> [*Ya'alzu ḥasidim be-khavod / yeranenu 'al mishkavotam / romemot 'el bi-gronam ve-ḥerev pifiyot be-yadam / la'asot nekama ba-goyim / toḥakhot ba-le'umim la'asor malkheyhem be-'azikim / ve-nikhbadeyhem be-kivlei barzel*].[113]

In the biblical context, this is a psalm about the people of Israel fighting as a politically independent nation against their enemies. If we interpret "Hasidim" as referring to the Eastern European Hasidic movement, the poem reads as an accusation of Hasidism as a political group seeking to destabilize the reigning government, to destroy the social and political order, to bind the king "with shackles" and the nobles "with chains of iron." To all the accusations in the satirical poem we can add one more—the accusation of Hasidism as a political threat, as a revolutionary group.

The adoption of a structure of secrecy also allows Tarler to invert the relations of power. This is the secret content they are purported to conceal in their books. The censor, in contrast, is forced to cipher this information in his poem, supposedly because of the imaginary dominance of this movement. The oppressor, the censor, thus present himself as the censored, the oppressed.

Finally, reinstating the state provides another layer to our understanding of the symbolic directionality of the poem. The text visually contrasts two points of view about the Hasidism, two competing perspectives, from left to right, and from right to left. If we read it from right to left, the way Hebrew usually does, it reflects the common Jewish view of Hasidism. If, in contrast, we read it from left to right, it exposes the machinations and corruption of the Hasidic movement. Reading from left to right was a practice of particular significance, of reading in Latin letters, in the language of the state. Exposing the corruption of the Hasidic movement, reading from left to right, signified embracing the perspective of the censor, that is, the point of view of the state.

"Ya'alzu ḥasidim be-khavod," the 1845 Hebrew poem by Peter (Joseph) Tarler, the Habsburg censor of Lemberg, hearkens back to the book's introduction. The privileged relationship between Tarler, the Habsburg censor, and the Galician maskilim is analogous to Shalom Abramovitsh's exchange with Vladimir Fedorov (Hirsh Grinboym), the censor of the Chancellery of the Governor-General of Kiev, Podolia, and Volhynia. The persistence of these modes of politico-literary collaboration and denunciation into the second half of the nineteenth century highlights the longevity of the genre I have described as the *fiction of the state*, reaching beyond the confines of this study's time frame. In this sense, the book's introduction may also serve as its conclusion, bringing the study full circle. Together, the opening and conclusion of this monograph invite further research that extends my findings chronologically and geographically, gesturing toward new scholarly horizons and new points of departure.

Notes

Introduction

1. James C. Scott, *Seeing Like a State: How Certain Schemes to Improve the Human Condition Have Failed* (New Haven: Yale University Press, 1998), 2. Eugene M. Avrutin was the first to apply and develop the concept of imperial legibility in the context of the Russian partition of Poland. See his *Jews and the Imperial State: Identification Politics in Tsarist Russia* (Ithaca: Cornell University Press, 2010), 21–53. Johannes Czakai applied the concept of legibility in his study of Habsburg surname identification policies in Galicia: *Nochems neue Namen: Die Juden Galiziens und der Bukowina und die Einführung deutscher Vor- und Familiennamen, 1772–1820* (Göttingen: Wallstein Verlag, 2021).

2. A copy of Shalom Abramovitsh's correspondence with the authorities is preserved in the YIVO Archive Sutzkever-Kaczerginski Collection, RG 223.2, folder 456. The letters dated 1864–1865 are copied at the bottom of page 3 and the top of page 4. It is possible that this document is based on Abramovitsh's diary, in which he transcribed letters addressed to him. The diary was lost during World War II. See Arn Vorobeytshik, "Tsu der frage vegen mendeles literarishe yerushe," in *Mendele un zayn tsayt: Materyaln tsu der geshikhte fun der yidisher literatur in XIX yorhundert,* ed. Arn Gurshteyn (Moscow: Melukhe-farlag "Der Emes," 1940), 58–59.

3. Prior to this exchange, Nikolai Annenkov, the governor-general of the southwestern gubernias (Kiev, Podolia, and Volhynia), published the questions included in this letter in the Kiev-based, Russian-language periodical *Kievlianin* on November 12, 1864. See John D. Klier, "*Kievlianin* and the Jews: A Decade of Disillusionment, 1864–1873," *Harvard Ukrainian Studies* 5, no. 1 (March 1981): 83–101, esp. 91–92. For a chronology of

Abramovitsh's career in the 1860s, see Dan Miron, "Reshime fun publikatsyes un geshe'en-ishen, 1857–1869," in Abramovitsh *Limdu heitev*, by Sholem Yankev Abramovitsh, ed. Dan Miron (New York: YIVO, 1969), 89–100.

4. YIVO RG 233.2, Folder 456; Shalom Ya'akov ben Ḥaim Moshe Abramovitsh, *'Ein mishpat* (Zhitomir: A.Sh. Shadov, 1867), 44 [*sic*], 60 [*sic*].

5. Abramovitsh, *'Ein mishpat*, 43–44. According to Abramovitsh's personal correspondence, he had initially written his response to the government in Hebrew and later commissioned a professional translation into Russian. See his letter to Yehuda Leib Binshtok, dated December 15, 1864, in *Dos Mendele bukh: Briv un oytobiografishe notitsn*, ed. Nachman Mayzel (New York: Ikuf, 1959), 79–80. The introduction to *'Ein mishpat* offers a different account, stating that Abramovitsh had submitted the Hebrew manuscript to the Russian authorities, who then provided a Russian translation and returned the document to him. See Abramovitsh, *'Ein mishpat*, 60.

6. Abramovitsh, *'Ein mishpat*. For a full bibliographical account of Abramovitsh's Ha-melits publications, see Eliezer Raphael Malach, "Ha-bibliografya shel mendele," *Ha-toren* 4, no. 44 (January 18, 1918): 12.

7. Abramovitsh, *'Ein mishpat*, 51.

8. Israel Zinberg (Tsinberg), *A History of Jewish Literature*, 12 vols. (Cincinnati: Ktav Publishing House, 1978), 12:138–42.

9. This argument draws on Amnon Raz-Krakotzkin's study of church censorship as a cultural force shaping the early modern Jewish canon in *The Censor, the Editor, and the Text: The Catholic Church and the Shaping of the Jewish Canon in the Sixteenth Century* (Philadelphia: University of Pennsylvania Press, 2007), and on Marta Fik's analysis of censorship as coauthorship in "Cenzor jako współautor," in *Literatura i władza*, ed. Bożena Wojnowska (Warsaw: IBL, 1996), 131–48.

10. The aforementioned correspondence between Abramovitsh and the authorities preserved in YIVO RG 233.2 contains additional information, for example, the signature of V. Tagarev, another employee of the Kiev, Podolia, and Volhynia chancellery who corresponded with Abramovitsh.

11. On Vladimir Fedorov's bureaucratic career, see Vassili Schedrin, *Jewish Souls, Bureaucratic Minds: Jewish Bureaucracy and Policymaking in Late Imperial Russia, 1850–1917* (Detroit: Wayne State University Press, 2016), 74. For a biographical account of Fedorov's relationship with Hebrew writers, see Shaul Gintsburg, *Meshumodim in tsarishn rusland: Forshungen un zikhroynes vegn yidishn lebn in amolikn rusland* (New York: Shaul Gintsburg Shriftn Komitet, 1946), 251–63; Zinberg, *A History of Jewish Literature*, 133–38.

12. Ahuva Sheler, "'Avraham Uri Kovner – reshita shel ha-bikoret ha-'ivrit ha-ḥadasha" (PhD diss., Tel Aviv University, 2003), 106–13.

13. Abramovitsh's letter to Yehuda Leyb Binshtok, dated March 15, 1867, in Mayzel, *Dos mendele bukh*, 84–85.

14. N[aḥum] S[okolov], "Ha-tsefira ve-ha-mevakrim mi-ta'am." *Ha-tsefira sefer ha-yovel* (1912): 8–10.

15. See Moshe ben Menaḥem (Moses Mendelsohn), *Yerushalaim* (Vienna: Perets ben moshe smolenskin, 1877).

16. Mayzel, *Dos mendele bukh.*

17. Joseph Klausner, for example, misrepresents the circumstances surrounding the writing of *'Ein mishpat* in his *Historiyah shel ha-sifrut ha-'ivrit ha-ḥadasha* (Jerusalem: Aḥiasaf, 1960), 6:403–7. Similarly, Amir Banbaji's otherwise masterful analysis of *'Ein mishpat* overlooks its Russian imperial context; see Amir Banbajai, *Mendele ve-ha-sipur hale'umi* (Or Yehuda: Kinneret, Zmora-Bitan, Dvir, 2009), 42.

18. Ya'akov Fichman, *Sofrei 'odesa: 'Amat ha-binyan* (Jerusalem: Mosad Bialik: Jerusalem, 1951), 10. For a similar shift in Abramovitsh's political vision, see the shift in the author's representation of the Russian army in the different versions of *Dos kleyne mentshele.* See Shalom Lurie, introduction to Abramovitsh*Ha-'ishon ha-katan = Dos kleyne mentshele,* by Shalom Ya'akov Abramovitsh (Haifa: Hotsa'at ha-Sefarim shel Universitat Ḥefa, 1984), 30–31.

19. Klausner, *Historiyah shel ha-sifrut,* 6:407.

20. Sholem Yankev Abramovitsh, *Di takse, oder, di bande shtot bale toyves* (Zhitomir: A. Sh. Shadov, 1869), 3–4.

21. Ruth R. Wisse, "The Jewish Informer as Extortionist and Idealist," in *Insiders and Outsiders: Dilemmas of East European Jewry,* ed. Richard I. Cohen, Jonathan Frankel, and Stefani Hoffman (Portland: Littman Library of Jewish Civilization, 2010), 195–96.

22. Abramovitsh, *Di takse,* 20.

23. Abramovitsh, *Di takse,* 76.

24. Shmuel Werses, "Beyn dimyon le-metsi'ut ba-maḥaze shel mendele *di takse,*" *Ḥulyot* 10 (Winter 2007): 12–14.

25. S(olomon) M(oiseevich) Abramovich (Abramovitsh, Shalom Ya'akov), *Taksa, t. e. Korobochnyi sbor: Komediia v 5-ti deistviiakh* (Belaia Tserkov': M. Mezhybovskii, 1884). Abramovitsh expressed dissatisfaction with the translation in his autobiographical "Reshimot le-toldotai," in *Sefer zikaron le-sofrei yisrael ha-ḥayim 'itanu kayom,* ed. Naḥum Sokolov (Warsaw: Meir Yeḥiel Alter, 1889), 122.

26. Christopher Alan Bayly, *Empire and Information: Intelligence Gathering and Social Communication in India, 1780–1870* (Cambridge: Cambridge University Press, 1996), 2.

27. On the 1863 Polish uprising in Kiev and its surroundings, see Piotr S. Wandycz, *The Lands of Partitioned Poland, 1795–1918* (Seattle: University of Washington Press, 1974), 177–89. On Berdichev, see *Wspomnienia z powstania 1863 r. w powiecie berdyczowskim* (manuscript, Rps 6536 III, National Library of Poland). On the Russian imperial policies in Kiev, Podolia, and Volhynia in response to the Polish insurrection of 1863, see Edward C. Thaden, *Russia's Western Borderlands, 1710–1870* (Princeton: Princeton University Press, 1984), 117–43.

28. The letter from Nikolai Annenkov is cited according to Fabian Baumann, *Dynasty Divided: A Family History of Russian and Ukrainian Nationalism* (Ithaca: Cornell

University Press, 2023), 28. On the relationship between *Kievlianin* and the provincial authorities, see Klier, "*Kievlianin*," 85–91; Baumann, *Dynasty Divided*, 27–33; Iuliia Polovynchak, *Hazeta "Kievlianin" i ukrainstvo: dosvid natsional'noi samoidentyfikatsii: Monohrafiia* (Kyiv: Natsionalna biblioteka imeni V.I. Vernadskoho NAN Ukrainy, 2008), 3–7.

29. Baumann, *Dynasty Divided*, 28.

30. Shalom Abramovitsh and Osip Levin to Yehuda Leyb Binshtok, January 14, 1871, in Mayzel, *Dos Mendele bukh*, 97–98.

31. Abramovitsh, *'Ein mishpat*, 5, 24.

32. Yiśra'el Bartal, "Ha-lo-yehudim ve-ḥevratam be-sifrut 'ivrit ve-yidish be-mizraḥ 'eropah ben ha-shanim 1856–1914" (PhD diss., Hebrew University of Jerusalem, 1980), 83.

33. Sholem Yankev Abramovitsh, "The Little Man; or, Portrait of Life," in *Classic Yiddish Stories of S. Y. Abramovitsh, Sholem Aleichem, and I. L. Peretz*, trans. and ed. Ken Frieden (Syracuse: Syracuse University Press, 2004), 3–5. On the changes in the 1879 edition, see 2, 3.

34. As Gadi Sagiv and Ada Rapoport-Albert pointed out, the Hebrew and Yiddish term for Poland, Poyln/Polin was in continuous use throughout the nineteenth century and in some cases designated territories that were never under Polish rule. See Gadi Sagiv and Ada Rapoport-Albert, "Ḥabad keneged ḥasidut 'polin': Le-toledotav shel dimuy," in *Ḥabad – historia, hagut ve-dimuy*, ed. David Assaf (Jerusalem: Merkaz Zalman Shazar, 2017), 224–26.

35. Sholem Yankev Abramovitsh, *Dos kleyne mentshele: Oder A lebensbashraybung fun yitskhok avrom takif, gor in gantsen oyf dos nay ibergemakht* (Vilna: Bi-defus Rom, 1879), 3–4.

36. See Dan Miron, "Abramovitsh, Sholem Yankev," *YIVO Encyclopedia of Jews in Eastern Europe*, YIVO Institute for Jewish Research, https://encyclopedia.yivo.org/article/1039; Dan Miron, *A Traveler Disguised: The Rise of Modern Yiddish Fiction in the Nineteenth Century* (New York: Schocken, 1973), 130-249; Gershon Shaked, *Mendele lifanav ve'aḥarav* (Jerusalem: Magnes Press, 2005); Banbaji, *Mendele ve-ha-sipur ha-le'umi*; Irene Tucker, *A Probable State: The Novel, the Contract, and the Jews* (Chicago: University of Chicago Press, 2000); Todd Hasak-Lowy, *Here and Now: History, Nationalism, and Realism in Modern Hebrew Fiction* (Syracuse: Syracuse University Press, 2008); Lilach Netanel, "Zman mendele: 'al ha-poetika shel ha-merḥak ha-ḥal ba-nusaḥ ha'ivri shel abramovitsh ve'ad ha-roman ha-'ivri-vina'i shel fogel," *'Iyunim be-tkumat israel* 26 (2016): 1–21; Naomi Seidman, *A Marriage Made in Heaven: The Sexual Politics of Hebrew and Yiddish*, Contraversions 7 (Berkeley: University of California Press, 1997), 40–67.

37. Hannan Hever, *Hasidism, Haskalah, Zionism: Chapters in Literary Politics* (Philadelphia: University of Pennsylvania Press, 2023), 53.

38. I am indebted to Gayatri Spivak for this insight. The quote is from Pierre Bourdieu, *On the State: Lectures at the Collège de France, 1989–1992* (Cambridge: Polity Press, 2014), 36–37.

39. Larry Wolff, *The Idea of Galicia: History and Fantasy in Habsburg Political Culture* (Stanford: Stanford University Press, 2010), 17.

40. Timothy Mitchell, "Society, Economy, and the State Effect," in *State/Culture: State-Formation After the Cultural Turn*, ed. George Steinmetz (Ithaca: Cornell University Press, 1999), 77–78.

41. Naḥman of Bratslav, *The Tales*, trans. Arnold Band (New York: Paulist Press, 1978), 118.

42. Lubomír Doležel, *Heterocosmica: Fiction and Possible Worlds*, Parallax: Re-Visions of Culture and Society (Baltimore: Johns Hopkins University Press, 1998), 16.

43. Thomas Pavel, "Immersion and Distance in Fictional Worlds," *Itinéraires*, no. 1 (2010): 99–109.

Chapter 1

1. Francis Morgan Nichols, *The Epistles of Erasmus from His Earliest Letters to His Fifty-First Year Arranged in Order of Time: English Translations from the Early Correspondence with a Commentary Confirming the Chronological Arrangement and Supplying Further Biographical Matter* (London: Longmans, Green, 1901), 366. For a theorization of the panegyric genre, see Rebecca Gould's "The Much-Maligned Panegyric: Toward a Political Poetics of Pre-modern Literary Form," *Comparative Literature Studies* 52, no. 2 (2015): 254–88.

2. Bernard Bate, "Political Praise in Tamil Newspapers: The Poetry and Iconography of Democratic Power," in *Everyday Life in South Asia*, 2nd ed., ed. Diane P. Mines and Sarah Lamb (Bloomington: Indiana University Press, 2010), 356.

3. For an account of the Russian historical background of Eastern European Hebrew panegyrics, consult Haim Borodinski (Ben-Dayan), "Di loyblider lekoved Katerine II un zayere mekhabrim, a bletl kultur geshikhte," *Historishe Shriftn* 2 (1937): 532–33; David Fishman, *Russia's First Modern Jews: The Jews of Shklov* (New York: NYU Press, 1995), 80–84; Alex Averbuch, "Jewish Solicitory Poetry in the Eighteenth-Century Russian Empire: Materiality, Poetics, Diplomacy," *AJS Review* 49, no. 1 (2025): 1–29.

4. On *Ha-noten teshu'a*, see Barry Schwartz, "Hanoten teshua': The Origin of the Traditional Jewish Prayer for the Government," *Hebrew Union College Annual* 57 (1986): 113–20. On practices related to this prayer in eighteenth-century Poland, see Pinkhas Kohn, "Di fayerung lekoved stanislav oygust poniatovski in der vilner shtot shul (1764)," *Historishe Shriftn* 1 (1929): 763–64. On a similar practice in Krakow, see Eugeniusz Müller, *Żydzi w Krakowie w drugiej połowie XIV-stulecia* (Krakow: Druk. Czasu, 1906), 52. Alex Averbuch ("Jewish Solicitory Poetry," 3) argues that medieval Iberian-Jewish panegyrics served as a source of inspiration for the emergence of Hebrew praise poetry in Tsarist Russia. While this possible connection is certainly intriguing, it is worth noting that medieval Jewish panegyric poetry was addressed exclusively to Jewish dignitaries, not to non-Jewish rulers, and thus cannot readily serve as a model for Hebrew praise poems dedicated to non-Jewish sovereigns.

5. Harsha Ram, *The Imperial Sublime: A Russian Poetics of Empire* (Madison: University of Wisconsin Press, 2003), 32.

6. On panegyric poetry dedicated to Catherine the Great, see Ram, *The Imperial Sublime*, 63–121. See also the special issue of *Russian Literature* 75 nos. 1–4 (Winter 2014, ed. Joachim Klein) dedicated to Russian panegyric poetry; and Joachim Klein, "Herrscherlob: Panegyrische Dichtung und russischer Absolutismus," *Zeitschrift für Slavische Philologie* 70, no. 2 (2014): 257–93.

7. For the text of the poems, see *Freudengesang der Judenschaft zu Sclow beym Durchzuge Ihrer Kayserlichen Majestät Katharina II, Selbstbeherrscherinn Aller Reussen* (n.p., 1780); *Lob- und Danklied der Judengemeine zu Mohilow beym einzuge Ihrer Kayserlichen Majestät Katharina II, Selbstbeherrscherinn aller Reussen* (n.p., 1780); *Bey der höchsterfreulichen Durchreise der Allerdurchlauchtigsten und Grossmächtigsten Kaiserin und Frau Catharina Alexiewna, Selbstherrscherin aller Reussen* [. . .] *überreichte mit allerunterthänigster Devotion die Judengemeine in Poloczko folgenden Gesang* (Königsberg: G. L. Hartung, 1780).

8. Moshe Pelli, "'La-menatseaḥ ba-neginot maskil' – melekhet ha-shir ve-tofa'at ha-shira ba-me'asef, ktav ha-'et ha-rishon shel ha-haskala ha-'ivrit," *Dappim le-meḥkar be-safrut* 12 (1999–2000): 65–116.

9. The identification of Wessely and Mendelsohn follows Valentin Heinrich Schmidt and Daniel Gottlieb Gebhard Mehring, *Neuestes gelehrtes Berlin: oder literarische Nachrichten von jetztlebenden Berlinischen Schriftstellern und Schriftstellerinnen* (Berlin: Friedrich Mauer, 1795), 2:261–63. For an analysis of Wessely's panegyric poetry, see Moshe Pelli, *Bikurei ha-'itim – Bikurei ha-haskala: An Annotated Index to Bikurei ha-'itim, the Hebrew Journal of the Haskalah in Galicia, 1820–1831* (Jerusalem: Magnes Press, 2005), 107–9. For an analysis of the Shklov poem, see Fishman, *Russia's First Modern Jews*, 82. Fishman argues convincingly that the poem preempts a call for Jewish legal emancipation.

10. See Yosef Klausner, *Historiyah shel ha-sifrut ha-'ivrit ha-ḥadasha* [History of modern Hebrew literature] (Jerusalem: Magnes Press, 1960), 1:149. For a history of Hebrew poems dedicated to Alexander I, see Olga Minkina, *"Syny Rakhili": Evreiskie deputaty v Rossiiskoi imperii, 1772–1825* (Moscow: Novoe literaturnoe obozrenie, 2011), 259–60.

11. Fishman, *Russia's First Modern Jews*, 81–84. See Arjun Appadurai, "Topographies of the Self: Praise and Emotion in Hindu India," in *Language and the Politics of Emotion*, ed. Catherine A. Lutz and Lila Abu-Lughod (Cambridge: Cambridge University Press, 1990), 92–112.

12. Mendel Lefin, "Divre todah be-tse't 'adat yisra'el poh de-k"k mikolayov le-kabel pnei gevirtenu ha-dukasit 'izabelah tsharteriska be-'elul taksa"h (1805), National Library of Israel, Jerusalem, Arc 4° 1153/8; On Lefin's ties to his patrons, the Czartoryskis, see Majer Bałaban, "Mendel Lewin i książę Adam Czartoryski (Notatka historyczna), *Chwila* 5313 (January 7, 1934): 10; 5314 (8 Apr. 1934): 11; Nancy Sinkoff, *Out of the Shtetl: Making Jews Modern in the Polish Borderlands* (Providence: Brown University Press, 2004), 50–112.

13. *Freudengesang*, 2. This description dovetails with Catherine's practice of accepting a select group of local communal leaders. See Fishman, *Russia's First Modern Jews*, 80; Averbuch, "Jewish Solicitory."

14. *Freudengesang*, 4.

15. Richard Butterwick-Pawlikowski, *Polish-Lithuanian Commonwealth, 1733–1795: Light and Flame* (New Haven: Yale University Press, 2021), 121.

16. *Sotrudniki Rossiiskoi natsional'noi biblioteki: Deiateli nauki i kultury; Biograficheskii slovar'* (St. Petersburg: Izd-vo Rossiiskoi natsionalnoi biblioteki, 2005), 120. For a similar entry on Moshe Elḥanan, see Iakov Meerovich Shulman, *Goroda i liudi evreiskoi diaspory v Vostochnoi Evrope do nachala XX veka: Ukraina. Berdichev, Vinnitsa, Zhitomir, Kamenets-Podol'sk, Tul'chin* (Moscow: TLS Faktors, 2007), 176.

17. Moïse Elkana (Moshe Elḥanan), *Hymne addressée à sa Majesté l'Empereur Alexandre I* (Munich: Imprimerie J. Sidler, 1811). The French text was reproduced in Nikolai Nikolaevich Golitsyn, *Istoriia russkogo zakonodatel'stva o evreiakh* (St. Petersburg: Tip. ministerstva vnutrennikh del, 1886), 989–91.

18. Moshe Elḥanan, correspondence, Family Collection Moritz Moses Gottschalk Lewy, P 253/1, Central Archives for the History of the Jewish People, Jerusalem.

19. Dov Ber (Birkenthal) of Bolechów, *Divre binah/zikhronot*, vol. 2, *Zikhronot*, ed. Gershon Hundert (Jerusalem: Mosad Bialik, 2023); Heinrich Loewe, ed., *Memoiren eines polnischen Juden: Lebenserinnerungen von Mosche Wasserzug* (Berlin, 1911). Wasserzug's birth and death dates are according to Anna Michałowska-Mycielska, "Jewish Autobiographical Writing: Memoirs of Moses Vasertsug (c. 1760–1832)," *Acta Poloniae Historica* 128 (2023): 249–76. See also Uriel Gellman's reconstruction of the biography of Moshe Kerner (1762–1836) in "Between Worlds: The Miserable Life of an Itinerant Preacher on the Eve of Modernity," *Jewish Quarterly Review* 109, no. 1 (January 1, 2019): 54–83.

20. "Ob opredelenii ravvina Moiseya El'kana v chislo pochetnykh bibliotekarei," National Library of Russia, St. Petersburg, Department of Archival Documents, collection 1, file 9 (Copy: CAHJP RU-2058).

21. Isaac Hirsch Weiss, *Zikhronotay me-yalduti 'ad mel'ot li shemonim shanah* (Warsaw: Bi-dfus ha-Aḥim Shuldberg, 1895), 73.

22. On the students of Yechezkel Landau, see Michael Miller, *Rabbis and Revolution: The Jews of Moravia in the Age of Emancipation* (Stanford: Stanford University Press, 2011), 63. Eleazar Fleckeles's first position was in Goitein, Moravia, and Moses Minz's in Alt-Ofen, Hungary. Mordecai Benet (1753–1829) was the rabbi of Nikolsburg in Moravia.

23. On Stanisław Szczęsny Feliks Potocki (1754–1805), see Emanuel Rostworowski, "Potocki Stanisław Szczęsny (Feliks) herbu Pilawa," in *Polski Słownik Biograficzny*, 55 vols., ed. Emanuel Rostworowski (Warsaw: Zakład Narodowy im. Ossolińskich, Polska Akademia Nauk, 1984–1985), 28:183–202. On the Potockis and the Tulczyn court, see Jerzy Łojek, *Potomkowie Szczęsnego: Dzieje fortuny Potockich z Tulczyna, 1799–1921* (Lublin: Lubelskie, 1983).

24. "W sprawie pretensji pieniężnej rabina Daszowskiego Zundela do kahału i pospólstwa m. Daszów; oświadczenie świadków-Żydów m-ka Daszów, podpisany przez Mosesa Elkana Josepha, Rabina Generalnego; również – Pretensja kahalu Kalnickiego do rabina m. Kalnik z wykazem Żydów," Central State Historical Archives of Ukraine, Kyiv (TsDIAK), *fond* 49, inventory 1, file 2121, copy at CAHJP HM2-7925.1.

25. "Shir ve-shevaḥ la-'adoneinu ha-melekh ha-gadol stanislas, nitḥaber 'al-yedei 'avdo ha-ne'eman moshe elḥanan, 'av beyt din de-ha-medina," *Recueil de littérature, Stanisław August*, call no. 938, Czartoryski Library, Kraków, fols. 733–34. I thank Kamil Kijek and Paweł Wierzbicki for their assistance in the reproduction of the manuscript. The dating rests both on the dates of the remainder of the texts in the manuscript, as well as on the fact that Moshe Elḥanan signed the poem with his title of a provincial rabbi, which he gained after he moved to Tulczyn (1789) and lost in 1793.

26. "Pismo Awigdora Rabina z Pińska i Mosze Elechanan Rabina z Tulczyna do Kahału Pińskiego" (December 2, 1791), in *Materiały do dziejów Sejmu Czteroletniego*, 6 vols., ed. Arthur Eisenbach et al. (Wrocław: Zakład Narodowy im. Ossolińskich, 1969), 6:380–81. The Hebrew original is appended to the volume.

27. On Barukh ben Yechiel of Międzybóż, see Tsippi Kauffman, "Rabi barukh ve-shoshelet mezhibozh," *Tarbits* 87, no. 1 (2019): 99–143.

28. This speculation was first proposed by Jacob Goldberg in *Ha-ḥevrah ha-yehudit be-mamlekhet Polin–Lita* (Jerusalem: Zalman Shazar, 1999), 223. I have not been able to determine the precise chronology of Barukh of Międzybóż's rabbinic tenure in Tulczyn.

29. In his novel *Dos Shterntikhl*, Isroel Aksenfeld adduces a tradition, according to which Graf Potocki expelled Barukh ben Yechiel from Tulczyn in light of a complaint from the wealthiest man in town. Szczęsny Potocki died in 1805, so if one considers this a reliable tradition, then the event may have transpired while Moshe Elḥanan was living in Tulczyn. See Isroel Aksenfeld, *Dos shterntikhl: Oder, shabes khanuke in mezhibizh* (Leipzig: C. W. Vollrath, 1862), 68–69. For a detailed discussion on the evidence concerning Barukh ben Yechiel's location, see Rayah Haran, "Belil 'igarot ve-'igeret le-darkhei ha-'atakah shel 'igrot ḥasidim," *Tsiyon* 56, no. 3 (1991): 304–6.

30. Nadav, *The Jews of Pinsk*, 315–16.

31. Nadav, *The Jews of Pinsk*, 315–16.

32. Antoni Chrząszczewski, *Pamiętnik oficjalisty Potockich z Tulczyna* (Wrocław: Zakład Narodowy im. Ossolińskich, 1976), 107, 117.

33. Moshe Elḥanan's wife, Sara Horowitz, was the daughter of the Vilnius doctor Itzhak Horowitz. She was buried in Odessa in 1839. See her epitaph in Ya'akov Eichenboym, *Tsiyunim metsuyanim be-vate ha-kevarot ha-yashan ve-he-ḥadash 'asher le-'adat yisra'el be-'ir odessa* (Warsaw: n.p., 1888), 12.

34. On the history of the garden, see, e.g., Roman Włodzimierz Aftanazy, "Humań i Zofiówka," in his *Dzieje rezydencji na dawnych kresach Rzeczypospolitej* (Wrocław: Zakład Narodowy im. Ossolińskich, 1996), 10:110–19; Ekaterina Shif, *Mify i skazaniia v parke "Sofievka"* (Kiev: Mystetstvo, 2007).

35. Naḥman's saying is cited in *Ha-'aliyah: Sipur korot ha-'aliyah le-tsiyon shel rabenu ha-kadosh ve-ha-nora' naḥman nove'a mekor ḥokhma* (Jerusalem, 1988), 44. On Naḥman of Bratslav and the Sophia gardens, see Yehuda Tsvi Shapira, *Ze sefer ha-derekh le-tsadik . . . 'al 'ir 'Uman* (Jerusalem: n.p., 2000), 44–47. Israel Belfer and Maoz Kahana argue that Naḥman's encounter with the garden exerted a significant influence on his theology. See

"Thinking Through Gardens: Park Sofijówka at the Crossroads of Jewish Messianism and Polish Noble Culture in Partitioned Poland" (forthcoming)

36. Auguste Louis Charles de Lagarde-Chambonas, *The Journal of a Nobleman: Being a Narrative of his Residence at Vienna during the Congress* (Philadelphia: Key and Biddle, 1833), 73, 81. The most substantial study of the Tulczyn estate to date is Oksana Lobko, "Pomishchyts'ki maietky Pravoberezhzhia v umovakh sotsial'no-ekonomichnoi transformatsii 1831–1917 rokiv (za materialamy volodin' hrafiv Potots'kykh)." (PhD diss., Kyiv University, 2008).

37. Stanisław Filip Krzyżanowski, *Tulczyn: Monografia.* (Kraków: Wielogłowski, 1862), 14–16; Giovanni Battista Lampi files, RF 2378, RF 2389, RF 1980.49, Louvre Museum, Center for Studies and Documentation, Paris.

38. On French aristocrats finding refuge in Tulczyn, see, e.g., Stanisław Schabowski, "Przedstawiciele rodu Polignaców i ich dzienniki w zbiorach Muzeum Zamku w Łańcucie," *Studia Wilanowskie* 24 (2017): 115–28.

39. Przemyslaw B. Witkowski, "Jean Potocki et le théâtre de Tulczyn," in *Jean Potocki à nouveau*, ed. Émilie Klene, Emiliano Ranocchi, and Przemyslaw B. Witkowski (Amsterdam: Rodopi, 2010), 53–54.

40. Jan Potocki, *Oeuvres,* ed. François Rosset and Dominique Triaire (Louvain: Peeters, 2004), 5:296.

41. On Stanisław Trembecki's final years in Tulczyn, see Roman Kaleta, "Grób Trembeckiego," *Oświeceni i Sentymentalni; Studia Nad Literatura i Życiem w Polsce w Okresie Trzech Rozbiorów* (Wrocław: Zakład Narodowy im. Ossolińskich, 1971), 399–411.

42. In addition to Yekutiel Grunem, Moshe Elḥanan had two daughters, Rivka-Raḥel and Pesya-Le'a (Elena), and another son, Aleksandr (Yuzefovich), who graduated from the University of Heidelberg in 1848; he was a physician by training. On Moshe Elḥanan's family, see "Ob opredelenii rabbina Moiseya El'kana"; Andrei Andreev, *Russkie studenty v nemetskikh universitetakh XVIII—pervoi poloviny XIX veka* (Moscow: Novoe literaturnoe obozrenie, 2005).

43. Auguste Louis Charles de LaGarde-Chambonas, *Voyage dans quelques parties de l'Europe* (London: Harding, Triphook, and Lepard, 1825), 100–1.

44. On Allan in Tulczyn, see Jeremy Howard and Andrzej Szczerski, "William Allan, Greek Beauty, and Polish Romanticism," *Apollo* (June 2001): 47–55; Godfrey Evans, "The 10th Duke of Hamilton and William Allan in Russia and the Ukraine," *Journal of the Scottish Society for Art History* 19 (2014): 15–26. For additional materials, see William Allan's letter to the Marquis of Douglas, St. Petersburg, January 16, 1812, quoted in Godfrey Evans, "Alexander, 10th Duke of Hamilton (1767–1852) as Patron and Collector" (PhD diss., University of Edinburgh, 2008), 675–77; *Letters Chiefly to Sir William Allan, Member of the Royal Academy of Arts, Historical Painter, 1808–1848, undated,* MS. 6294, fols. 62–156, Archives and Manuscripts, National Library of Scotland.

45. The full title is according to the 1815 summer exhibition of the Royal Academy of London. See *The Exhibition of the Royal Academy, MDCCCXV* (London: B. McMillan,

Bow-Street, Covent Garden, 1815), 4. I am grateful to Adam Waterton of the Royal Academy of London for providing this information. Allan offered the painting for sale at his 1819 solo exhibition at McIntosh's Gallery, London, for one hundred guineas. See the annotated copy preserved at the Royal Scottish Academy, *Catalogue of Pictures Painted by William Allan, as Exhibited at Mr. McIntosh's Gallery, 49 Princes Street* (Edinburgh, 1819). I would like to thank Robin H. Rodger from the Royal Scottish Academy of Art and Architecture for his assistance in locating this catalog.

46. John Gibson Lockhart, *Peter's Letters to His Kinsfolk: To Which Is Added, Postscript Addressed to Samuel T. Coleridge* (New York: Collins & Hannay, 1820), 286–87. As Lockhart notes elsewhere in this letter, Allan was unwell that day, and the two did not meet in person. Perhaps for this reason, while the description of the painting is highly valuable, the interpretation is inaccurate.

47. Witkowski, "Jean Potocki," 53–54.

48. Stanisław Trembecki, *Zofiówka w sposobie topograficznym opisana przez Stanisława Trembeckiego* (Leipzig: n.p., 1806).

49. The citation is according to the scholarly edition: Stanisław Trembecki, *Sofijówka*, ed. Jerzy Snopek (Warsaw: Instytut Badań Literackich, Pro Cultura Litteraria, 2000), 22, 31.

50. An excerpt from *Sofijówka* was first published under the title "Wyjątek z opisu Sofiówki przez Stanisława Trembeckiego," in *Tygodnik Wileński* 1, no. 13 (July 16, 1804): 182–86. The roughly parallel French title to Moshe Elḥanan's poem was "Hymne addressée à sa Majesté l'Empereur Alexandre Ier par Moïse Elkana Rabbin, traduite en vers français par le Chevalier de Messence." The most significant difference here was the use of the term for "hymn" in French; the cover also included the name of the translator.

51. Daniel Beauvois, *Pouvoir russe et noblesse polonaise en Ukraine, 1793–1830* (Paris: CNRS Éditions, 2003), 16–17.

52. Trembecki, *Sofijówka*.

53. For an analysis of *Sofijówka*'s political imaginary, see Erik Martin, "Das Imperium und der Garten: Die metapoetische Rolle der Panegyrik in Stanisław Trembeckis *Sofijówka* (1806)," *Zeitschrift für Slavische Philologie* 77, no. 1 (2021): 97–121.

54. There are a few indications of an interest in Judaism and Jewish mysticism in the Tulczyn court. Jan Potocki (1761–1815) incorporated Hebrew words in an Ashkenazi pronunciation into his philological writings, which, according to him, he learned through his communication with rabbis. See Jan Potocki, *Principes de chronologie pour les temps antérieurs aux olympiades* (St. Petersburg: A. Pluchart et comp., 1810), 60–61; and Jan Potocki, *Voyage dans les steppes d'Astrakhan et du Caucase: Histoire primitive des peuples qui ont habité anciennement ces contrées. Nouveau périple du Pont-Euxin . . . Ouvrages publiés et accompagnés de notes et tables*, vol. 2 (Paris: Merlin, 1829), 253. On Potocki's support for the education of Jewish students, see Viktoriia Kolesnyk, *Vidomi poliaky v istorii vinnychchyny: Biohrafichnyi slovnyk* (Vinnytsia: VMHO "Rozvytok," 2007), 596. Between 1804 and 1805, Tadeusz Grabianka (1740–1807), a Polish mystic and self-assigned "king" of *New Israel*, resided in Tulczyn and greatly influenced the Potocki court. This episode may indicate an

interest among the court members in mysticism and messianism. See Robert Collis and Natalie Bayer, *Initiating the Millennium: The Avignon Society and Illuminism in Europe* (New York: Oxford University Press, 2020), 156–91.

55. Gould, "The Much-Maligned Panegyric," 282.

56. Elkana, *Hymne*, 3.

57. For an analysis of Homer's *Odyssey* on the design of *Sofijówka*, see Ivan Oleksandrovych Kosenko, "Materializatsiia obraziv Homerovoi *Odissei* v parkovykh kompozytsiiakh *Sofiivky* iak vershyna henial'nosti Liudvyha Mettselia," *Ogrody Czartoryskich: Międzynarodowa Konferencja Naukowa Ogrody Rezydencji Magnackich XVIII-XIX Ww. w Europie Środkowej i Wschodniej Oraz Problemy Ich Ochrony* (Warsaw: Ośrodek Ochrony Zabytkowego Krajobrazu, Narodowa Instytucja Kultury, 2001), 49–54.

58. Tetiana Dmytrivna Chubina, "Rid Potots'kykh v Ukraini (tul'chyns'ka liniia): suspil'no-politychni ta kulturolohichni aspekty," PhD diss., Cherkas'kyi Derzhavnyi Tekhnolohichnyi Universytet, 2008), 276.

59. "Opisanie umanskogo sada," reprinted in Pavlo Usenko, *Serpankova preliudiia "Sofiivky"—Potots'ki: pol's'kyi mozhnovladets' i hrets'ka superkrasunia v ukrains'komu prystanovyshchi zahal'noi istorii* (Kyiv: Instytut istorii Ukrainy NAN Ukrainy, 2010), 54–56.

60. Armand-Emmanuel de Vignerot du Plessis, 5th Duke of Richelieu, to Sophia Potocka, July 1809, in *Lettres d'Odessa du duc de Richelieu: 1803–1814* ed. Elena Polevchtchikova and Dominique Triaire (Ferney-Voltaire: Centre international d'étude du XVIIIe siècle, 2014), 175.

61. Michał Konarski to Józef Zawadzki Peczar (May 17, 1813), reproduced in "Wyjątki listów Pana Michała Konarskiego," *Dziennik Wileński* 118, no. 1 (1815): 181–87.

62. On Wittgenstein in Tulczyn, see Alla Krasko, *Zabytyi geroi voiny 1812 goda general-fel'dmarshal P. Kh. Vitgenshtein* (Moscow: Tsentrpoligraf, 2012), 54–87; Ekaterina Lebedeva, "Tul'chin vremeni dekabristov: nezamechennye istochniki," *Istoricheskii kur'er* 14, no. 6 (2020): 9–29.

63. On Biblicism in the Russian court, see Stephen K. Batalden, *Russian Bible Wars: Modern Scriptural Translation and Cultural Authority* (Cambridge: Cambridge University Press, 2013).

64. Damiano Rebecchini, "An Influential Collector: Tsar Nicholas I of Russia," *Journal of the History of Collections* 22, no. 1 (May 2010): 45–67; Irina Marisina, "'Smart Travels': The Encounters of Grand Duke Nicholas with British Art and Artists, 1816–17," in *Courtly Gifts and Cultural Diplomacy: Art, Material Culture, and British-Russian Relations*, ed. Louise Hardiman, Russian History and Culture 24 (Paderborn: Ferdinand Schöningh, Brill Deutschland, 2023), 253–69; Hermitage Museum, "Digital Collection: Allan, Sir William (1782–1850), *The Bashkirs (The Bashkirs Escorting Prisoners)*," https://www.hermitagemuseum.org/digital-collection/40338?lng=en.

65. Ia. D. Baum, "Evrei-dekabrist. Grigorii Abramovich Peretts: Biograficheskii ocherk po arkhivnym materialam," *Katorga i ssylka*, no. 4 (1926): 121–22.

66. Jean-Henry Schnitzler, *Secret History of the Court and Government of Russia under the Emperors Alexander and Nicholas* (London: Richard Bentley, 1847), 2:3.

67. Bernard Natanson, *Sefer ha-zikhronot: Divre yeme ḥayye yitzḥak ber levinzohn, tekhunat sefarav, merots ha-'igrot beno u-ven ḥakhmei doro be-noge'a le-haskalat ha-yehudim be-'artsot rusya* (Warsaw: Y. Goldman, 1890), 151.

Chapter 2

1. *General Civil Code: For all the German Hereditary Provinces of the Austrian Monarchy*, trans. Joseph M. Chevalier de Winiwarter (Vienna: n.p., 1866), 5.

2. Natanson, *Sefer ha-zikhronot,* 150–51.

3. Shelomo Yehuda Leib Rapoport, *Kol nehi u-mispad mar: 'al mot . . . landes-gouverneur fun galitsien frants freiherr von hauer be-yom 12 le-ḥodesh kislev 5583* (Lemberg: Schnaider Joseph, 1822); Shmuel Yosef Bick, *dema'ot le-zikhron yashar: hi 'azkarat ha-nefesh . . . frants frayherr fon hauer . . . me-'adat bnei yisra'el be-vet ha-kneset ha-gedola di-k. k. brod* (Lemberg: Grosman, 1822); Me'ir Letteris, *pelage mayim: . . . 'al mot . . . netsiv ha-aretz . . . frants freiherr von hoyer: et 'asher safad vayekonen 'alav . . .* (Lemberg: Grosman, 1822).

4. *Sefer shivḥei ha-besht* (Kopys: Dfus Israel Yafe, 1815); Naḥman of Bratslav, *Sefer sipurei ma'asiyot she-zakhinu lishmo'a mi-pi rabeynu ha-kadosh moharan zutsakal* (Ostraha: n.p., 1815).

5. Dan Miron, *From Continuity to Contiguity, Toward a new Jewish Literary Thinking* (Stanford: Stanford University Press, 2010), 342.

6. Immanuel Etkes, "Haskalah," trans. Jeffrey Green, in *YIVO Encyclopedia of Jews in Eastern Europe*, 2010, https://encyclopedia.yivo.org/article/10.

7. For a survey of the interrelation between Maskilic and Hasidic literature, see David Assaf, "Son'im sipur 'ahava? Hitpatḥuyot be-meḥkar yaḥasey ha-gomlin beyn ḥasidut ve-ha-haskala," in *Ha-haskala li-gvaneyha: 'Iyunim ḥadashim be-toldot ha-haskala u-ve-safruta,* ed. Israel Bartal and Shmuel Feiner (Jerusalem: Magnes Press, 2005), 183–200.

8. On Joseph von Sonnenfels, see Simon Karstens's biography: *Lehrer – Schriftsteller – Staatsreformer, Die Karriere des Joseph von Sonnenfels (1733–1817)* (Vienna: Böhlau Verlag, 2008). See also Robert Kann, *A Study in Austrian Intellectual History from Late Baroque to Romanticism* (New York: Praeger, 1960), 146–259; Josef Karniel, "Joseph von Sonnenfels," *Jahrbuch des Instituts für Deutsche Geschichte* 6 (1978): 111–58.

9. Jonathan Israel, *Democratic Enlightenment: Philosophy, Revolution, and Human Rights 1750–1790* (Oxford: Oxford University Press, 2011), 286.

10. See the chapter devoted to Sonnenfels as a legal reformer in Karstens, *Lehrer – Schriftsteller – Staatsreformer,* 281–345.

11. On Sonnenfels's literary theory, see Hilde Haider-Pregler, "Die Schaubühne als 'Sittenschule' der Nation: Joseph von Sonnenfels und das Theater," *Josef von Sonnenfels,* ed. Helmut Reinalter (Vienna: Verlag der dsterreichischen Akademie der Wissenschaft, 1988), 191–244.

12. Cited in Ernst Wangermann, "'By and By We Shall Have an Enlightened Populace': Moral Optimism and the Fine Arts in Late-Eighteenth-Century Austria," *Austrian History Yearbook* 30 (1999): 8.

13. Joseph von Sonnenfels, *Grundsätze aus den Polizei Handlungs und Finanzwissenschaften* (Vienna: Joseph Edlen von Kurzbek, 1768–1786), 2:94.

14. See von Sonnenfels, *Grundsätze aus den Polizei,* 1:122.

15. Imperial laws were at the center of many of the studies early in the century concerning the history of Galician Jewry. See, e.g., the studies of Avraham Ya'akov Brawer: *Galizien, wie es an Österreich kam: Eine historisch-statistische Studie über die inneren Verhältnisse des Landes im Jahre 1772* (Vienna: F. Tempsky, 1910), 104–7, and the expanded Hebrew edition: *Galitsya ve-yehudeha: Meḥkarim be-toldot galitsya ba-me'ah ha-shemoneh-'esreh* (Jerusalem: Mosad Bialik, 1964), 141–97. See also Filip Friedman, "Dzieje Żydów w Galicji (1772–1914)," in *Żydzi w Polsce odrodzonej działalność społeczna, gospodarcza, oświatowa i kulturalna*, ed. Ignacy Schiper et al. (Warsaw: Nakl. Wydawn. "Żydzi w Polsce Odrodzonej," 1932–1933), 1:372–412.

16. For an overview of the legal status of the Jewish population in Galicia, see Svjatoslav Pacholkiv, "Galizische Judengemeinden unter Maria Theresia und Joseph II," *Bulletin der Polnischen Historischen Mission* (2014): 93–123; Anthony Polonsky, *The Jews in Poland and Russia, vol. 1 (1350–1881),* (Oxford: Oxford University Press, 2010), 248–73. See also Israel Bartal, *The Jews of Eastern Europe 1772–1881* (Philadelphia: University of Pennsylvania Press, 2006), 71–81.

17. Werner Ogris, "The Habsburg Monarchy in the Eighteenth Century: The Birth of the Modern Centralized State," in *Legislation and Justice*, ed. Antonio Padoa-Schioppa (Oxford: Oxford University Press, 1997), 333.

18. Ogris, "The Habsburg Monarchy," 329.

19. Gershon David Hundert, *The Jews in a Polish Private Town: The Case of Opatów in the Eighteenth Century* (Baltimore: Johns Hopkins University Press, 2019), xi.

20. Charles Tilly, *Contention and Democracy in Europe, 1650–2000* (Cambridge: Cambridge University Press, 2004), 66.

21. Thomas Ertman, *Birth of the Leviathan: Building States and Regimes in Medieval and Early Modern Europe* (Cambridge: Cambridge University Press, 1997), 265.

22. Tomasz Opas, "Miasta prywatne a Rzeczpospolita," *Kwartalnik Historyczny* 78, no. 1 (1971): 28–29.

23. Adam Teller, "The Legal Status of the Jews on the Magnate Estates of Poland-Lithuania in the Eighteenth Century," *Gal-Ed* 15–16 (1997): 41.

24. Max Weber, *From Max Weber: Essays in Sociology,* ed. Hans Heinrich Gerth and Charles Wright Mills (New York: Oxford University Press, 1946), 239.

25. Jacob Goldberg, *Jewish Privileges in the Polish Commonwealth: Charters of Rights Granted to Jewish Communities in Poland-Lithuania in the Sixteenth to Eighteenth Centuries: Critical Edition of Original Latin and Polish Documents with English Introductions and Notes* (Jerusalem: Israel Academy of Sciences and Humanities, 1985), 1.

26. Jacob Goldberg, "The Role of the Jewish Community in the Socio-Political Structure of the Polish-Lithuanian Commonwealth," *Polin* 22 (2010): 146–47.

27. Lauren Benton and Richard J. Ross, "Empires and Legal Pluralism: Jurisdiction, Sovereignty, and Political Imagination in the Early Modern World," in *Legal Pluralism and*

Empires, 1500–1850, ed. Lauren Benton and Richard J. Ross (New York: NYU Press, 2013), 1–18.

28. On the serfs' right to lodge complaints against landowners, see Kai Struve, *Bauern und Nation in Galizien. Über Zugehörigkeit und soziale Emanzipation im 19. Jahrhundert*, Schriften des Simon-Dubnow-Instituts 4 (Göttingen: Vandenhoeck & Ruprecht, 2005), 71–77. On complaints lodged by Ukrainian-speaking serfs, see Jan Fellerer, "Discourse and Hegemony: The Case of the Ukrainian Language in Galicia under Austrian Rule," in *Diglossia and Power: Language Policies and Practice in the 19th Century Habsburg Empire*, ed. Rosita Rindler Schjerve (Berlin: Mouton de Gruyter, 2003), 116; Andrii Zaiarniuk, *Idiomy emansypatsii: "Vyzvol'ni" proiekty i halyts'ke selo v seredyni XIX stolittia* (Kyiv: Krytyka, 2007). On complaints lodged by Polish-speaking serfs, see Piotr Wandycz, "The Poles in the Habsburg Monarchy," *Austrian History Yearbook* 3, no. 2 (1967): 265. See also two seminal studies on serfdom in Galicia: Ludwig von Mises, *Die Entwicklung des gutsherrlich-bäuerlichen Verhältnisses in Galizien (1772–1848)* (Vienna: Franz Deuticke, 1902); Roman Rozdolski, *Stosunki poddańcze w dawniej Galicji*, 2 vols. (Warsaw: Panstwowe Wydawn. Naukowe, 1962).

29. For example, in 1777, the delegates of Potocki, the owner of the city of Brody, announced in the local synagogue his intention to take the monopoly of alcohol production from Jewish hands, annulling a 1699 privilege. This, to be sure, was not the first time in which the Potocki family had announced legal changes of major implications on the Jewish population. At this historical point, however, four years after Brody fell under Austrian rule, the residents of the private city were legally subject both to the town owner and the laws of the land, as well as to the imperial law. The Jewish community appealed, in response, for legal protection, a *Schutzdekret*, from the Austrian authorities, against what they perceived as a persecution on part of the city owner. See Nathan Michael Gelber, *Toldot yehudei brodi*, Vol. 6 of *'Arim ve-'imahot be-yisra'el*, ed. Judah Leyb Maimon, 7 vols. (Jerusalem: Mosad ha-rav kuk, 1956), 6:132. On the concept of royal alliance, see Yosef Hayim Yerushalmi, *Servants of Kings and Not Servants of Servants: Some Aspects of the Political History of the Jews*, Tenenbaum Family Lecture Series in Judaic Studies (Atlanta: Emory University, 2005), 7–29.

30. Ernst Wangermann, *From Joseph II to the Jacobin Trials: Government Policy and Public Opinion in the Habsburg Dominions in the Period of the French Revolution* (London: Oxford University Press, 1959), 23.

31. Abraham Trebitsch, *Korot ha-'itim* (Brünn: Joseph Rossmann, 1801), 29–30.

32. For a review of the sources of legal knowledge in Poland before the partition, see Zdzisław Kaczmarczyk and Bogusław Leśnodorski, *Historia państwa i prawa polskiego* (Warsaw: Państwowe Wydawn. Naukowe, 1965), 2:84–89. On the Volumina Legum project, see Jerzy Lukowski, *Liberty's Folly: The Polish Lithuanian Commonwealth in the Eighteenth Century, 1697–1795* (London: Routledge, 1991), 94.

33. *Sammlung aller k.k. Verordnungen u. Gesetze vom Jahre 1740 bis 1780, Die unter der Regierung des Kaisers Joseph des II. theils noch ganz bestehen, theils zum Theile abgeändert*

sind, als ein Hilfs- und Ergänzungsbuch zu dem Handbuche aller unter der Regie, 2 vols. (Vienna: Mößle, 1787).

34. *Sammlung aller k.k. Verordnungen,* 2:896.

35. *Sr. k.k. Majestät Franz des Ersten politische Gesetze und Verordnungen für Sämmtliche Provinzen des Österreichischen Kaiserstaates mit Ausnahme von Siebenbürgen* (Vienna: K.K. Hof- u. Staats-Aeralial- Druckerey, 1811), 34:96. For the official form, see p. 528.

36. Iryna Vushko, "Enlightened Absolutism, Imperial Bureaucracy and Provincial Society: The Austrian Project to Transform Galicia, 1772–1815" (PhD diss., Yale University, 2008), 53.

37. *Edicta et mandata universalia Regnis Galiciæ & Lodomeriæ a die initiæ possessionis promulgata: Rozkazy i ustawy powszechne Krolestwom Galicyi i Lodomeryi od dnia obięcia possessyi ogłoszone* (Lemberg: n.p., 1791), 65:73–74. The edict contains further instructions for smaller cities, villages, and other forms of settlements. On legal publications in Galicia, see Stanisław Grodziski, *Historia ustroju społeczno politycznego Galicji, 1772–1848* (Wrocław: Zakład Narodowy im. Ossolińskich, 1971), 133–44. Jan Fellerer, *Mehrsprachigkeit im Galizischen Verwaltungswesen (1772–1914): Eine Historisch-soziolinguistische Studie zum Polnischen und Ruthenischen (Ukrainischen)* (Cologne: Böhlau, 2005), 65–103.

38. Franciszek Karpiński, "List do J.L. C. P.W.Ks. L. z Krasnegostawu," in *Dzieła Franciszka Karpińskiego* (Warsaw: W Druk. Stereotypowey, 1830), 177–78.

39. Grodziski, *Historia ustroju,* 32. On the Habsburg policy concerning translations of legal documents, see Wilhelm Neder, "Die Übersetzungen von Gesetzen in der Habsburgmonarchie" (Working Paper No. 7, Donau-Institut, Budapest, 2013).

40. The promotion of translation of laws and statues into Polish was in decline between 1815 and 1848. For example, between 1819 and 1827 the compendium of laws for Galicia (*Provinzial Gesetzsammlung des Königreichs Galizien und Lodomerien*) was published without translation into Polish. For statistics on translations into Latin and Polish, see Jan Fellerer, *Mehrsprachigkeit im galizischen,* 67–75; Zdzisław Kaczmarczyk and Bogusław Leśnodorski, *Historia Państwa i Prawa Polski* (Warsaw: Państwowe Wydawn. Naukowe, 1965), 2:184–89.

41. Rudolf Mark, *Galizien unter österreichischer Herrschaft: Verwaltung, Kirche, Bevölkerung* (Marburg: Herder-Institut, 1994), 64.

42. Fellerer, "Discourse and Hegemony," 141–43. There was, however, a limited attempt to translate legal documents into Galician Church Slavonic. Jan Fellerer (*Mehrsprachigkeit im galizischen,* 126–32) located six legal documents in Galician church Slavonic published between 1772 and 1848: five documents containing rules for ecclesiastical schools, and an 1827 "subjects duties to the sovereign" (*Povinnosti poddanych ko icy monarchy*).

43. *Iberzetsung der fun unzern allergnedigsten keyzar: Und bahershter aller raysen, in 54 punktn, iber di aynrikhtung un farbeserung der yehudim be-medinat rusiya* (Vilnius: n.p., 1804). I thank Israel Bartal for bringing this document to my attention.

44. Bodleian Library, Oxford-Neubauer no. N2215(1).

45. Bernhard Friedberg, *Toldot ha-defus ha-'ivri be-polanya: me-reshit hitpatḥuto be-shnat 297 [1537], hishtalemuto, divre yamav ve-hishtalsheluto 'ad ha-yom* (Antwerp: n.p., 1932), 86. According to Friedberg, the text was printed only as late as 1790. The Hebrew manuscript "Words of Wisdom" [Divre binah], authored by Dov ber Birkenthal (1723–1805), explicitly mentions laws that were "explained in the Emperor's (Juden) system" [*shmevo'ar ba-system me-ha-kirah*]. In reference to these laws, Birkenthal uses the terminology in the German text, followed by a legal term from the Hebrew translation, which may suggest he had access to both. See Gershon David Hundert, "The Introduction to Divre binah by Dov Ber of Bolechów: An Unexamined Source for the History of Jews in the Lwów Region in the Second Half of the Eighteenth Century," *AJS Review* 33 (2009): 264.

46. On the project of the "Germanization" of Galician Jewry, see Hendrika Johanna (Tehilah) van Luit, "Paths of Modernity in Traditions' Strongholds the German Jewish Schools as a Playground between the Austrian Absolutist Welfare State and the Galician Kahal" (PhD diss., Hebrew University of Jerusalem, 2011), 121–61.

47. Cited according to Henry E. Strakosch, *State Absolutism and the Rule of Law: The Struggle for the Codification of Civil Law in Austria 1753–1811* (Sydney: Sydney University Press, 1967), 195.

48. *General Civil Code*, 5.

49. Cited according to Damiano Canale, "The Many Faces of the Codifications of the Law in Modern Continental Europe," in *A Treatise of Legal Philosophy and General Jurisprudence*, ed. Damiano Canale et al. (New York: Springer, 2005), 9:138.

50. *General Civil Code*, 4; *Allgemeines bürgerliches Gesetzbuch für die gesammten deutschen Erbländer der Oesterreichischen Monarchie* (Vienna: k.k. Hof- und Staatsdruckerey, 1811).

51. On the historical origins of the principle, see Rollin M. Perkins, "Ignorance and Mistake in Criminal Law," *University of Pennsylvania Law Review and American Law Register* 88, no. 1 (November 1939): 35–70; Sharon L. Davies, "The Jurisprudence of Willfulness: An Evolving Theory of Excusable Ignorance," *Duke Law Journal* 48, no. 3 (December 1998): 341–427.

52. In his commentary on this law, Franz von Zeiller (1751–1828), one of the principal drafters of the ABGB, elaborated on the vision of an efficient, universal circulation of legal texts as a means of disseminating knowledge about the state. See von Zeiller's *Commentar über das allgemeine bürgerliche Gesetzbuch: Für die gesamten deutschen Erbländer der österreichischen Monarchie* (Vienna: Geistinger, 1811), 34.

53. *Gesetzbuch über Verbrechen und Schwere Polizey-Uebertretungen* (Vienna: Hof-und Staats-Aerarial-Druckerey, 1815). For a history of Austrian criminal law, see Christian Neschwara, "Zur Genese des österreichischen Strafgesetzes von 1803," in *Strafrechtsgeschichte im „langen" 19. Jahrhundert: Forschungen und Perspektiven*, ed. Martin P. Schennach (Vienna: Verlag Österreich, 2020), 37–60; and Thomas Olechowski, "Zur Entstehung des österreichischen Strafgesetzes 1852," in *Grundlagen der österreichischen Rechtskultur: Festschrift für*

Werner Ogris zum 75. Geburtstag, ed. Alina Lengauer, Christian Neschwara, and Thomas Olechowski (Vienna: Böhlau Verlag, 2010), 319–41.

54. Chone Shmeruk, introduction to *Maʿasiyot ve-ʾigrot mi-tsadikim amitiyim u-meʾanshei shelomenu*, by Joseph Perl, ed. Chone Shmeruk and Shmuel Werses (Jerusalem: Ha-ʾAkademya ha-leʾumit ha-Yisraʾelit le-Madaʿim, 1969), 15, 41. For a study of the relationship between Perl's *Tales and Letters* and Naḥman of Bratslav's tales, see Jeremy Asher Dauber, *Antonio's Devils: Writers of the Jewish Enlightenment and the Birth of Modern Hebrew and Yiddish Literature* (Stanford: Stanford University Press, 2004), 228–57.

55. Dan Miron, "Lifnei shaʿar ha-ḥok," *Kivunim ḥadashim*, December 29, 2013, 88.

56. Arye Avnun-Broynshtayn, "Tarnopol be-khol yemot ha-shana" in *ʾEnsiklopedya shel galuyot: Sifre zikaron le-ʾartsot ha-gola ve-ʿedoteha*, 12 vols., ed. Yeruḥam Kongrin (Jerusalem: Ḥevrat 'entsiklopedyah shel galuyot, 1955), 3:331.

57. Nathan Michael Gelber, "Tarnopol," in *ʾEnsiklopedya shel galuyot*," 3:58.

58. On legends about Joseph Perl's meetings with Joseph II, see Michael Ha-kohen Brawer, "Lifnei me'a shana," *Ha-hed* 12 (1933): 30. See also Meir (Max) Weissberg, "Die neuhebräische Aufklärungsliteratur in Galizien," *Monatsschrift für die Geschichte und Wissenschaft des Judentums* 36, nos. 1–2 (1928): 83.

59. Y. H. Koren, "Kol ʿale nidaf, Kislon ben parnakh ha-parʿatoni, mishpat ʿami," *Ha-kol* 32 (August 13, 1880): 487.

60. "Takanot ve-hamlatsot bi-dvar ha-pulḥan ha-dati shel yehudei galitsya, 1789," National Library of Israel, Joseph Perl's Archive, ARC. 4* 1153/101.

61. *Edicta et mandata universalia Regnis Galiciae et Lodomeriae* (Lemberg: Joseph Piller, 1789), 90.

62. The document references *Sr. k.k. Majestät Franz des Ersten*, 6.

63. A number of Joseph Perl's denunciation letters were published. See, e.g., Joseph Nacht, "Ein unveröffentlichtes Aktenstück von Josef Perl," *Monatsschrift für Geschichte und Wissenschaft des Judentums* 7–8 (July–August 1927): 308–11; Raphael Mahler, *Ha-ḥasidut ve-ha-haskala be-galitsya u-ve-polin ha-kongresaʾit ba-maḥatsit ha-rishona shel ha-meʾa ha-tesha ʿesre* (Merḥavyah: Sifriyat poʿalim, 1961), 397–463. Rachel Manekin, "Sefer ḥok le-Yisrael ve-hitpashtut ha-ḥasidut: Teʿudah meʾet yosef perl," in *Yashan mi-pnei ḥadash: Meḥkarim be-toldot yehudei mizraḥ eropa ve-tarbutam, shay le-ʿimanuel ʾetkes*, ed. David Assaf and Ada Rappaport, 2 vols. (Jerusalem: Merkaz Zalman Shazar, 2009), 2:345–55. For an example of a communication regarding Jewish education, see Perl's 1835 request from the government to allocate money for training Jewish teachers: k.k. Kreisamt, Kreisamt 13084, No. 127 1695 VII 23 G Tarnopol, AVA, Sthk. 23E Tarnopol, December 23, 1835. Perl also appealed to the Austrian authorities on personal matters; in 1823, he requested a permission to become a member of the Berlin Society for Jewish Culture and Science (Verein fur die Kultur und Wissenschaft der Juden). See HHStA, StK, *Noten an die Polizeihofstelle*, December 9, 1822, and March 28, 1823.

64. On the 1789 Edict of Tolerance, see Josef Karniel, "Das Toleranzpatent Kaiser Josephs II. für die Juden Galiziens und Lodomeriens," *Jahrbuch des Instituts für Deutsche Geschichte* 11 (1982): 55–89.

65. On the network of state-sponsored German-Jewish schools in Galicia, see Isabel Röskau-Rydel, *Kultur an der Peripherie des Habsburger Reiches: Die Geschichte des Bildungswesens und der kulturellen Einrichtungen in Lemberg von 1772 bis 1848* (Wiesbaden: Harrassowitz, 1993); Dirk Sadowski, "Maskilisches Bildungsideal und josephinische Erziehungspolitik: Herz Homberg und die jüdisch-deutschen Schulen in Galizien, 1787–1806," *Leipziger Beiträge zur jüdischen Geschichte und Kultur* 1 (2003): 145–68; "The Jewish German Schools in Galicia (1782–1806)—School Reality and Corporate Resistance," *Jewish Culture and History* 13, nos. 2–3 (2012): 153–72.

66. Joseph Perl, "Takanot ve-hamlatsot bi-dvar ha-pulḥan ha-dati shel yehudei galitsya, 1789" (Annotated Judenpatent), NLI Arc 4* 1153/101.

67. Rachel Manekin, "Hasidism and the Habsburg Empire, 1788–1867," *Jewish History* (2013): 280; Shimon Bernfeld, "Zikhronot," *Reshumot* 4 (1927): 184.

68. In the 1814 Galicia Schematismus, directory of imperial official, there is a list of five Jewish police supervisors: Samuel Reitz, Saul Landes, Leiser Dettersdorf, Abraham Unter, and David Ulrich. See *Schematismus des Königreiches Galizien und Lodomerien* (Lemberg: Joseph Johann Piller, 1814), 57. For a discussion on state rabbis, see Haim Gertner, *Ha-rav ve-ha-ʿir ha-gedola, ha-rabanut be-galitsiya u-mifgasha im ha-moderna 1816–1867* (Jerusalem: Merkaz Zalman Shazar, 2013).

69. On the Russian rule of Tarnopol and its administration, see Jan Leszczyński, *Rządy rosyjskie w kraju Tarnopolskim*, 1809–1815 (Krakow: Druk W. L. Anczyca, 1903).

70. For information on Jews in Tarnopol and Zaleszyk purchasing houses from Christians under Russian rule, see *Jüdische Einwohner von Tarnopol und Zaleszyk um Belassung im Besitze der während des russischen Besitzes von Christen erkauften Häusern*, 1818, State Chancellery, Court and State Archives, Vienna (HHStA), Staatsratsindex 1818, no. 1545 (Copy CAHJP HM-3245).

71. On Perl's educational activities, see Filip Friedman, "Yoysef perl vi a bildungs-tuer un zayn shul in tarnopol (125 yor nokh ir grindung)," *YIVO-Bleter* 31–32 (1948): 131–90; Sinkoff, *Out of the Shtetl*, 225–37 and Kazimierz Rędziński, "Szkoła Józefa Perla w Tarnopolu (1813–1939)," in *Prace Naukowe Gliwickiej Wyższej Szkoły Przedsiębiorczości, Społeczne konteksty edukacji, Pedagogika*, ed. Kazimierza Rędzińskiego and Mirosława Łapota (Gliwice: Gliwicka Wyższa Szkoła Przedsiębiorczości, 2009), 225–45.

72. Franciszek Korytowski (1763–1833) inherited from his uncle Felicyan Korytowski considerable financial resources in 1809. See Adam Bonieck, *Herbarz polski: Wiadomości historyczno-genealogiczne o rodach szlacheckich* (Warsaw: Gebethner i Wolff, 1899–1913), 9:214. Turning to the Polish landowner for support of public institutions was certainly not an exception: It was fairly common among magnates to finance projects for the welfare of their residents, particularly educational institutions. For example, Maciej Lanckoroski financed a school in Zakliczna in 1788, and Wit Żeleński sponsored a school in Brzesko in 1834. See Łukasz Jewuła, *Galicyjskie miasta i miasteczka oraz ich mieszkańcy w latach 1772–1848* (Krakow: Towarzystwo Wydawnicze "Historia Iagellonica," 2013), 116–17.

73. The letter from Ignatz Theyls to Josef Perl was published in Joseph Perl, *Yoysef perls yidishe ksovim*, ed. Zelig Kalmanovitch (Vilnius: Yivo-bibliotek, filologishe sektsye, 1937), xx–xxi.

74. See the letter from Ignatz Theyls to Joseph Perl published in *Shulamit* 2 (1812): 422–23.

75. Leszczyński, *Rządy rosyjskie*, 31–33.

76. Raphael Mahler, *Ha-ḥasidut ve-ha-haskala*, 402.

77. To provide one example, Joseph Perl personally contributed to the creation of a Galician reserve squadron, paying two hundred golden rubles from his own funds; by comparison, the Jewish community of Tarnopol collectively provided three hundred silver rubles in October 1815. See *Gazeta Lwowska* 95 (November 28, 1815): 1.

78. Joseph Perl, *'Al mahut kat ha-ḥasidim*, ed. Avraham Rubinshtayn (Jerusalem: ha-'Akademya ha-le'umit ha-yisra'elit le-mada'im, 1977), 133.

79. See, e.g., Mordechai Vilenski, *Ḥasidim u-mitnagdim: Le-toldot ha-pulmus she-benehem ba-shanim tak–taka* (Jerusalem: Mosad bialik, 1990), 1:230–65.

80. Arthur Green, *Tormented Master: The Life and Spiritual Quest of Rabbi Naḥman of Bratslav* (Tuscaloosa: University of Alabama Press, 1979), 339.

81. Dauber, *Antonio's Devils*, 233.

82. Naḥman of Bratslav, *The Tales*, 91.

83. Perl, *Ma'asiyot ve-'igrot mi-tsadikim 'amitiyim u-me'anshei shelomenu*, ed. Chone Shmeruk and Shmuel Werses (Jerusalem: Ha-'Akademya ha-le'umit ha-Yisra'elit le-Mada'im, 1969), 91.

84. Perl, *Ma'asiyot ve-'igrot*, 223

85. For a review of literature concerning the context in which the tale was told, see Yoav Elstein, *Pa'amei bat melekh* (Ramat Gan: Universitat Bar Ilan, 1984), 104–8.

86. Naḥman of Brastlav, *The Tales*, 55.

87. Cited according to Naḥman of Bratslav, *Sefer sipurei ma'asiyot*, 14.

88. Perl, *Ma'asiyot ve-'igrot*, 188

89. See Perl, *Ma'asiyot ve-'igrot*, 138–39.

90. The manuscript is part of the YIVO Sutzkever-Kaczerginski collection, RG 223.2.

91. For a detailed analysis of the story in relation to Joseph Perl's political vision, see Chone Shmeruk, "Ḥazono ha-maskili shel yosef perl," in *Ma'asiyot ve-'igrot mi-tsadikim 'amitiyim u-me'anshei shelomenu*, by Joseph Perl, ed. Chone Shmeruk and Shmuel Werses (Jerusalem: ha-'Akademya ha-le'umit ha-yisra'elit le-Mada'im, 1969), 36–42.

92. Perl, *Ma'asiyot ve-'igrot*, 55.

93. Perl, *Ma'asiyot ve-'igrot*, 211.

94. Perl, *Ma'asiyot ve-'igrot*, 222.

95. Manekin, "Hasidism and the Habsburg Empire," 272.

96. Naḥman of Bratslav, *The Tales*, 99.

97. Konstanty Słotwiński, *Katechizm poddanych galicyjskich: o prawach i powinnościach ich względem Rządu, Dworu i samych siebie* (Lviv: n.p., 1832).

98. Me'ir Letteris, *Sefer mikhtavei bnei kedem: kolel 'igrot u-mikhtevim be-leshon ʿavar ve-ʾashkenaz* (Vienna: Y. Shlosberg, 1866), 146.

99. This reconstruction builds on Rachel Manekin's "Ha-ḥerem be-lemberg bishnat 1816, ravrevanut maskilit ve-historiya yehudit," *Tsiyon* (2008): 173–98; Gertner, *Harav ve-haʿir ha-gedola,* 39–46.

100. Shmuel Feiner, *Haskalah and History: The Emergence of a Modern Jewish Historical Consciousness* (Portland: Littman Library of Jewish Civilization, 2002), 75.

101. Manekin, "Ha-ḥerem," 197.

102. Jacob Katz, *Tradition and Crisis; Jewish Society at the End of the Middle Ages* (New York: Schocken Books, 1961), 84–86. See also Jonas Weisner, *Der Bann in seiner geschichtlichen Entwicklung auf dem Boden des Judenthums* (Leipzig: Leiner, 1864): 88–89.

103. Michael Silber, "Shorshe ha-pilug be-yahadut hungariya: tmurot tarbutiyot ve-ḥevratiyot mi-yemey yosef ha-sheni ʿad-ʿerev mahapekhat 1848" (PhD diss., Hebrew University of Jerusalem, 1985), 109. See also Manekin, "Ha-ḥerem."

104. *Provinzial-Gesetzsammlung des Königreichs Galizien und Lodomerien für das Jahr 1823* (Lemberg: Peter Piller, 1824), 141–42.

105. Mary Gallagher, "Mobilizing the Law in China: 'Informed Disenchantment' and the Development of Legal Consciousness," *Law & Society Review* 40, no. 4 (December 2006): 792–93.

106. Perl, *Yidishe Ksovim,* xxxii–xxxi.

107. Richard L. Abel, "What We Talk About When We Talk About Law," in *The Law and Society Reader,* ed. Richard L. Abel (New York: NYU Press, 1995), 3.

108. Perl, *Yidishe Ksovim,* xxxii–xxxi.

109. Naḥman Krochmal, *Kitvei Rabi Naḥman Krokhmal,* ed. Shimʿon Ravidovits (ʿEnot, 1924), 416–18. The translation is from Raphael Mahler, *Hasidism and the Jewish Enlightenment: Their Confrontation in Galicia and Poland in the First Half of the Nineteenth Century* (Philadelphia: Jewish Publication Society of America, 1985), 80.

110. For an interpretation of the idiom *genarte velt,* see Dov Sadan, *A vort bashteyt: Shpatsirn tsvishn shprakh un literatur* (Tel Aviv: Farlag Y. L. Perets, 1975), 223–25.

111. Meir Viner, *Bibliologisher zamelbukh* 1 (1929): 140–47; Meir Viner, ed., *Di genarte velt: Komedye fun an umbakantn avtor inem tsveytn yortsendlik funem nayntsntn yorhundert* (Moscow: Melukhe-farlag "Der Emes," 1940), 3–47; A. Mukdoyni [pseud. Aleksander Kapel], "Di ershte yidishe komedye," *Yidishe Kultur* 9 (September 1947): 42–43; Yudl Mark, "Di shprakh fun der komedye di genarte velt," *Yidishe Shprakh* (May–June 1943): 68–86; Chone Shmeruk, "Nosaḥ bilti yadu'a shel ha-komediya ha'anonimit 'Di genarte velt,'" *Kiryat Sefer* 54 (1979): 802–16; Jeremy A. Dauber, "Between Two Worlds: Antitheatricality and the Beginnings of Modern Yiddish Theatre," in *Inventing the Modern Yiddish Stage: Essays in Drama, Performance, and Show Business,* ed. Joel Berkowitz and Barbara Henry (Detroit: Wayne State University Press, 2012), 27–39.

112. See the introduction to the 1863 version of the play in Dauber's translation, "Between Two Worlds," 27.

113. Viner, *Di genarte velt*, 103.

114. Solomon Ettinger, *Ale Ksovim* (Vilnius: B. Kletskin, 1925), xxviii.

115. Sheryl Kroen, *Politics and Theater: The Crisis of Legitimacy in Restoration France, 1815–1830* (Berkeley: University of California Press, 2000), 3.

116. Joel Berkowitz and Jeremy Asher Dauber, eds., *Landmark Yiddish Plays: A Critical Anthology* (Albany: State University of New York, 2006), 110.

117. Chone Shmeruk, "Nosaḥ bilti yadu'a."

118. Chone Shmeruk, *Sifrut yidish: perakim le-toldoteha* (Tel Aviv: Mifʿalim Universita'iyim le-Hotsa'ah la-'or, 1978), 110.

119. *Di genarte velt oder shverer me nemt zikh fir, griner helft got* (Lemberg: J. Madfes, 1865).

120. *Di genarte velt* (Moscow: Melukhe-farlag "Der Emes," 1940), 31.

121. Meir Viner, *Tsu der geshikhte fun der yidisher literatur in 19-tn yorhundert (etyudn un matiryaln)* (New York: Ikuf, 1945): 53.

122. Dauber, "Between Two Worlds," 38.

123. Manekin, "Ha-ḥerem," 198.

124. Joseph Perl, *Boḥen tsadik: Bo muva deʿot ʿal ha-sefer megale temirin* (Prague: M. J. Landau, 1838), 53.

125. *Di genarte velt* (1940), 54.

126. *Di genarte velt* (1940), 98.

127. Murray Jay (Moshe) Rosman, *The Lords' Jews: Magnate-Jewish Relations in the Polish-Lithuanian Commonwealth During the Eighteenth Century* (Cambridge: Harvard University Press, 1990), 146–47.

128. *Di genarte velt oder shverer me nemt zikh fir, griner helft got*, 28.

129. On the profession of a bookseller in relation to the figure of Mendele Moykher Sforim, see Dan Miron, *A Traveler Disguised*, 187–88.

130. On Bikurei ha-ʿitim, see Feiner, *Haskalah and History*, 72–74.

131. *Bikurei ha-ʿitim* (1821), 211.

132. Frank MS. Hebrew fol 11. (Merzbacher 64). For more information about this personal notebook, see Efraim Kupfer, "Ya'akov shemu'el bik le-'or te'udot ḥadashot," *Gal-Ed* 4–5 (1978): 535–47.

133. *"Magistrat m. Lwowa, Kreisschreiben vom k.k. Galizischen Landesgubernium betr: Der jüdischen Kleidung und Aufhebung des Gebrauches der hebraischen und sogenannten jüdischen Sprache und Schrift in allen öffentlichen gerichtlechen und außergerichtlichen Handlungen, 1814,"* State Archive of Lviv Oblast, Lviv (DaLO), collection 3, inventory 1, file 601 (Copy CAHJP HM2-8283.8).

134. See Simcha Katz, "'Igrot maskilim bi-gnutam shel ha-ḥasidim," *Mozna'im* 10 (1940): 273.

Chapter 3

1. This article was published as Ofer Dynes, "How to Read Naḥman of Bratslav's Tales in Their Historical Context," *Jewish Social Studies* 29, no. 3 (2024): 61–85. No part of it may be reproduced, stored in a retrieval system, transmitted, or distributed in any form, by any means, electronic, mechanical, photographic, or otherwise, without the prior permission of Indiana University Press. For education reuse, please contact the Copyright Clearance Center http://www.copyright.com/. For all other permissions, contact IU Press at http://iupress.indiana.edu/rights/.

2. Nathan Sternhartz, *Sefer ḥayei moharan: ḥayav . . . shel rabi naḥman mi-bratslav . . . ʿim hashmatot me-ha-rav* [*ʾalter*] *mi-teplik ve-hosafot me-ha-rav sh. horowitz* (Beyt Shemesh: Nekudotot Tovot, 2008), 369. The translation is from Reb Noson of Breslov (Nathan Sternhartz), *Tzaddik: A Portrait of Rebbe Nachman*, trans. Avraham Greenbaum (Jerusalem: Breslov Research Institute, 2019), 399 with slight modifications.

3. The one major exception, "The King Who Decreed Conversion," is discussed later.

4. Naḥman of Bratslav, *Sefer sipurei maʿasiyot*, introduction (unpaginated).

5. Yosef Dan, *Ha-sipur ha-ḥasidi* (Jerusalem: Keter, 1990), 137.

6. Arnold J. Band, *Studies in Modern Jewish Literature. JPS Scholar of Distinction Series* (Philadelphia: Jewish Publication Society, 2003), 13–38.

7. Ora Wiskind-Elper, *Tradition and Fantasy in the Tales of Reb Nahman of Bratslav* (Albany: State University of New York Press, 1998), 54.

8. Arthur Green, *Seek My Face, Speak My Name: A Contemporary Jewish Theology* (Northvale: J. Aronson, 1992), xvi.

9. Simcha Petrushka, "Makor polani le-sipurei maʿasiyot shel rabi naḥman mi-bratslav," *Ketuvim* 2, no. 42 (1928): 3; Avidav Lipsker, "'Hakala ve-shivʿat ha-kabtsanim': Le-she'elat me-korotav shel sipur ha-misgeret shel 'maʿaseh me-ha-zain betler,'" *Meḥkarei yerushalayim be-folklor yehudi* 13–14 (1991): 229–48; Martin Irving Mantel, "Rabbi Naḥman of Bratzlav's [*sic*] Tales: A Critical Translation from the Yiddish with Annotations and Commentary" (PhD diss., Princeton University, 1977); Chone Shmeruk, "Alegorizatsiya yehudit shel yetsirot mi-folklor ha-amim," *Ha-kongres ha-ʾolami ha-sheni le-madaʿei ha-yahadut* (1957): 3; Chana Hendler, "Ha-sipur ha-ḥasidi bein ʿitsuv safruti le-ide'a ruḥanit, iyun be-shalosh girsa'ot shel ha-tema ʿotsar taḥat ha-gesher ke-degem meyatseg," in *Maʿaseh sipur*, ed. Avidav Lipsker and Rela Kushelevski (Ramat Gan: Universitat Bar Ilan), 1:147–67.

10. Wiskind-Elper, *Tradition and Fantasy*, 155–56; Aryeh Kaplan, *Rabbi Nachman's Stories* (Brooklyn: Breslov Research Institute, 1985), 128.

11. David Roskies, "The Master of Prayer: Rabbi Naḥman of Bratslav," in *God's Voice from the Void: Old and New Studies in Bratslav Hasidism*, ed. Shaul Magid (Albany: State University of New York Press, 2002), 67–102, and esp. 80; Yizhak Lewis, *A Permanent Beginning: R. Nachman of Bratslav and Jewish Literary Modernity* (Albany: State University of New York Press, 2020), 59.

12. Roskies, "Master of Prayer," 82.

13. The only exception is "The Rabbi's Son," which comments on Naḥman's dispute with Aryeh Leyb of Shpola (Shpoler Zeyde, 1725–1815). Shpola is the Polish Szpoła, today in Ukraine. See Mendel Piekarz, *Ha-hanhaga ha-ḥasidit: Samkhut ve-emunat tsadikim be-as-paklaryat sifurtah shel ha-ḥasidut* (Jerusalem: Mosad Bialik, 1999), 202–4.

14. For a general notion of common themes in folktales, compare Hans-Jorg Uther, *The Types of International Folktales: A Classification and Bibliography, Based on the System of Anttii Aarne and Stith Thompson*, 3 vols. (Helsinki: Suomalainen Tiedeakatemia, Academia Scientiarum Fennica, 2004). Compare the group of nineteenth-century Hasidic tales that Dvir-Goldberg collected, in which the *tzaddik* is a prince. Strikingly, in all the tales she brings, "king" and "prince" can be replaced by "father" and "son" without further changes in the meaning of the tale. See Rivka Dvir-Goldberg, *Ha-tsadik ha-ḥasidi ve-armon ha-livyatan, ʿiyun be-sipurei maʿasiyot mi-pi tsadikim* (Tel Aviv: ha-Kibuts ha-Meʾuḥad, 2003), 51–65. See also the list of themes in Gedalyah Nigal, *The Hasidic Tale* (Oxford: Littman Library of Jewish Civilization, 2008).

15. Marc Zvi Brettler, "God Is King: Understanding an Israelite Metaphor," *Journal for the Study of the Old Testament*, supplement series 76 (Sheffield: JSOT Press, 1989). On God as king in the midrash, see Ignaz Ziegler, *Die Königsgleichnisse des Midrasch, beleuchtet durch die römische Kaiserzeit* (Breslau: S. Schottlaender, 1903). On the relationship between the image of God and kingship in early Kabbalah, see Arthur Green, *Keter: The Crown of God in Early Jewish Mysticism* (Princeton: Princeton University Press, 1997).

16. On the husband-wife relationship, see Tsippi Kauffman, "Ha-shkhina ha-mitḥape-set: Perek be-te'ologiya be-shtianit," *Da'at* 78 (2015): 151–70. More broadly, see Moshe Idel, *Ben: Sonship and Jewish Mysticism* (London: Continuum, 2008), 531–85.

17. Band, *Studies in Modern Jewish Literature*, 13–38; Dan, *Ha-sipur ha-ḥasidi*, 7; Wis-kind-Elper, *Tradition and Fantasy*, 58. The citation is from Angus Fletcher, *Allegory: The Theory of a Symbolic Mode* (Ithaca: Cornell University Press, 1964), 2.

18. Maureen Quilligan, *The Language of Allegory, Defining the Genre* (Ithaca: Cornell University Press, 1979), esp. 27–28.

19. Naḥman of Bratslav, *The Tales*, 154–55. See also Nathan Sternhartz, *Siḥot ha-ran* §28. *Rateirin* (Yiddish) is a plural form of *Rater* or *Roter*, "councillor." See Menashe Unger, "Yidishe verter in loshn koydeshn tekst fun sipurey mayses," *Yidishe shprakh* 28 (1967): 20.

20. Naḥman's allusion to Italian politics may have been inspired by the critique of Yitzḥak Arama (1420–94). See Yitzḥak Arama, *Ḥazut kasha* (Pressburg: Franz Edlen von Schmid, 1859), 29–32. I thank Avraham Oriyah Kalman for this idea.

21. On the relationship between Orthodox Judaism and absolutist monarchism, and more broadly, between conservative groups in Eastern Europe across religious and ethnic lines, see Israel Bartal, *The Jews of Eastern Europe*, 124–33, and Immanuel Etkes, *Rabbi Shneur Zalman of Liady: The Origins of Chabad Hasidism* (Waltham: Brandeis University Press, 2014), 259–80.

22. In 1816, Joseph Perl showed how *Likutei moharan* §61 [Naḥman of Bratslav, *Likutei moharan mahadura le-limud ve-ʿiyun, hugʿa ʿal-pi defus moharnat, be-hashvaʿah le-shaʿar*

defusim, kerekh meyuḥad li-khvod mata'im shanah le-histalkut rabeinu (Jerusalem: n.p., 2011)] is a response to the 1804 statute of the Jews; see Perl, *'Al mahut kat ha-ḥasidim*, 136–37. Following is a selective list of scholarly works that have interpreted Naḥman's response to the 1804 law: Raphael Mahler, *A History of Modern Jewry 1780–1815* (New York: Schocken Books, 1971), 514–17; Mendel Piekarz, *Ḥasidut Bratslav: Perakim be-ḥayei me-ḥolela, bi-ktaveha uve-sefiḥe'a* (Jerusalem: Mosad bialik, 1972), 194–95; Amram Bloy, "Gerush ha-kfarim be-rusiya bi-yemei reshit ha-ḥasidut, yaḥasam u-fo'alam shel gedolei ha-ḥasidut le-gezirat ha-gerush," *Heikhal ha-besht* 13 (2006): 133–57; Avraham Avish Shur, "Yaḥas ged-olei ha-ḥasidut la-shilton ve-ha-kesher bein ha-'aliyah l-'erets isra'el le-halukat polin," *Kovets ḥitse giborim* 10 (April 2017): 1026–28; and Lewis, *Permanent Beginning*, index.

23. See, e.g., Wiskind-Elper, *Tradition and Fantasy*, 30; David Assaf, "When the Rabbis 'Met' Napoleon," *Tradition* 54, no. 2 (2022): 55–62; and Hever, *Hasidism, Haskalah, Zionism*, 8–52.

24. On the legal status of these individual locals, see Filip Sulimierski, Bronisław Chlebowski, and Władysław Walewski, *Słownik geograficzny królestwa Polskiego i innych krajów Słowiańskich* (Warsaw: nakł. Filipa Sulimierskiego i Władysława Walewskiego, 1880–1902); Petro Tymofilovych Tronko, *Istoriia mist i sil Ukrainy v konteksti rehional'nnykh doslidzhen': Dosvid, problemy, perspektyvy* (Kyiv: Instytut istorii Ukrainy NAN Ukrainy, 1967–1973).

25. The one notable exception is a section titled "Conversation Related to the Tales" in Sternhartz, *Ḥayei moharan* §70–77, which documented some of the responses of Naḥman students to the tale, mostly their expressions of misunderstanding and confusion. For a posthumous source, see Nathan Sternhartz's letter to his son, which touches on his interpretation of "The Loss of the Princess," Nathan Sternhartz, *'Alim li-trufa* (Warsaw: Hotsa'at Braslav, 1930), 7–8.

26. Joseph Perl, *Ma'asiyot ve-'igrot*, 117–223. For a discussion of Joseph Perl's engagement with Hasidic sources, Tsippi Kauffman, "Thoughts on the Seam Between Hasidic Literature and Haskalah Literature: The Works of Joseph Perl," *Prooftexts* 38, no. 2 (2020): 347–68; Joseph Perl, *Megale temirin*, ed. Jonathan Meir, 3 vols. (Jerusalem: Mosad bialik, 2013), 3:381–463.

27. Yoav Elstein, *Pa'amei bat melekh*, 191nn248–49. On dualism in Bratslav thought, see Joseph George Weiss, "Mystical Hasidism and the Hasidism of Faith: A Typological Analysis," in *God's Voice from the Void: Old and New Studies in Bratslav Hasidism*, ed. Shaul Magid, Series in Judaica (Albany: State University of New York Press, 2002), 277–85.

28. Isaiah Tishby, *Pirkei zohar: Mivḥar ma'amarei ha-zohar me-turgamim le-'ivrit be-tseruf mevo'ot ubi-urim* (Jerusalem: Mosad Bialik, 1969), 1:209, my translation.

29. Eliott R. Wolfson, *Luminal Darkness: Imaginal Gleanings from Zoharic Literature* (Oxford: Oneworld, 2007), 38.

30. On the general atmosphere in the tale, see the comment by Yehudit Kuk, *Rabi naḥman mi-bratslav 'iyunim be-sipurav* (Jerusalem: Feldheim, 1994), 78.

31. Sternhartz, *Ḥayei moharan* §428, 364 echoing Isaiah 1:22. The English is after Avraham Greenbaum's translation in Sternhartz, *Tzaddik*, 39. Naḥman's pun on "dross," *sigim*, which he changed to *sig* (Hebrew: *na'asa hama'ot ve-ha-kesef sig*) likely alludes to the Russian

assignatsia, or assignation bills. For an accusation against a Bratslav Jew, Hershko Moskovich, of counterfeiting, and the use of an assignation bill, see "Po obvineniiu Itska Gershkovicha, arendatora s. Strel'chintsy, v sozhitel'stve so sluzhivshei u nego russkoi devkoiu Evdokiei rodivshei mladentsa," 1805, collection 120, inventory 1, file 344, State Archives of Khmelnytskyi Oblast, Khmelnytskyi (Copy CAHJP CD-412.04). On assignation, see Rosman, *The Lords' Jews*, 128–30.

32. Perl, *'Al mahut kat ha-ḥasidim*, 133–41.

33. Zvi Mark, *Megilat setarim: Ha-ḥazon ha-meshiḥi ha-sodi shel r. naḥman mi-braslav* (Ramat Gan: Universitat Bar-Ilan, 2006), 54–55.

34. Strikingly, the political vision of the scroll also resonated with older Messianic literature, for example, with Nathan of Gaza's letter to Raphael Joseph. See Jacob Sasportas, *Tsitsat novel tsevi*, ed. Isaiah Tishby (Jerusalem: Mosad Bialik, 1954), 7–12.

35. Geoffrey Ellis, *The Napoleonic Empire* (New York: Bloomsbury Academic, 2003), 54–58.

36. Marianne Schleicher, *Intertextuality in the Tales of Rabbi Nahman of Bratslav: A Close Reading of Sipure ma'asiyot* (Leiden: Brill, 2007), 260–72.

37. Zvi Mark, *Mysticism and Madness: The Religious Thought of Rabbi Nachman of Bratslav* (New York: Continuum, 2009), 260–79.

38. Arthur Green, *Tormented Master*, 355–60; *Seek My Face*, xvii; "Ga'agu'ei ha-'elohim el ha-'adam, 'al ma'aseh mi-melekh 'anav, ha-sipur sheli," in *Ha-ḥayim kega'agu'a, keriyot ḥadashot be-sipurei ma'asiyot shel rabi Naḥman mi-braslav*, ed. Roee Horen (Tel Aviv: Miskal-Yedioth Ahronoth Books and Chemed Books, 2010), 91–99.

39. Green, *Tormented Master*, 356, with modifications.

40. On Naḥman's difficulty crossing the border between the Russian and the Austrian partitions of Poland, see Green, *Tormented Master*, 232–33.

41. Ya'akov Yosef mi-Polnoye, *Ben Porat Yosef* (Lemberg: n.p., 1866), 60B, 94A–94B, 105B. The English translation is from Idel, *Ben*, 545–46. Another version was recorded in Moshe Ḥaim Efraim of Sudlikow, *Degel maḥane efrayim* (Jerusalem: Makhon ha-Ktav, 1987), 222–23, 229. For a comparison, see Iris Brown, "Shelosha gilgulim shel meshal ha-ḥomot,'" *Meḥkare Yerushalayim be-sifrut 'ivrit* 23 (2009): 99–132. See also Tsippi Kauffman, "Hasidic Performance: Establishing a Religious (Non)Identity in the Tales about Rabbi Zusha of Annopol," *Journal of Religion* 95, no. 1 (2015): 51–71.

42. Iris Brown, "Shelosha gilgulim," 99.

43. Green, *Tormented Master*, 356, with minor modifications.

44. Naḥman Goldstein (Naḥman of Tcherin), *Sefer rimze ha-ma'asiyot* (Bnei Brak: Keren Hadpasa ve-Hafatsa le-Sifrei Ḥasidut Braslav, 1995), 7. The English translation is from Mark, *Mysticism and Madness*, 262.

45. See Yosef Dan's evaluation of Naḥman of Tcherin's interpretation of the tales in Dan, *Ha-sipur ha-ḥasidi*, 137.

46. Sternhartz, *Ḥayei moharan* §119, §154.

47. See also *Siḥot haran* §63.

48. See Zvi Mark, *Kol sipurei rabi naḥman mi-braslav, ha-ma'asiyot, ha-sipurim ha-sodi-yim, ha-ḥalomot ve-ha-ḥezyonot* (Jerusalem: Mosad Bialik, 2014), 235.

49. Green, *Tormented Master*, 356–57, with minor modification.

50. Kaiser Friedhelm Berthold, *Die russische Justizreform von 1864: Zur Geschichte der russischen Justiz von Katharina II. bis 1917* (Leiden: Brill, 1972), 10–20; Isabel de Madariaga, *Russia in the Age of Catherine the Great* (New Haven: Yale University Press, 1981), 282–87.

51. Daniel Beauvois, *Pouvoir russe et noblesse polonaise en Ukraine, 1793–1830* (Paris: CNRS Éditions, 2003), 74–75; Kryvosheia, *Shliakhta Umanshchyny*.

52. For example, in the years 1802–1803, Itsik Nusimovich from Nemirov appealed against the Potockis for lease violation. See the court file titled "Po zhalobe arendatorov Abramka Mortkovicha Panicha iz Bratslava, Itsko Nusimovicha iz Nemirova i Itsko Khaimovicha iz Brailova," 1798–1803, collection 120, inventory 1, file 1724, State Archives of Khmelnytskyi Oblast. For similar appeals in Galicia (Copy CAHJP *CD-193.07)*; See Nathan Michael Gelber, *'Arim ve-'imahot*, 6:132. See also *Siḥot haran*, §175.

53. Mark, *Mysticism and Madness*, 249; Green, *Tormented Master*, 357–58.

54. Evgenii Trefilov and Julia Leikin, "Proof of Sincere Love for the Tsar: Popular Monarchism in the Age of Peter the Great," *Kritika* 18, no. 3 (2017): 461–85; Daniel Beer, "To a Dog, a Dog's Death!": Naïve Monarchism and Regicide in Imperial Russia, 1878–1884," *Slavic Review* 80, no. 1 (2021): 112–32, at 113–14. On nineteenth-century popular monarchism, see also Germain de Lagny, *Le knout et les russes, moeurs et organisation de la Russie* (Paris: D. Giraud, 1853), 275–77. I am grateful to Gershon Hundert (z"l) for the idea that "The Humble King" is a response to Russian popular monarchism.

55. Maureen Perrie, "The Popular Image of Ivan the Terrible," *SEER* 56, no. 2 (1978): 275–86, at 277.

56. See Shneur Zalman's depiction of Paul I in his letter to Pinḥas Horowitz of Frankfurt in Shalom Duber Levin, *'Igrot kodesh* (Brooklyn: Kehot, 2002), 113–14, and Etkes, *Rabbi Shneur Zalman*, 259–80. On Chabad's politics in nineteenth-century Russia, see Ilia Lurie, *Milḥamot lyubavitch, ḥasidut ḥabad be-rusiya ha-tsarit* (Jerusalem: Merkaz Zalman Shazar, 2018), 180–205.

57. See the account on the tale "The Master of Prayer" in Sternhartz, *Ḥayei moharan,* §72.

58. See Sternhartz, *'Alim li-terufa*, 8.

59. Avraham Ḥazan, *'Avaneha barzel* (Jerusalem: Yeshivat Braslav le-Tora u-Tefila, 1935), 29–30. The translation is from Zvi Mark, *The Scroll of Secrets: The Hidden Messianic Vision of R. Nachman of Breslav* (Boston: Academic Studies Press, 2010), 28.

60. My analysis of Naḥman's messianic temporality is based on Ada Rapoport-Albert's account of the different stages of Naḥman's messianism. "He'arot le-ma'amaro shel yehuda *liebes,*" *Tsiyon* 46 (1981): 346–51.

61. Sternhartz, *Ḥayei moharan* §115; Sternhartz, *Yemei moharanat*, §38.

62. Green, *Tormented Master*, 356.

63. Joseph George Weiss, *Meḥkarim be-ḥasidut braslav* (Jerusalem: Mosad Bialik, 1974), 200.

64. On the conditions of crossing the Bug, see Adam Stanisław Naruszewicz, *Dziennik podróży króla Stanisława Augusta na Ukraine i do innych ziem koronnych* (Warsaw: Instytut Badań Literackich PAN. Wydawnictwo, 2019), 546–47. According to Marta Wiraszka, the survey of Bratslav was conducted in 1799. See Marta Wiraszka, *Rozwój Przestrzenny I Zabudowa Miast Guberni Podolskiej w Czasach Imperium Rosyjskiego* (Warsaw: Neriton, 2008), 89–90.

65. Serhii Anatoliiovych Kopylov and Andrii Zadorozhniuk, eds., *Opysy Podil's'koi hubernii kintsia XVIII – pochatku XIX st.* (Kamianets-Podilskyi: Aksioma, 2011), 91.

66. On district towns, see Susan Smith-Peter, *Imagining Russian Regions, Subnational Identity, and Civil Society in Nineteenth-Century Russia* (Leiden: Brill, 2018), 23–58.

67. On Naḥman's mystical intervention in politics, see Shaul Magid, *Hasidism Incarnate: Hasidism, Christianity, and the Construction of Modern Judaism* (Stanford: Stanford University Press, 2015), 1–27.

68. See Sternhartz, *Ḥayei moharan* §115.

69. For a description of the area of Bratslav adjacent to the river in the seventeenth century, see the travel notes of Ulrich von Werdum, *Das Reisejournal des Ulrich von Werdum (1670–1677): Kritische Edition eines Reiseberichtes*, ed. Silke Cramer (Frankfurt am Main: Peter Lang, 1990), 485–86.

70. This information is based on the 1799 land survey of Podolia: *Topohrafichnyi opys Podil'skoi hubernii 1799 r.: Vinnyts'kyi, Iampil's'kyi, Bratslavs'kyi povity*, ed. Iurii Lehun (Vinnytsia: Nilan, 2017), 257–380.

71. According to the 1799 land survey, in Bratslav "there are craftsmen . . . but their skills are simple and suitable only for Jewish [clients]: 2 silversmiths, 4 coppersmiths, 13 tailors, 8 shoemakers, 12 hatmakers, 8 furriers, 2 braiders, and one bookbinder." In Tulczyn, by way of comparison, "[there were] two Jews in foreign trade, and the rest were craftsmen with an excellent quality of work: 39 tailors, 8 furriers, 9 braiders, 9 silversmiths, 6 coppersmiths, 14 shoemakers, 3 saddlers, 2 watchmakers, one bookbinder, and a miller." *Topohrafichnyi opys*, 258–80.

72. Murphy, *From Citizens to Subjects*, 192.

73. According to Oleksandr Petrenko, the number of male residents in the viceroyalty was 404,578. The number of female residents was presumably equal or slightly higher than that of males, bringing the total population to just over eight hundred thousand. For a historical survey of the Bratslav viceroyalty, see Oleksandr Petrenko, "Bratslavs'ka huberniia i Bratslavs'ke namisnytstvo," *Kyivs'ka starovyna* 1 (2000): 44–61. It is worth noting that Bratslav already enjoyed a prominent administrative position under Polish rule as the capital of the Bratslav voivodeship (Polish: *województwo*).

74. On the formation of the Bratslav and Podolia eparchy in 1795, see "No. 17,318. Ob uchrezhdenii v trekh prisoedinennykh ot Pol'shi Guberniiakh i v Kamenetskoi Oblasti po odnomu muzheskomu i odnomu zhenskomu monastyriu (12 Apr. 1795)," Polnoe sobranie zakonov Rossiiskoi imperii, ser. 1, 45 vols. (St. Petersburg, 1830), 23:663–64. On the 1799 name change of the eparchy, see Pavel Vikul, "Podol'skie arkhipastyri (1795–1895 gg.),"

Trudy Podol'skago eparkhial'nago istoriko-statisticheskago komiteta (Kamianets-Podilskyi: Tipografiia podol'skago gubernskago pravleniia, 1897), 8:1–160. On the location of the cathedral, see "No. 19,156. O privedenii Eparkhial'nykh granits soobrazno granitsam Gubernii i ob uchrezhdenii novykh Eparkhii (16 Oct. 1799)," *Polnoe sobranie zakonov Rossiiskoi imperii*, ser. 1, 45 vols. (St. Petersburg, 1830), 25:813–21.

75. Green, *Tormented Master*, 136.

76. Naḥman of Bratslav, *Likutei moharan*, §44.

77. Sternhartz, *Ḥayei moharan*, §115.

78. Sternhartz, *Ḥayei moharan*, §115, §§148–49.

79. Sternhartz, *Ḥayei moharan*, §55.

80. Arthur Green, *Tormented Master*, 135–36; Sternhartz, *Ḥayei moharan* §1, §§7–8; and Naḥman of Bratslav, *Likutei moharan* §48.

81. For instance, the Russian authorities invited delegates from the Jewish community in the provincial capital Kamenets Podol'skii to discuss the draft statute prior to its issuance in 1804. This process was recorded in Kamenetskii magistrat, "O vyborakh v Kamentse deputatov v Peterburg dlia uchastiia v rabote Komissii po ustroistvu evreev. Zdes' zhe 'Polozhenie o evreiakh' 1804 g," State Archives of Khmelnytskyi Oblast, Khmelnytskyi, collection 46, inventory 1, file 30 (Copy CAHJP, HM2-8865.5). Similarly, the rabbi of Bratslav, in his role as district rabbi, was involved in numerous judicial processes in cooperation with the local authorities. "Po obvineniiu zhitelia m-ka Nemirova Itska Duvidovicha i drugikh razboinikov v ograblenii v Bratslave dubossarskogo kuptsa Nikolaia Muratova (s opis'iu ukradennykh veshchei i protokolami doprosov svidetelei, postradavshego i obviniaemykh)," Podol'skii glavnyi sud, 1805–1807, f. 120, State Archives of Khmelnytskyi Oblast, Khmelnytskyi, collection 120, inventory 1, file 524 (Copy CAHJP CD-412.11).

82. Green, *Tormented Master*, 228.

83. Mendel Piekarz elaborated on the chronology surrounding Naḥman's turn to storytelling in *Ḥasidut Bratslav*, 56–82.

84. Mark, *Kol sipurei*, 204–8.

85. Mark's *Kol sipurei* is the most ambitious attempt to reconstruct the chronology of Naḥman's tales (see the commentary on each tale). See also Piekarz, *Ḥasidut Bratslav*, 151–54.

86. The information on the road is from the 1806 Podolia land survey, published in Sergei Kopylov and Zadorozhniuk, *Opysy Podil's'koi*, 78.

87. Sternhartz, *Ḥayei moharan* §114. On Barukh of Międzybórz, see Tsippi Kauffman, "R. barukh." On his tenure in Tulczyn, see Shlomo Avish, *Sefer zikaron 'ir mivtsar: Toldot ha-'ir "mezhibozh" mivtsar ha-torah veha- ḥasidut: bo yeto'ar toldot ha-'ir, 'admoreha ve-rabaneha* (Brooklyn: Makhon Zikhron ba-Sefer, 2010), 243.

88. Naḥman of Bratslav, *The Tales*, 207.

89. Józef Ignacy Kraszewski, *Wspomnienia Odessy, Jedysanu i Budżaku* (Vilnius: T. Glücksberg, 1845), 1:74–75. Israel Belfer and Maoz Kahana offered a different interpretation, which associates this sculpture with Sofijówka. See Belfer and Kahana, "Thinking through Gardens," 1-2.

90. Kopylov and Zadorozhniuk, *Opysy Podil's'koi*, 78. On a visit to Bratslav by a European traveler on his way to Tulczyn, see Gian Pietro Vieusseux, *Journal-Itinéraire de mon voyage en Europe, 1814–1817: Con il carteggio relativo al viaggio*, ed. Lucia Tonini (Florence: L. S. Olschki, 1998), 96.

Chapter 4

1. Andreas Glaeser, *Political Epistemics: The Secret Police, the Opposition, and the End of East German Socialism* (Chicago: University of Chicago Press, 2010), 159.

2. Joseph Perl, *Revealer of Secrets* (Boulder: Westview Press, 1997), 13–14.

3. Christopher Bayly, *Empire and Information*, 315–38. For a classical account of the shift from enlightened absolutism to political repression, see Ernst Wangermann, *From Joseph II to the Jacobin Trials: Government Policy and Public Opinion in the Habsburg Dominions in the Period of the French Revolution* (London: Oxford University Press, 1959).

4. A 1773 memorandum cited in Avraham Ya'akov Brawer, *Galitsyah ve-yehudeha*, 23.

5. For a survey of studies on cameralism, see Andre Wakefield, *The Disordered Police State: German Cameralism as Science and Practice* (Chicago: University of Chicago Press, 2009). For a study of how cameralism shaped state policies toward the Jews, see Ari Joskowicz, "Toleration in the Age of Projects: Cameralism, German Police Science, and the Jews," *Jewish Social Studies* 22, no. 2 (2017): 1–37.

6. Marc Raeff, *The Well-Ordered Police State: Social and Institutional Change Through Law in the Germanys and Russia, 1600–1800* (New Haven: Yale University Press, 1983); John T. Alexander, *Catherine the Great: Life and Legend* (New York: Oxford University Press, 1989), 79–82; Claus Scharf, *Katharina II Deutschland und die Deutschen* (Mainz: P. von Zabern, 1995), 119–30.

7. For a conceptual history of the term "police," see Karolina Zobel, "Polizei: Geschichte und Bedeutungswandel des Wortes und seiner Zusammensetzungen" (PhD diss., University of Munich, 1952). On the changing meanings of the term in the early nineteenth century, see Keith Tribe, *Governing Economy: The Reformation of German Economic Discourse, 1750–1840* (Cambridge: Cambridge University Press, 1988), 161–63.

8. Isabel de Madariaga, *Russia in the Age of Catherine the Great* (New Haven: Yale University Press, 1981), 292–95.

9. Keith Tribe, *Strategies of Economic Order* (Cambridge: Cambridge University Press, 2006), 20–21.

10. The citation derives from the 1786 *Secret Police Instructions* reproduced in August Fournier, *Historische Studien und Skizzen* (Prague: E. Tempsky, 1885), 3:7–16. On the development of the Austrian police and secret police, and the relationship between the two, see Anna Hedwig Benna, "Die Polizeihofstelle: Ein Beitrag zur Geschichte der österreichischen Zentralverwaltung" (PhD diss., University of Vienna, 1942); Hermann Leitner, "Der geheime Dienst der Polizei in seinen Anfängen zur Zeit des österreichischen Absolutismus" (PhD diss., University of Vienna, 1994); Michal Chvojka, *Josef Graf Sedlnitzky als Präsident der Polizei- und Zensurhofstelle in Wien (1817–1848): Ein Beitrag zur Geschichte*

der Staatspolizei in der Habsburgermonarchie (Frankfurt: Peter Lang, 2010); and Donald E. Emerson, *Metternich and the Political Police: Security and Subversion in the Habsburg Monarchy, 1815–1830* (The Hague: Martinus Nijhoff, 1968). For studies of the Russian secret police, see Sidney Monas, *The Third Section: Police and Society in Russia under Nicholas I* (Cambridge: Cambridge University Press, 1968); Andrei Gavrilovich Chukarev, *Tainaia Politsiia Rossii, 1825–1855* (Zhukovskii: Kuchkovo Pole, 2005).

11. Monas, *The Third Section*, 26.

12. For an analysis of the "Song of the Polish Legions" in its historical context, see Larry Wolff, "Revising Eastern Europe: Memory and the Nation in Recent Historiography," *Journal of Modern History* 78, no. 1 (March 2006): 93–118.

13. Cited in Iryna Vushko, *The Politics of Cultural Retreat: Imperial Bureaucracy in Austrian Galicia, 1772–1867* (New Haven: Yale University Press, 2015), 83–105.

14. Friedrich Schembor, *Galizien im ausgehenden 18. Jahrhundert: Aufbau der österreichischen Verwaltung im Spiegel der Quellen* (Bochum: Verlag Dr. Dieter Winkler, 2015), 216.

15. Schembor, *Galizien im ausgehenden*, 276.

16. Simon Schwarzfuchs, *Napoleon, the Jews and the Sanhedrin* (London: Routledge & Kegan Paul, 1979), 24.

17. Nathan Michael Gelber, "La police autrichienne et le Sanhédrin de Napoléon," *Revue des Études Juives* 83 (1927): 1–19, 121–45; Gershon Wolf, *Geschichte der Juden in Wien 1156–1876* (Vienna: A. Hölder, 1876), 113–20. For additional materials collected by Gelber, see CAHJP RP083, folder I/44, titled "Sanhedrin 1806; verschiedene Abschriften aus den 1806 Sammlungen vom Haus-, Hof- und Staatsarchiv, Wien."

18. Wolf, *Geschichte der Juden*, 113–16.

19. Dawid Kandel, "Hymn do Napoleona," *Kwartalnik poświęcony badaniu przeszłości Żydów w Polsce* 1, no. 2 (1912–1913): 122.

20. François Guesnet, "The Turkish Cavalry in Swarzędz, or: Jewish Political Culture at the Borderlines of Modern History," in *Jahrbuch des Simon-Dubnow-Instituts / Simon Dubnow Institute Yearbook: Schwerpunkt / Special Issue: Early Modern Culture and Haskalah*, ed. Dan Diner (Leipzig: Vandenhoeck & Ruprecht, 2007), 234.

21. Barukh Mevorakh, *Napoleon u-tekufato: Reshumot ve-ʿeduyot ʿivriyot shel bnei ha-dor* (Jerusalem: Mosad Byalik, 1968), 31.

22. Ronald Schechter, *Obstinate Hebrews, Representations of Jews in France, 1715–1815* (Berkeley: University of California Press, 2003), 200.

23. Wolf, *Geschichte der Juden*, 114–15.

24. Gelber, "La police autrichienne."

25. "Sanhedrin 1806: Verschiedene Abschriften aus den 1806 Sammlungen vom Haus-, Hof- und Staatsarchiv, Wien," Private Collection N. M. Gelber, P 83 I/44, CAHJP.

26. Gelber, "La Police autrichienne," 131.

27. Aleksander Fredro, *Trzy Po Trzy* (1880; Warsaw: Państwowy Instytut Wydawniczy, 2023), 74.

28. Markian Prokopovych, *Habsburg Lemberg: Architecture, Public Space, and Politics in the Galician Capital, 1772–1914* (West Lafayette: Purdue University Press, 2008), 203. There are similar testimonies from other cities—for example, in Freiburg, where local citizens reportedly shouted "Vive la nation! Vive la république!" to avert potential violence from the invading troops. See Leighton S. James, *Witnessing the Revolutionary and Napoleonic Wars in German Central Europe* (Houndmills: Palgrave Macmillan, 2013), 133.

29. Vushko, *Enlightened Absolutism*, 146, 281.

30. "Eine Liste der Deportierten aus Österreich, darunter auch Juden, im Zusammenhang mit dem Vorwurf der Spionage und Strafanzeigen," Central State Historical Archives of Ukraine, Lviv (TsDIAL), collection 146, inventory 7, file 572, pp. 1–11, 1810 (Copy CAHJP HM3-893)

31. Alexander Grab, *Napoleon and the Transformation of Europe* (New York: Palgrave Macmillan, 2003), 18.

32. See Benyamin (Veniamin) Lukin, "'Sluzhba naroda evrejskogo i ego kagalov': Evrei i Otechestvennaja Vojna 1812 goda," *Lechaim* 187 (2007): 38–43. "Kagaly tainye i iavnye: Evreiskie obshchiny v voine 1812 goda," *Lechaim* 238 (2012); "'Bditel'noe oko pravitel'stva': k istorii uchastiia rossiiskikh evreev v voine 1812 goda," *Lechaim* 248 (2012). The most famous Jewish spy, Moshe Meislish (1759–1844), described later in his life how he was "summoned to the house of the Tsar, who was then in Vilna." He was ordered to "join up with the army of Bonaparte,' so that [he] would make a faithful friend . . . know all the secrets and recount them to the Czar." Alexander Marks, "Mikhtav r. moshe meizelsh Le-eli'ezer ha-levi," *Zion: Me'asef ha-ḥevra ha-'erets-yisra'elit le-historya ve-'etnografya* 4 (1930): 39–43.

33. Boerries Kuzmany, *Brody, Eine galizische Grenzstadt im langen 19. Jahrhundert* (Vienna: Böhlau, 2011), 252.

34. "Die Untersuchung unter der Anschuldigung der Juden in der Spionage und Verbindungen mit ausländischen Armeen," Central State Historical Archives of Ukraine, Lviv (TsDIAL), collection 146, inventory 7, file 570, 571, 1810–11, 1814 (Copy CAHJP HM3-893.04)

35. Majer Bałaban, *Shalshelet ha-yaḥas shel mishpaḥat Orenshtein-Broda: ('al smakh kitvei yad u-mekorot nidpasim)* (Warsaw: Monolit, 1931), vi. On Ya'akov Ornstein, see Hayim Natan Dembitzer, *Kelilat yofi: Kolel toldot ha-rabanim ba'ir lvov* (Krakow: Yosef Fisher, 1888–1893), 1:140(b)–152(b); Salomon Buber, *'Anshei shem, ge'oney Israel, 'adirei ha-tora, rabanim, 'asher shimshu ba-kodesh ba'ir lvov mi-shnat ha-ras ad ha-taran* (Krakow: n.p., 1895.), 111–12; Bałaban, *Shalshelet ha-yaḥas*, 30–32; Gertner, *Ha-Rav ve-ha-'ir*, 37–66; Yosef Mordekhai Dubavik, "Toledotav u-darkei limudo shel ba'al ha-yeshu'ot Ya'akov," *Yeshuron* 37 (2019): 419–65.

36. Joseph Rossi, *Denkbuch für Fürst und Vaterland* (Vienna: B. Wallishausser, 1814–1815), 2:271; Majer Bałaban, *Dzieje Żydów w Galicyi i w Rzeczypospolitej krakowskiej 1772–1868* (Lwow: Nakl. Księg. Polskiej B. Połonieckiego, 1914), 86–88.

37. An earlier version of this section was published under the title "Yiddish for Spies, or the Secret History of Jewish Literature, Lemberg 1814," *Naharaim: Journal of German-Jewish Literature & Cultural History* 10, no. 2 (2016): 195–213.

38. Johann Eduard Sack, *Schloime Klappzümbels treuherzige Beschreibung der von der Lemberger Judenschaft abgehalten wordenen letzten Friedensfeier – Seinem innig geliebten Freunde Hersch Schmeckpuedele als ein Denkmahl des dabei genossenen unvergesslichen Freudengefühls dargebracht* (Lemberg: n.p., 1814).

39. Filip Friedman, "Shlomo klaptsimbels bashraybung fun der sholem-fayrung in Lemberg: A yidish lid fun yor 1814," *Fun noentn over* (1937–1938): 123–30. Gelber's copy of the manuscript, formerly held in the Austrian Censorship Office, is preserved in the CAHJP, Private Collection N. M. Gelber, P 83, "Sack, Johann Eduard: *Schloime Klappzümbels treuherzige Beschreibung* . . . in der galizisch-deutsch-jüdischen Volkssprache abgefasst, Lemberg, 1814. *Biblioteka Uniwersytetu Lwowskiego*, rkp. 880," (copy) G/21.

40. Grodziski, *Historia Ustroju*, 158; *Schematismus des Königreiches Galizien und Lodomerien* (Lemberg: Joseph Johann Piller, 1814), 42.

41. Claus Jürgen Hutterer, "Ein 'deutschmerisches' Denkmal des Jiddischen aus Lemberg," in *Deutsche Sprache in Raum und Zeit: Festschrift für Peter Wiesinger zum 60. Geburtstag*, ed. Peter Ernst and Franz Patocka (Vienna: Edition Praesens, 1998), 503–15.

42. Andreas Glaeser, "Collective Intentionality, Belonging and the Production of State Paranoia: Stasi in the Late GDR," in *Off Stage/On Display: Intimacies and Ethnographies in the Age of Public Culture*, ed. Andrew Shryock (Stanford: Stanford University Press, 2004), 244.

43. Dov Sadan, *Kheyn grivalakh: Tsu der biografie fun vort un vertl* (Buenos Aires: Altveltekher yidisher kultur kongres, 1971), 212.

44. Shlomo Yehuda Rapoport, *Tekhunat 'ir pariz: Godla, maḥlakoteha, mispar yoshveha u-nimusehem, tekhunat armonoteha . . . reḥovoteha u-shukeha, gam aklima, ve-ḥavrah lah gam tekhunat 'i alba godlo, yevulo ve-aklimo, mispar 'arav u-mivtsarav, mispar yoshavav, misḥaram ve-khol ma'ase yedeyhem* (Lemberg: Herz Grossman, 1814). On *Tekhunat 'ir pariz*, see Nathan Shifriss, *Shir Ḥadash: Shelomo Yehuda Rapoport: Rabanut, Haskala, Le'umiyut* (Jerusalem: Merkaz Zalman Shazar, 2021), 25–29.

45. On the wartime Austrian censorial constraints, see Norbert Bachleitner, *Censorship of Literature in Austria 1751–1848* (Leiden: Brill, 2022), 81–112.

46. Friedman, "Shlomo klaptsimbels," 123.

47. Arthur Haas, *Metternich, Reorganization and Nationality, 1813–1818; a Story of Foresight and Frustration in the Rebuilding of the Austrian Empire* (Wiesbaden: F. Steiner, 1963), 12–13.

48. Johann Wendrinsky, ed., *Kaiser Josef II. Ein Lebens- und Charakterbild zur hundertjährigen Gedenkfeier seiner Thronbesteigung* (Vienna: Braumüller, 1880), 152–57. For an English translation, see "The Jewish Patents," in *The Habsburg and Hohenzollern Dynasties in the Seventeenth and Eighteenth Centuries*, ed. Carlile Aylmer Macartney (New York: Harper & Row, 1970), 164–69.

49. Dirk Sadowski, *Haskala und Lebenswelt. Herz Homberg und die jüdischen deutschen Schulen in Galizien 1782–1806* (Göttingen: Vandenhoeck & Ruprecht, 2010), 177.

50. Gottfried Selig, *Lehrbuch zur gründlichen Erlernung der jüdisch-deutschen Sprache für Beamte, Gerichtsver-wandte, Advocaten und insbesondere für Kaufleute; mit*

einem vollständigen Hebräisch und jüdisch-deutschen Wörterbuche (Leipzig: Votz und Leo, 1792).

51. Joseph Errington, *Linguistics in a Colonial World: A Story of Language, Meaning, and Power* (Malden: Blackwell Pub., 2008), 4.

52. The omission of Lemberg's rabbi may alternatively be a reflection of censorial constraints. The Austrian censorship often discouraged authors from publicly discussing public religious figures in their writings. See Norbert Bachleitner, *Censorship of Literature in Austria,* 97.

53. Johann Eduard Sack, however, published at least one more Yiddish text: a letter by a local Lemberg Jew describing his impressions of an opera concert. See *Schreiben des Rebb Jossel Pippik aus Anlass von Madame Catalani hier gegebenen Vokal Konzerte: An seinen Freund Rebb Simche Hoyker* (Lemberg, 1820).

54. Scott, *Seeing Like a State,* 2.

55. Mahler, *Ha-ḥasidut ve-ha-haskala,* 397–398.

56. Bayly, *Empire and Information,* 7.

57. Adam Zamoyski, *Phantom Terror: The Threat of Revolution and the Repression of Liberty 1789–1848* (London: William Collins, 2015). On this transition, see Michal Chvojka, "Die gespannteste Aufmerksamkeit gefragt . . . : Habsburger Vertraute, Spione und Denunzianten in Mähren und Schlesien zwischen Napoleonischen Kriegen und Vormärz," in *Hinter vorgehaltener Hand: Studien zur historischen Denunziationsforschung,* ed. Anita Krätzner-Ebert (Göttingen: Vandenhoeck & Ruprecht, 2014), 21–36.

58. Charles Sealsfield (Karl Postl), *Austria as It Is or Sketches of Continental Courts by an Eyewitness* (London: Hurst, Chance, and Co., 1828), 87, 133, 186; Haas, *Metternich,* 167. For a similar description, see William Henry Stiles, *Austria in 1848–49: Being a History of the Late Political Movements in Vienna, Milan, Venice, and Prague: With Details of the Campaigns of Lombardy and Novara: A Full Account of the Revolution in Hungary* (London: Harper & brothers, 1852), 1:89–90.

59. "Vortrag des Fürsten Metternich an Kaiser Franz über die Situation in Galizien und die von Graf Goess dazu Geäußerte Meinung," April 18, 1815. The document was reproduced in Haas, *Metternich, Reorganization and Nationality,* 167.

60. Alan Sked, *Metternich and Austria: An Evaluation* (Basingstoke: Palgrave Macmillan, 2008), 123–75; Pieter M. Judson, *The Habsburg Empire: A New History* (Cambridge: Harvard University Press, 2016), 131–34.

61. Judson, *The Habsburg Empire,* 132.

62. Bayly, *Empire and Information,* 7–17.

63. See Manekin, "Hasidism and the Habsburg Empire." On Jewish policemen, see Schembor, *Galizien im ausgehenden 18. Jahrhundert,* 221. On Christian theologian as expert on Polish Jewry, see the autobiography of Ignaz Aurelius Fessler, a Hungarian Ecclesiastic who served as a Hebrew censor in Galicia in the 1790s: *Dr. Fessler's Rückblicke auf seine siebzigjährige Pilgerschaft, ein Nachlass an seine Freunde und an seine Feinde* (Breslau: Wilhelm Gottlieb Korn, 1824).

64. *Anzeige über die Umtriebe der Juden in Galizien und das Selbe unter die Sekte der Carbonari zu zahlen sehen*, no. 1384 (Wien: Haus und Hauff, Staatsrats-Index, 1822); Raphel Mahler discussed the comparisons Austrian bureaucrats drew between Hasidism and Freemasonry in *Ha-ḥasidut ve-ha-haskala*, 400–4.

65. Mahler, *Ha-ḥasidut ve-ha-haskala*, 400–404; Avraham Rubinstein, introduction to *'Al Mahut*, 11–14. Many excerpts from *On the Essence of Hasidism* were incorporated into Peter Beer's *Geschichte, Lehren und Meinungen aller bestandenen und noch bestehenden religiösen Sekten der Juden und der Geheimlehre oder Cabbalah* (Brünn, 1822–1823) and Isaak Markus Jost's *Geschichte der Israeliten seit der Zeit der Maccabäer bis auf unsre Tage* (Berlin: In der Schlesingerschen Buch- und Musikhandlung, 1828). For further discussion, see Michael Brenner, "Between Haskala and Kabbalah: Peter Beer's History of Jewish Sects," in *Jewish History and Jewish Memory*, ed. Elisheva Carlebach, John M. Efron, and David N. Myers (Hanover: University Press of New England, 1998), 389–404.

66. Janet Gurkin Altman, *Epistolarity: Approaches to a Form* (Columbus: Ohio State University Press, 1982).

67. For a general review of scholarship on *Megale temirin*, see Shmuel Werses, "Shive'im shenot ḥeker yetsirato u-foalo shel yosef perl," *Ḥuliot* 7 (2002): 321–38; Yonatan Meir, "Meḥkar ktavav ha-'anti ḥasidiyim shel yosef perl," in Yosef Perl, *Megale temirin*, ed. Yonatan Meir (Jerusalem: Mosad Bialik, 2013), 15–19.

68. Dauber, *Antonio's Devils*, 263; Yonatan Meir, *Ḥasidut meduma: 'Iyunim bi-ketavav ha-satiriyim shel yosef perl* (Jerusalem: Mosad Bialik, 2013), 1:18–20.

69. Perl encoded the locations of the Hasidic courts, using gematria, a Hebrew numerical system. The geographical identification of these locations is based on the research of the following scholars: Avraham Rubinstein, "Midrash ha-shemot shel yosef perl," *Tarbiz* 43 (1974): 140–57; Chone Shmeruk, *Keri'a lenavi, meḥkare historia vesafrut* (Jerusalem: Ha-merkaz le-Ḥeker Toldot Yehudei Polin ve-Tarbutam. 2000), 144–55; Yonatan Meir, *Ḥasidut meduma* 3:363–81.

70. Perl, *Ma'asiyot ve-'igrot*, 211.

71. Perl, *Megale temirin*, 246–71.

72. Miron, "Lifne sha'ar ha-ḥok," 40.

73. Israel Davidson, *Parody in Jewish Literature* (New York: Columbia University Press, 1907), 63–64.

74. *Chvojka*, *"Die gespannteste Aufmerksamkeit gefragt . . . ,"* 22.

75. On the gloss of "secretary" as "secret holder," see Perl, *Megale temirin*, 72. Yonatan Me'ir discussed the Bratslav sources in *Ḥasidut meduma*, 1:79.

76. On the accusation of Judaism as a form of a "state within a state," see Jacob Katz, "A State Within a State: The History of an Anti-Semitic Slogan," in *Proceedings of the Israel Academy of Sciences and Humanities* (Jerusalem: The Israel Academy of Sciences and Humanities, 1969), 4:29–58; Magda Teter, "Delegated Governance: Rethinking the Idea of Premodern Jewish Autonomy," *Shofar: An Interdisciplinary Journal of Jewish Studies* 43, no. 1 (2025): 215–29.

77. Ritchie Robertson, "Freemasons Versus Jesuits: Conspiracy Theories in Enlightenment Germany," *Times Literary Supplement*, October 12, 2012, 14.

78. From this point onward, I cite the Hebrew original from Perl, *Megale temirin* (ed. Yonatan Meir), and the English translation from *Revealer of Secrets*, trans. Dov Taylor (Boulder: Westview Press, 1997) in the following format: [§(letter number), Hebrew x, English (Taylor), x].

79. On the *bukh*, see Barukh Kurzweil, "'Al ha-satira shel yosef perl," in *Bema'avak al 'erkhey ha-yahadut* (Jerusalem: Shocken, 1970), 68–86; Me'ir, *Ḥasidut meduma*, 1:80–85.

80. The first to identify the *bukh* with Perl's *On the Essence of the Hasidic Sect* was Simon Dobnow, "Der ershter kamf fun haskole kegen khsides, veygn a ksav yad fun yor 1816," *Yivo Bletter* 1 (1931), 4–8. See also Avraham Rubinstein, "Ktav hayad 'al mahut kat ha-ḥasidim'," *Kiryat Sefer* 38 (1963): 263–72, 415–24; 39 (1964): 117–36. Olga Litvak has suggested that the *bukh* may in fact correspond to *The Revealer of Secrets* rather than *On the Essence of the Hasidic Sect*. This reading, however, is open to question, as the novel indicates that the *bukh* is written in German rather than Hebrew. See *Haskalah: The Romantic Movement in Judaism* (New Brunswick: Rutgers University Press, 2012), 113–30.

81. For a historical account of how Habsburg policies toward Hasidism were shaped, see Rachel Manekin's "Hasidism and the Habsburg Empire" and "Hasidism and the State," *Marginalia* (2018), https://themarginaliareview.com/hasidism-and-the-state-2/.

82. See Gertner, *Harav ve-ha'ir*, 100–109.

83. Perl, *Revealer of Secrets*, 44.

84. Yonatan Me'ir, *Megale temirin*, 1:208–9.

85. Barukh Kurzweil, "'Al ha-satira," 76. On Raphael Mahler's visit to the Austrian State Archives, see his letters to Jacob Shatzky, YIVO Archives, RG 356 (Jacob Shatzky Papers), folder 14. On his scholarship on Hasidism in Galicia, see Raphael Mahler, *Ha-ḥasidut ve-ha-haskala*.

86. Daniel Jütte, *The Age of Secrecy: Jews, Christians, and the Economy of Secrets, 1400–1800* (New Haven: Yale University Press, 2015), 2

87. Jütte, *The Age of Secrecy*, 224–25.

88. Elaine Freedgood, "Fictional Settlements: Footnotes, Metalepsis, the Colonial Effect," *New Literary History* 41, no. 2 (Spring 2010): 398.

89. Marc Caplan, "Science Fiction in the Age of Jewish Enlightenment," *Prooftexts* 19, no. 1 (1999): 94.

90. Svetlana Natkovich, *Questionable People: Inventing Modern Jewish Selves in the Russian Empire, 1860–1890*, Judaic Traditions in Literature, Music, and Art (Syracuse: Syracuse University Press, 2025), 88.

91. Chone Shmeruk, "Dvarim ke-havayatam u-devarim she-ba-dimyon be-megale temirin shel yosef perl," *Tsiyon* 21 (1957): 92–99.

92. Mahler, *Hasidism and the Jewish Enlightenment*, 83.

93. For example, "Ha'ataka shel mikhtav me'et miriam ḥavah, 'eshet rabbi yosef tsviling 'el marat hanile," Joseph Perl Archive Arc. 4* 1153/58, NLI; "Ha'ataka mikhtav shel ha-ḥasid shlomo eliezer ben yehuda lev me-diburbovni," Joseph Perl Archive Arc. 4* 1153 / 99, NLI.

94. Yonatan Me'ir, *Ḥasidut meduma*, 3:373.

95. Litvak, *Haskalah*, 116.

96. Joseph Perl, *Sound an Alarm! Joseph Perl's Revealer of Secrets, Megaleh Temirin, and Testing the Righteous, Boḥen Tsadik,* 2 vols., trans. Dov Taylor (Cincinnati: Hebrew Union College Press, 2024), 1:129.

97. Simkha Katz, "Naye materialn fun dem perl-arkhiv," *YIVO-Bleter* 12 (1938): 560–61.

98. Perl, *Sound an Alarm!*, 129.

99. Natkovich, *Questionable People*, 91.

100. Perl, *Sound an Alarm!*, 44.

101. Miron, *A Traveler Disguised.*

102. Shelomo Yehuda Rapoport, "Mikhtav yud," *Kerem Ḥemed* 4 (1839): 45–57.

103. Katz, "'Igrot maskilim."

104. Katz, "'Igrot maskilim," 270.

105. Katz, "'Igrot maskilim," 270–72.

106. Joseph Perl (pseud. Ovadia), *'Mikhtav d'*, in *Kerem Ḥemed* 3 (1838): 61.

107. Joseph (Peter) Tarler, "Ya'alzu ḥasidim be-khavod." *Yerushalaim* 2 (1845): 95–96.

108. See Meir Weissberg, "Józef Kohn Zedek, Ostatni publicysta nowohebrajski galicyjskiej haskali," *Rocznik Żydowski* 6 (1906): 256.

109. Michael Taussig, *Defacement: Public Secrecy and the Labor of the Negative* (Stanford: Stanford University Press, 1999), 56.

110. Gilbert Herdt, "Secret Societies and Secret Collectives," *Oceania* 60, no. 4 (June 1990): 360–81.

111. On Joseph Tarler, see Israel Weinlos, "Yosl tarler einer von die ershten maskilim in galizien," *Morgen* (Lemberg), January 22, 1927, 3–4; Max Weissberg, *Die neuhebräische Aufklärungs-Literatur in Galizien: Eine Literar-Historische Charakteristik* (Leipzig: M. Breitenstein, 1898), 184–85; Bernfeld, "Zikhronot," 185–86. On Tarler in Hasidic legends, see Gedalyah Nigal, *Ha-siporet ha-ḥasidit: Toldotehah ve-nosaḥeha* (Jerusalem: J. Marcus, 1981), 212. A letter from Yitzḥak Erter to Joseph Tarler was printed in Yitzḥak Erter, *Ha-tsofe le-veyt yisrael ve-nispeḥu 'elav mikhtavim 'igrot ve-shirim* (Warsaw: Y. Alapin, 1908), 123–26.

112. It is possible that Tarler was alluding to a well-worn joke about the gluttony of the Hasidic movement. According to Dov Sadan, a maskilic pun renders the biblical verse *ya'alazu ḥasidim be-khavod* into the Yiddish expression *khsidim fresen zikh on mit leber* (Hasidim gorge themselves on liver). The pun plays simultaneously on *ya'alazu* (rejoice) and the Yiddish *yilasu* (to munch), as well as on *kavod* (Ashkenazi pronunciation "koved") and *kaved* (liver). It is unclear whether the pun inspired the poem or, perhaps, the other way around. See Dov Sadan, "Kal u-kaved: Le-darko shel pitgam," in *Studies in Jewish Bibliography, History, and Literature: in Honor of Edward Kiev*, ed. Charles Berlin (New York: Ktav Publishing House, 1971), 115–16.

113. Psalm 149:5–8.

Bibliography

1. Primary Sources: Archives

Central Archives for the History of the Jewish People, Jerusalem (CAHJP)

- Family Collection Moritz Moses Gottschalk Lewy
  - Moshe Elḥanan, family correspondence, P 253/1
- Private Collection N. M. Gelber, P 83
  - Sack, Johann Eduard. *Schlojme* [*sic*] *Klappzinbels* [*sic*] *treuherzige Beschreibung . . . in der galizisch-deutsch-jüdischen Volkssprache abgefasst,* Lemberg, 1814. Biblioteka Uniwersytetu Lwowskiego, rkp. 880 (Copy), G/21.
  - *Sanhedrin 1806: verschiedene Abschriften aus den 1806 Sammlungen vom Haus-, Hof- und Staatsarchiv, Wien* (Copy), I/44.

Central State Historical Archives of Ukraine, Kyiv (TsDIAK)

- Archiwum Potockich z Tulczyna
  - "W sprawie pretensji pieniężnej rabina Daszowskiego Zundela do kahału i pospólstwa m. Daszów; oświadczenie świadków-Żydów m-ka Daszów, podpisany przez Mosesa Elkana Josepha, Rabina Generalnego; również – Pretensja kahalu Kalnickiego do rabina m. Kalnik z wykazem Żydów," *fond* 49, inventory 1, file 2121 (Copy CAHJP CD-392.07).

Central State Historical Archives of Ukraine, Lviv (TsDIAL)

- "Eine Liste der Deportierten aus Österreich, darunter auch Juden, im Zusammenhang mit dem Vorwurf der Spionage und Strafanzeigen," Collection 146, inventory 7, file 572, 1810 (Copy CAHJP HM3-893).
- "Die Untersuchung unter der Anschuldigung der Juden in der Spionage und Verbindungen mit ausländischen Armeen," Collection 146, inventory 7, files 570–571, 1810–1811, 1814 (Copy CAHJP HM3-893.04).

Czartoryski Library, Kraków

- "Shir ve-shevaḥ la-ʾadoneynu ha-melekh ha-gadol stanislas, nitḥaber ʿal-yedei ʿavdo ha-neʾeman moshe elḥanan, ʾav beyt din de-ha-medina," Recueil de littérature, Stanisław August, call no. 938, fols. 733–734.

Louvre Museum, Center for Studies and Documentation, Paris

- Giovanni Battista Lampi: RF 2378; RF 2389; RF 1980.49.

National Galleries of Scotland, Edinburgh

- Photographic Archive, William Allan folder.

National Library of Israel, Jerusalem (NLI)

- Joseph Perl Archive
  - Mendel Lefin, *Divrei toda be-tseʾt ʿadat yisraʾel*... (1805), Arc 4° 1153/8.
  - Joseph Perl, "Takanot ve-hamlatsot bi-dvar ha-pulḥan ha-dati shel yehudei galitsya, 1789" (Annotated Judenpatent), Arc 4° 1153/101.
  - "Haʿataka shel mikhtav meʾet miriam ḥavah, ʾeshet rabbi yosef tsviling, ʾel marat hanile," Arc 4° 1153/58.
  - "Haʿataka mikhtav shel ha-ḥasid shlomo eliezer ben yehuda lev me-diburbovni," Arc 4° 1153/99.

National Library of Russia, Saint Petersburg

- "Ob opredelenii ravvina Moiseia El'kana v chislo pochetnykh bibliotekarei," Department of Archival Documents, Collection 1, file 9 (Copy CAHJP RU-2058).
- [Map of Bratslav (c. 1799)], Podolia 1806 Land Survey, OP F.IV.605.

National Library of Scotland, Archives and Manuscripts

- Letters chiefly to Sir William Allan, Member of the Royal Academy of Arts, Historical Painter, 1808–1848, undated, MS 6294, fols. 62–156.

Royal Scottish Academy, Edinburgh

- Catalogue of Pictures Painted by William Allan, as Exhibited at Mr. McIntosh's Gallery, 49 Princes Street (Edinburgh, 1819), annotated copy.

State Archives of Khmelnytskyi Oblast, Khmelnytskyi (DAKhMO)

- "Po obvineniiu Itska Gershkovicha, arendatora s. Strel'chintsy, v sozhitel'stve so sluzhivshei u nego russkoi devkoiu Evdokiei rodivshei mladentsa," 1805, Collection 120, inventory 1, file 344 (Copy CAHJP CD-412.04).
- "Po zhalobe arendatorov Abramka Mortkovicha Panicha iz Bratslava, Itsko Nusimovicha iz Nemirova i Itsko Khaimovicha iz Brailova," 1798–1803, Collection 120, inventory 1, file 1724 (Copy CAHJP CD-193.07).
- "O vyborakh v Kamentse deputatov v Peterburg dlia uchastiia v rabote Komissii po ustroistvu evreev. Zdes' zhe 'Polozhenie o evreiakh' 1804 g," Collection 46, inventory 1, file 30 (Copy CAHJP HM2-8865.5).
- "Po obvineniiu zhitelia m-ka Nemirova Itska Duvidovicha i drugikh razboinikov v ograblenii v Bratslave dubossarskogo kuptsa Nikolaia Muratova (s opis'iu ukradennykh veshchei i protokolami doprosov svidetelei, postradavshego i obviniaemykh)," Podol'skii glavnyi sud, 1805–1807, Collection 120, inventory 1, file 524 (Copy CAHJP CD-412.11).

State Archive of Lviv Oblast, Lviv (DALO)

- "Magistrat m. Lwowa, Kreisschreiben vom k.k. Galizischen Landesgubernium betr. Der jüdischen Kleidung und Aufhebung des Gebrauches der hebraischen und sogenannten jüdischen Sprache und Schrift in allen öffentlichen gerichtlechen und außergerichtlichen Handlungen, 1814," Collection 3, inventory 1, file 601 (Copy CAHJP HM2-8283.8).

Haus-, Hof- und Staatsarchiv, Vienna (HHStA)

- *Anzeige über die Umtriebe der Juden in Galizien und das Selbe unter die Sekte der Carbonari zu zahlen sehen*, Staatsratsindex 1822, Nr. 1384 (Copy HM-3250).
- Noten an die Polizeihofstelle, December 9, 1822, and March 28, 1823, HHStA, StK.
- Jüdische Einwohner von Tarnopol und Zaleszyk um Belassung im Besitze der während des russischen Besitzes von Christen erkauften Häusern, 1818, Staatsratsindex 1818, Nr. 1545 (Copy CAHJP HM-3245).

University Library of Frankfurt

- "Ha-tsadik ha-'amiti," Frank MS Hebrew fol. 11.

YIVO Archives

- Sutzkever–Kaczerginski Collection, RG 223.2, folder 456
  - Shalom Ya'akov Abramovitsh, correspondence.
- Jacob Shatzky Papers, RG 356, folder 14
  - Raphael Mahler, correspondence.

2. Printed Materials

Abel, Richard L. "What We Talk About When We Talk About Law." In *The Law and Society Reader*, edited by Richard L. Abel, 1–12. New York: NYU Press, 1995.

Abramovitsh, Shalom Ya'akov (Sholem Yankev) ben Ḥaim Moshe. *'Ein mishpat.* Zhitomir: A. Sh. Shadov, 1867.

———. *Di takse, oder, di bande shtot bale toyves.* Zhitomir: A. Sh. Shadov, 1869.

———. *Dos kleyne mentshele: oder A lebensbeshreybung fun yitskhok Avrom Takif, gor in gantsen oyf dos nay ibergemakht.* Vilnius: Bi-defus Rom, 1879.

———. "Reshimot le-toldotai." In *Sefer zikaron le-sofrei yisrael ha-ḥayim 'itanu kayom*, edited by Naḥum Sokolov, 122. Warsaw: Meir Yeḥiel Alter, 1889.

———. "The Little Man; or, Portrait of Life." In *Classic Yiddish Stories of S. Y. Abramovitsh, Sholem Aleichem, and I. L. Peretz*, translated and edited by Ken Frieden, 3–5. Syracuse: Syracuse University Press, 2004.

Abramovich, S(olomon) M(oiseevich) (Abramovitsh, Shalom Ya'akov). *Taksa, t. e. Korobochnyi sbor: Komediia v 5-ti deistviiakh.* Belaia Tserkov': M. Mezhybovskii, 1884.

Aftanazy, Roman Włodzimierz. "Humań i Zofiówka." In *Dzieje rezydencji na dawnych kresach Rzeczypospolitej*, 10:110–19. Wrocław: Zakład Narodowy im. Ossolińskich, 1996.

Aksenfeld, Isroel. *Dos Shterntikhl: Oder, shabes khanuke in mezhibizh.* Leipzig: C. W. Vollrath, 1862.

Alexander, John T. *Catherine the Great: Life and Legend.* New York: Oxford University Press, 1989.

Allgemeines bürgerliches Gesetzbuch für die gesammten deutschen Erbländer der Oesterreichischen Monarchie. Vienna: K. K. Hof- und Staatsdruckerey, 1811.

Altman, Janet Gurkin. *Epistolarity: Approaches to a Form.* Columbus: Ohio State University Press, 1982.

Andreev, Andrei. *Russkie studenty v nemetskikh universitetakh XVIII—pervoi poloviny XIX veka.* Moscow: Novoe literaturnoe obozrenie, 2005.

Appadurai, Arjun. "Topographies of the Self: Praise and Emotion in Hindu India." In *Language and the Politics of Emotion*, edited by Catherine A. Lutz and Lila Abu-Lughod, 92–112. Cambridge: Cambridge University Press, 1990.

Arama, Yitzḥak. *Ḥazut kasha.* Pressburg: Franz Edlen von Schmid, 1859.

Assaf, David. "Son'im sipur 'ahava? Hitpatḥuyot be-meḥkar yaḥasey ha-gomlin beyn ḥasidut ve-ha-haskala." In *Ha-haskala li-gvaneyha: 'Iyunim ḥadashim be-toldot ha-haskala u-ve-safruta*, edited by Israel Bartal and Shmuel Feiner, 183–200. Jerusalem: Magnes Press, 2005.

———. "When the Rabbis 'Met' Napoleon." *Tradition* 54, no. 2 (2022): 55–62.

Averbuch, Alex. "Jewish Solicitory Poetry in the Eighteenth-Century Russian Empire: Materiality, Poetics, Diplomacy." *AJS Review* 49, no. 1 (2025): 1–29.

Avish, Shlomo. *Sefer zikaron 'ir mivtsar: Toldot ha-'ir "mezhibozh" mivtsar ha-torah ve-ha-ḥasidut: bo yeto'ar toldot ha-'ir, 'admoreha ve-rabaneha.* Brooklyn: Makhon Zikhron ba-Sefer, 2010.

Avnun-Broynshtayn, Arye. "Tarnopol be-khol yemot ha-shana." In *'Ensiklopedya shel galuyot: Sifre zikaron le-'artsot ha-gola ve-ʿedoteha*, 12 vols., edited by Yeruḥam Kongrin, 3:331. Jerusalem: Ḥevrat 'Entsiklopedyah Shel Galuyot, 1955.

Avrutin, Eugene M. *Jews and the Imperial State: Identification Politics in Tsarist Russia*. Ithaca: Cornell University Press, 2010.

Bachleitner, Norbert. *Censorship of Literature in Austria 1751–1848*. Leiden: Brill, 2022.

Bałaban, Majer. *Dzieje Żydów w Galicyi i w Rzeczypospolitej krakowskiej 1772–1868*. Lviv: Nakl. Księg. Polskiej B. Polonieckiego, 1914.

———. "Mendel Lewin i książę Adam Czartoryski (Notatka historyczna)." *Chwila* 5313 (January 7, 1934): 10; 5314 (April 8, 1934): 11.

———. *Shalshelet ha-yaḥas shel mishpaḥat Orenshtein-Broda: (ʿAl semakh kitvei yad u-mekorot nidpasim)*. Warsaw: Monolit, 1931.

Banbaji, Amir. *Mendele ve-ha-sipur hale'umi*. Or Yehuda: Kinneret, Zmora-Bitan, Dvir, 2009.

Band, Arnold J. *Studies in Modern Jewish Literature*. JPS Scholar of Distinction Series. Philadelphia: Jewish Publication Society, 2003.

Bartal, Israel. "Ha-lo-yehudim ve-ḥevratam be-sifrut ʿivrit ve-yidish be-mizraḥ 'eropah ben ha-shanim 1856–1914." PhD diss., Hebrew University of Jerusalem, 1980.

———. *The Jews of Eastern Europe 1772–1881*. Philadelphia: University of Pennsylvania Press, 2006.

Batalden, Stephen K. *Russian Bible Wars: Modern Scriptural Translation and Cultural Authority*. Cambridge: Cambridge University Press, 2013.

Bate, Bernard, "Political Praise in Tamil Newspapers: The Poetry and Iconography of Democratic Power." In *Everyday Life in South Asia*, 2nd ed., edited by Diane P. Mines and Sarah Lamb, 354–70. Bloomington: Indiana University Press, 2010.

Baum, Ia. D. "Evrei-dekabrist. Grigorii Abramovich Peretts: Biograficheskii ocherk po arkhivnym materialam." *Katorga i ssylka*, no. 4 (1926): 121–22.

Baumann, Fabian. *Dynasty Divided: A Family History of Russian and Ukrainian Nationalism*. Ithaca: Cornell University Press, 2023.

Bayly, Christopher. *Empire and Information: Intelligence Gathering and Social Communication in India, 1780–1870*. Cambridge: Cambridge University Press, 1996.

Beauvois, Daniel. *Pouvoir russe et noblesse polonaise en Ukraine, 1793–1830*. Paris: CNRS Éditions, 2003.

Beer, Daniel. "'To a Dog, a Dog's Death!': Naïve Monarchism and Regicide in Imperial Russia, 1878–1884." *Slavic Review* 80, no. 1 (2021): 112–32.

Beer, Peter. *Geschichte, Lehren und Meinungen aller bestandenen und noch bestehenden religiösen Sekten der Juden und der Geheimlehre oder Cabbalah*. Brünn: n.p., 1822–1823.

Belfer, Israel and Kahana, Maoz. "Thinking Through Gardens: Park Sofijówka at the Crossroads of Jewish Messianism and Polish Noble Culture in Partitioned Poland." *Forthcoming*.

Benna, Anna Hedwig. "Die Polizeihofstelle: Ein Beitrag zur Geschichte der österreichischen Zentralverwaltung." PhD diss., University of Vienna, 1942.

Benton, Lauren, and Richard J. Ross, "Empires and Legal Pluralism: Jurisdiction, Sovereignty, and Political Imagination in the Early Modern World." In *Legal Pluralism and Empires, 1500–1850*, edited by Lauren Benton and Richard J. Ross, 1–18. New York: NYU Press, 2013.

Berkowitz, Joel, and Jeremy Asher Dauber, eds. *Landmark Yiddish Plays: A Critical Anthology*. Albany: State University of New York, 2006.

Bernfeld, Shimon. "Zikhronot." *Reshumot* 4 (1927): 145–93.

Berthold, Kaiser Friedhelm. *Die russische Justizreform von 1864: zur Geschichte der russischen Justiz von Katharina II. bis 1917*. Leiden: Brill, 1972.

Bey der höchsterfreulichen Durchreise der Allerdurchlauchtigsten und Grossmächtigsten Kaiserin und Frau Catharina Alexiewna, Selbstherrscherin aller Reussen [. . .] *überreichte mit allerunterthänigster Devotion die Judengemeine in Poloczko folgenden Gesang*. Königsberg: G. L. Hartung, 1780.

Bick, Shmuel Yosef. *dema'ot le-zikhron yashar:hi 'azkarat ha-nefesh . . . frants frayherr fon hauer . . . me-'adat bnei yisra'el be-vet ha-kneset ha-gedola di-k. k. brod*. Lemberg: Grosman, 1822.

Birkenthal, Dov Ber of Bolechów, *Divrei binah/zikhronot*, edited by Gershon Hundert. Jerusalem: Mosad Bialik, 2023.

Bloy, Amram. "Gerush ha-kfarim be-rusiya bi-yemei reshit ha-ḥasidut, yaḥasam u-fo'alam shel gedolei ha-ḥasidut le-gezirat ha-gerush." *Heikhal ha-besht* 13 (2006): 133–57.

Bonieck, Adam. *Herbarz polski: Wiadomości historyczno-genealogiczne o rodach szlacheckich*. 9 vols. Warsaw: Gebethner i Wolff, 1899–1913.

Borodinski (Ben-Dayan), Haim. "Di loyblider lekoved Katerine II un zayere mekhabrim, a bletl kultur geshikhte." *Historishe Shriftn* 2 (1937): 532–33.

Bourdieu, Pierre. *On the State: Lectures at the Collège de France, 1989–1992*. Cambridge: Polity Press, 2014.

Brawer, Avraham Ya'akov. *Galizien, wie es an Österreich kam: Eine historisch-statistische Studie über die inneren Verhältnisse des Landes im Jahre 1772*. Vienna: F. Tempsky, 1910.

———. *Galitsya ve-yehudeha: meḥkarim be-toldot galitsya ba-me'ah ha-shemone-'esreh*. Jerusalem: Mosad Bialik, 1964.

Brawer, Michael Ha-kohen. "Lifnei me'a shana." *Ha-hed* 12 nos. 10–11 (1937): 30–31.

Brenner, Michael. "Between Haskala and Kabbalah: Peter Beer's History of Jewish Sects." In *Jewish History and Jewish Memory*, edited by Elisheva Carlebach, John M. Efron, and David N. Myers, 389–404. Hanover: University Press of New England, 1998.

Brettler, Marc Zvi. *God Is King: Understanding an Israelite Metaphor*. Journal for the Study of the Old Testament. Supplement Series 76. Sheffield: JSOT Press, 1989.

Brown, Iris. "Shelosha gilgulim shel meshal ha-ḥomot.'" *Meḥkare yerushalayim be-sifrut 'ivrit* 23 (2009): 99–132.

Buber, Salomon. *Anshei shem, ge'onei Yisrael, 'adirei ha-tora, rabanim, 'asher shimshu ba-kodesh ba'ir lvov mi-shnat ha-ras ad ha-taran*. Kraków: n.p., 1895.

Butterwick-Pawlikowski, Richard. *Polish-Lithuanian Commonwealth, 1733–1795: Light and Flame*. New Haven: Yale University Press, 2021.

Canale, Damiano. "The Many Faces of the Codifications of the Law in Modern Continental Europe." In *A Treatise of Legal Philosophy and General Jurisprudence*, vol. 9, edited by Damiano Canale et al., 135–81. New York: Springer, 2005.

Caplan, Marc. "Science Fiction in the Age of Jewish Enlightenment." *Prooftexts* 19, no. 1 (1999): 93–100.

Catalogue of Pictures Painted by William Allan, as Exhibited at Mr. McIntosh's Gallery, 49 Princes Street. Edinburgh: n.p., 1819.

Chrząszczewski, Antoni. *Pamiętnik oficjalisty Potockich z Tulczyna*. Wrocław: Zakład Narodowy im. Ossolińskich, 1976.

Chubina, Tetiana Dmytrivna. "Rid Potots'kykh v Ukraini (tul'chyns'ka liniia): suspil'-no-politychni ta kulturolohichni aspekty." PhD diss., Cherkas'kyi Derzhavnyi Tekhnolohichnyi Universytet, 2008.

Chukarev, Andrei Gavrilovich. *Tainaia Politsiia Rossii, 1825–1855*. Zhukovskii: Kuchkovo Pole, 2005.

Chvojka, Michal. *Josef Graf Sedlnitzky als Präsident der Polizei- und Zensurhofstelle in Wien (1817–1848): Ein Beitrag zur Geschichte der Staatspolizei in der Habsburgermonarchie*. Frankfurt: Peter Lang, 2010.

———. "Die gespannteste Aufmerksamkeit gefragt . . . : Habsburger Vertraute, Spione und Denunzianten in Mähren und Schlesien zwischen Napoleonischen Kriegen und Vormärz." In *Hinter vorgehaltener Hand: Studien zur historischen Denunziationsforschung*, edited by Anita Krätzner-Ebert, 21–36. Göttingen: Vandenhoeck & Ruprecht, 2014.

Collis, Robert, and Natalie Bayer. *Initiating the Millennium: The Avignon Society and Illuminism in Europe*. Oxford Studies in Western Esotericism. New York: Oxford University Press, 2020.

Czakai, Johannes. *Nochems neue Namen: Die Juden Galiziens und der Bukowina und die Einführung deutscher Vor- und Familiennamen, 1772–1820*. Göttingen: Wallstein Verlag, 2021.

Dan, Yosef. *Ha-sipur ha-ḥasidi*. Jerusalem: Keter, 1990.

———. Preface to *The Tales*, by Naḥman of Bratslav. Translated by Arnold Band. New York: Paulist Press, 1978.

Davidson, Israel. *Parody in Jewish Literature*. New York: Columbia University Press, 1907.

Davies, Sharon L. "The Jurisprudence of Willfulness: An Evolving Theory of Excusable Ignorance." *Duke Law Journal* 48, no. 3 (Dec. 1998): 341–427.

Dauber, Jeremy Asher. *Antonio's Devils: Writers of the Jewish Enlightenment and the Birth of Modern Hebrew and Yiddish Literature*. Stanford: Stanford University Press, 2004.

———. "Between Two Worlds: Antitheatricality and the Beginnings of Modern Yiddish Theatre." In *Inventing the Modern Yiddish Stage, Essays in Drama, Performance, and*

Show Business, edited by Joel Berkowitz and Barbara Henry, 27–39. Detroit: Wayne State University Press, 2012.

de LaGarde-Chambonas, Auguste Louis Charles. *The Journal of a Nobleman: Being a Narrative of his Residence at Vienna During the Congress*. Philadelphia: Key and Biddle, 1833.

———. *Voyage dans quelques parties de l'Europe*. London: Harding, Triphook, and Lepard, 1825.

———. *Le knout et les russes, moeurs et organisation de la Russie*. Paris: D. Giraud, 1853.

Dembitzer, Hayim Natan. *Kelilat yofi: Kolel toldot ha-rabanim ba'ir lvov*. Vol. 1. Kraków: Yosef Fisher, 1888–1893.

Di genarte velt. Moscow: Melukhe-farlag "Der Emes," 1940.

Di genarte velt oder shverer me nemt zikh fir, griner helft got. Lemberg: J. Madfes, 1865.

Dobnow, Simon. "Der ershter kamf fun haskole kegen khsides, veygn a ksav yad fun yor 1816." *Yivo Bletter* 1 (1931): 4–8.

Fessler, Ignaz Aurelius. *Dr. Fessler's Rückblicke auf seine siebzigjährige Pilgerschaft, ein Nachlass an seine Freunde und an seine Feinde*. Breslau: Wilhelm Gottlieb Korn, 1824.

Doležel, Lubomír. *Heterocosmica: Fiction and Possible Worlds*. Parallax: Re-Visions of Culture and Society. Baltimore: Johns Hopkins University Press, 1998.

Dubavik, Yosef Mordekhai. "Toledotav u-darkei limudo shel ba'al ha-yeshu'ot Ya'akov." *Yeshuron* 37 (2019): 419–65.

Dvir-Goldberg, Rivka. *Ha-tsadik ha-ḥasidi ve-'armon ha-livyatan, 'iyun be-sipurei ma'asiyot mi-pi tsadikim*. Tel Aviv: ha-Kibuts ha-Me'uḥad, 2003.

Dynes, Ofer. "How to Read Naḥman of Bratslav's Tales in Their Historical Context." *Jewish Social Studies* 29, no. 3 (2024): 61–85.

———. "Yiddish for Spies, or the Secret History of Jewish Literature, Lemberg 1814." *Naharaim: Journal of German-Jewish Literature & Cultural History* 10, no. 2 (2016): 195–213.

———. "On Romantic and Patriotic Love in the Russian Maskilic Imagination (1804–1863)." *European Journal of Jewish Studies* 19, no. 2 (2025): 1–18.

Edicta et mandata universalia Regnis Galiciae et Lodomeriae. Lemberg: Joseph Piller, 1789–1791.

Eichenboym, Ya'akov. *Tsiyunim metsuyanim be-vate ha-kevarot ha-yashan ve-he- ḥadash 'asher le-'adat yisra'el be-'ir odessa*. Warsaw: n.p., 1888.

Eisenbach, Arthur et al., eds. *Materiały do dziejów Sejmu Czteroletniego*. Vol. 6. Wrocław: Zakład Narodowy im. Ossolińskich, 1969.

Elkana, Moïse (Elḥanan, Moshe). *Hymne addressée à sa Majesté l'Empereur Alexandre I*. Munich: Imprimerie J. Sidler, 1811.

Ellis, Geoffrey. *The Napoleonic Empire*. New York: Bloomsbury Academic, 2003.

Elstein, Yoav. *Pa'amei bat melekh*. Ramat Gan: Universitat Bar-Ilan, 1984.

Emerson, Donald E. *Metternich and the Political Police: Security and Subversion in the Habsburg Monarchy, 1815–1830*. The Hague: Martinus Nijhoff, 1968.

Errington, Joseph. *Linguistics in a Colonial World: A Story of Language, Meaning, and Power*. Malden: Blackwell Pub., 2008.

Ertman, Thomas. *Birth of the Leviathan: Building States and Regimes in Medieval and Early Modern Europe*. Cambridge: Cambridge University Press, 1997.

Etkes, Immanuel. "Haskalah." Translated by Jeffrey Green. In *YIVO Encyclopedia of Jews in Eastern Europe*, 2010. https://encyclopedia.yivo.org/article/10.

———. *Rabbi Shneur Zalman of Liady: The Origins of Chabad Hasidism*. Waltham: Brandeis University Press, 2014.

Erter, Yitzḥak. *Ha-tsofe le-veyt yisrael ve-nispeḥu 'elav mikhtavim 'igrot ve-shirim*. Warsaw: Y. Alapin, 1908.

Ettinger, Solomon. *Ale Ksovim*. Vilnius: B. Kletskin, 1925.

Evans, Godfrey. "Alexander, 10th Duke of Hamilton (1767–1852) as Patron and Collector." PhD diss., University of Edinburgh, 2008.

———. "The 10th Duke of Hamilton and William Allan in Russia and the Ukraine." *Journal of the Scottish Society for Art History* 19 (2014): 15–26.

Feiner, Shmuel. *Haskalah and History: The Emergence of a Modern Jewish Historical Consciousness*. Portland: Littman Library of Jewish Civilization, 2002.

Fellerer, Jan. "Discourse and Hegemony. The Case of the Ukrainian Language in Galicia under Austrian Rule." In *Diglossia and Power. Language Policies and Practice in the 19th Century Habsburg Empire*, edited by Rosita Rindler Schjerve, 107–66. Berlin: Mouton de Gruyter, 2003.

———. *Mehrsprachigkeit im Galizischen Verwaltungswesen (1772–1914): Eine Historisch-soziolinguistische Studie zum Polnischen und Ruthenischen (Ukrainischen)*. Cologne: Böhlau, 2005.

Fichman, Ya'akov. *Sofrei 'odesa: 'Amat ha-binyan*. Jerusalem: Mosad Bialik, 1951.

Fik, Marta. "Cenzor jako współautor." *Literatura i władza*, edited by Bożena Wojnowska, 131–48. Warsaw: IBL, 1996.

Fishman, David. *Russia's First Modern Jews: The Jews of Shklov*. New York: NYU Press, 1995.

Fletcher, Angus. *Allegory: The Theory of a Symbolic Mode*. Ithaca: Cornell University Press, 1964.

Fournier, August. *Historische Studien und Skizzen*. Vol. 3. Prague: E. Tempsky, 1885.

Franaszek, Piotr, ed. *O nowoczesnym zarządzaniu majątkiem – rady dla potomnych Karola Belina Brzozowskiego, Źródła do dziejów gospodarstwa ziemiańskiego na Kresach w XIX wieku*. Kraków: Towarzystwo Wydawnicze "Historia Iagellonica," 2005.

Fredro, Aleksander. *Trzy Po Trzy*. 1880. Warsaw: Państwowy Instytut Wydawniczy, 2023.

Freedgood, Elaine. "Fictional Settlements: Footnotes, Metalepsis, the Colonial Effect." *New Literary History* 41, no. 2 (Spring 2010): 393–411.

Friedberg, Bernard (Ḥaim Dov Berish). *Toldot ha-defus ha-'ivri be-polanya: Me-reshit hitpatḥuto be-shnat 297 [1537], hishtalemuto, divrei yamav ve-hishtalsheluto 'ad ha-yom*. Antwerp: n.p., 1932.

Friedman, Filip. "Dzieje Żydów w Galicji (1772–1914)." In *Żydzi w Polsce odrodzonej działalność społeczna, gospodarcza, oświatowa i kulturalna*, edited by Ignacy Schiper et al. Warsaw: Nakł. Wydawn. "Żydzi w Polsce Odrodzonej," 1932–1933.

———. "Shlomo klaptsimbels bashraybung fun der sholem-fayrung in Lemberg: A yidish lid fun yor 1814." *Fun noentn over* (1937–1938): 123–30.

———. "Joseph perl vi a bildungs-tuer un zayn shul in tarnopol (125 yor nokh ir grindung)." *YIVO-Bleter* 31–32 (1948): 131–90.

Freudengesang der Judenschaft zu Sclow beym Durchzuge Ihrer Kayserlichen Majestät Katharina II, Selbstbeherrscherinn Aller Reussen. N.p., 1780.

Gallagher, Mary. "Mobilizing the Law in China: 'Informed Disenchantment' and the Development of Legal Consciousness." *Law & Society Review* 40, no. 4 (December 2006): 783–816.

Gelber, Nathan. "La police autrichienne et le Sanhédrin de Napoléon." *Revue des Études Juives* 83 (1927): 1–21, 113–45.

———.*Toldot yehudei brodi*. Vol. 6 of *'Arim ve-'imahot be-yisra'el*. 7 vols. Edited by Judah Leib Maimon. Jerusalem: Mosad ha-Rav Kuk, 1956.

———. "Tarnopol." In *'Ensiklopedya shel galuyot: Sifrei zikaron le-'artsot ha-gola ve-'edoteha*, edited by Yeruḥam Kongrin, 3:58. Jerusalem: Ḥevrat 'Entsiklopedyah Shel Galuyot, 1955.

Gellman, Uriel. "Between Worlds: The Miserable Life of an Itinerant Preacher on the Eve of Modernity." *Jewish Quarterly Review* 109, no. 1 (2019): 54–83.

General Civil Code: For all the German Hereditary Provinces of the Austrian Monarchy. Translated by Joseph M. Chevalier de Winiwarter. Vienna, n.p., 1866.

Gertner, Haim. *Ha-rav ve-ha-'ir ha-gedola, ha-rabanut be-galitsiya u-mifgasha 'im ha-moderna 1816–1867*. Jerusalem: Merkaz Zalman Shazar, 2013.

Gesetzbuch über Verbrechen und Schwere Polizey-Uebertretungen. Vienna: Hof-und Staats-Aerarial-Druckerey, 1815.

Gintsburg, Shaul. *Meshumodim in tsarishn rusland: Forshungen un zikhroynes vegn yidishn lebn in amolikn rusland*. New York: Shaul Gintsburg Shriftn Komitet, 1946.

Glaeser, Andreas. "Collective Intentionality, Belonging and the Production of State Paranoia: Stasi in the Late GDR." In *Off Stage/On Display: Intimacies and Ethnographies in the Age of Public Culture*, edited by Andrew Shryock, 244–76. Stanford: Stanford University Press, 2004.

———. *Political Epistemics: The Secret Police, the Opposition, and the End of East German Socialism*. Chicago: University of Chicago Press, 2010.

Goldberg, Jacob. *Ha-ḥevrah ha-yehudit be-mamlekhet polin–lita*. Jerusalem: Zalman Shazar, 1999.

———. *Jewish Privileges in the Polish Commonwealth: Charters of Rights Granted to Jewish Communities in Poland-Lithuania in the Sixteenth to Eighteenth Centuries*. Critical edition of original Latin and Polish documents with English introductions and notes. Jerusalem: Israel Academy of Sciences and Humanities, 1985.

———. "The Role of the Jewish Community in the Socio-Political Structure of the Polish-Lithuanian Commonwealth." *Polin* 22 (2010): 142–55.

Goldstein, Naḥman (Naḥman of Tcherin). *Sefer rimze ha-ma'asiyot*. Bnei Brak: Keren Hadpasa ve-Hafatsa le-Sifrei Ḥasidut Braslav, 1995.

Golitsyn, Nikolai Nikolaevich. *Istoriia russkogo zakonodatel' stva o evreiakh*. St. Petersburg: Tip. ministerstva vnutrennikh del, 1886.

Gould, Rebecca. "The Much-Maligned Panegyric: Toward a Political Poetics of Pre-Modern Literary Form." *Comparative Literature Studies* 52 no. 2 (2015): 254–288.

Grab, Alexander. *Napoleon and the Transformation of Europe*. New York: Palgrave Macmillan, 2003.

Green, Arthur. *Tormented Master: The Life and Spiritual Quest of Rabbi Nahman of Bratslav*. Judaic Studies Series. Tuscaloosa: University of Alabama Press, 1979.

———. *Seek My Face, Speak My Name: A Contemporary Jewish Theology*. Northvale: J. Aronson, 1992.

———. *Keter: The Crown of God in Early Jewish Mysticism*. Princeton: Princeton University Press, 1997.

———."Ga'agu'ei ha-'elohim el ha-'adam, al ma'ase mi-melekh 'anav, ha-sipur sheli." In *Haḥayim kega'agu'a, keriyot ḥadashot be-sipurei ma'asiyot shel rabi Naḥman mi-braslav*, edited by Roee Horen, 91–99. Tel Aviv: Miskal-Yedioth Ahronoth Books and Chemed Books, 2010.

Grodziski, Stanisław. *Historia ustroju społeczno politycznego Galicji 1772–1848*. Wrocław: Zakład Narodowy im. Ossolińskich, 1971.

Guesnet, François. "The Turkish Cavalry in Swarzędz; or, Jewish Political Culture at the Borderlines of Modern History." In *Jahrbuch des Simon-Dubnow-Instituts / Simon Dubnow Institute Yearbook: Schwerpunkt / Special Issue: Early Modern Culture and Haskalah*, edited by Dan Diner, 227–48. Leipzig: Vandenhoeck & Ruprecht, 2007.

Ha-'aliyah: sipur korot ha-'aliyah le-tsiyon shel rabenu ha-kadosh ve-ha-nora' naḥman nove'a mekor ḥokhma. Jerusalem: n.p., 1988.

Haas, Arthur G. *Metternich, Reorganization and Nationality, 1813–1818; a Story of Foresight and Frustration in the Rebuilding of the Austrian Empire*. Wiesbaden: F. Steiner, 1963.

Haider-Pregler, Hilde. "Die Schaubühne als 'Sittenschule' der Nation: Joseph von Sonnenfels und das Theater." In *Josef von Sonnenfels*, edited by Helmut Reinalter, 191–244. Vienna: Verlag der österreichischen Akademie der Wissenschaft, 1988.

Haran, Rayah. "Belil 'igarot ve-'igeret le-darkhei ha-ha'atakah shel 'igrot ḥasidim." *Tsiyon* 56, no. 3 (1991): 304–6.

Hasak-Lowy, Todd. *Here and Now: History, Nationalism, and Realism in Modern Hebrew Fiction*. Syracuse: Syracuse University Press, 2008.

Ḥazan, Avraham. *'Avaneha barzel*. Jerusalem: Yeshivat Braslav le-Tora u-Tefila, 1935.

Hendler, Chana. "Ha-sipur ha-ḥasidi bein 'itsuv safruti le-ide'a ruḥanit, iyun be-shalosh girsa'ot shel ha-tema 'otsar taḥat ha-gesher ke-degem meyatseg." In *Ma'aseh sipur*, edited by Avidav Lipsker and Rela Kushelevski, 1:147–67. Ramat Gan: Universitat Bar-Ilan.

Herdt, Gilbert. "Secret Societies and Secret Collectives." *Oceania* 60, no. 4 (June 1990): 360–81.

Hever, Hannan. *Hasidism, Haskalah, Zionism: Chapters in Literary Politics*. Philadelphia: University of Pennsylvania Press, 2023.

Howard, Jeremy, and Andrzej Szczerski. "William Allan, Greek Beauty, and Polish Romanticism." *Apollo* (June 2001): 47–55.

Hundert, Gershon David. "The Introduction to Divrei binah by Dov Ber of Bolechów: An Unexamined Source for the History of Jews in the Lwów Region in the Second Half of the Eighteenth Century." *AJS Review* 33 (2009): 225–69.

———. *The Jews in a Polish Private Town: The Case of Opatów in the Eighteenth Century*. Baltimore: Johns Hopkins University Press, 2019.

Hutterer, Claus Jurgen. "Ein 'deutschmerisches' Denkmal des Jiddischen aus Lemberg." In *Deutsche Sprache in Raum und Zeit: Festschrift für Peter Wiesinger zum 60. Geburtstag*, edited by Peter Ernst and Franz Patocka, 503–15. Vienna: Edition Praesens, 1998.

Idel, Moshe. *Ben: Sonship and Jewish Mysticism*. London: Continuum, 2008.

Israel, Jonathan. *Democratic Enlightenment: Philosophy, Revolution, and Human Rights 1750–1790*. Oxford: Oxford University Press, 2011.

James, Leighton S. *Witnessing the Revolutionary and Napoleonic Wars in German Central Europe*. Houndmills: Palgrave Macmillan, 2013.

Jewuła, Łukasz. *Galicyjskie miasta i miasteczka oraz ich mieszkańcy w latach 1772–1848*. Kraków: Towarzystwo Wydawnicze "Historia Iagellonica," 2013.

Joskowicz, Ari. "Toleration in the Age of Projects: Cameralism, German Police Science, and the Jews." *Jewish Social Studies* 22, no. 2 (2017): 1–37.

Jost, Isaak Markus. *Geschichte der Israeliten seit der Zeit der Maccabäer bis auf unsre Tage*. Berlin: In der Schlesingerschen Buch- und Musikhandlung, 1828.

Judson, Pieter M. *The Habsburg Empire: A New History*. Cambridge: Harvard University Press, 2016.

Jütte, Daniel. *The Age of Secrecy: Jews, Christians, and the Economy of Secrets, 1400–1800*. New Haven: Yale University Press, 2015.

Kaczmarczyk, Zdzisław, and Leśnodorski, Bogusław. *Historia państwa i prawa polskiego*. Vol. 2. Warsaw: Państwowe Wydawn. Naukowe, 1965.

Kądziela, Łukasz. *Od Konstytucji do Insurekcji: Studia nad dziejami Rzeczypospolitej w latach 1791–1794*. Warsaw: Wydawn. Neriton, 2011.

Kaleta, Roman. "Grób Trembeckiego." *Oświeceni i Sentymentalni: Studia Nad Literatura i Życiem w Polsce w Okresie Trzech Rozbiorów*. Wrocław: Zakład Narodowy im. Ossolińskich, 1971.

Kandel, Dawid. "Hymn do Napoleona." *Kwartalnik poświęcony badaniu przeszłości Żydów w Polsce* 1, no. 2 (1912–1913): 122.

Kann, Robert. *A Study in Austrian Intellectual History from Late Baroque to Romanticism.* New York: Praeger, 1960.

Kaplan, Aryeh. *Rabbi Nachman's Stories.* Brooklyn: Breslov Research Institute, 1985.

Karniel, Josef. "Joseph von Sonnenfels." *Jahrbuch des Instituts für Deutsche Geschichte* 6 (1978): 111–58.

———. "Das Toleranzpatent Kaiser Josephs II. für die Juden Galiziens und Lodomeriens." *Jahrbuch des Instituts für Deutsche Geschichte* 11 (1982): 55–89.

Karpiński, Franciszek . "List do J.L. C. P.W.Ks. L. z Krasnegostawu." In *Dzieła Franciszka Karpińskiego,* 177–78. Warsaw: W Druk. Stereotypowey, 1830.

Karstens, Simon. *Lehrer – Schriftsteller – Staatsreformer, Die Karriere des Joseph von Sonnenfels (1733–1817).* Vienna: Böhlau Verlag, 2008.

Katz, Jacob. *Tradition and Crisis: Jewish Society at the End of the Middle Ages.* New York: Schocken Books, 1961.

——— "A State Within a State: The History of an Anti-Semitic Slogan." In *Proceedings of the Israel Academy of Sciences and Humanities,* 4:29–58. Jerusalem: Israel Academy of Sciences and Humanities, 1969.

Katz, Simkha. "Naye materialn fun dem Perl-arkhiv." *YIVO-Bleter* 12 (1938): 560–61.

———. "'Igrot maskilim bi-gnutam shel ha-ḥasidim." *Mozna'im* 10 (1940): 266–76.

Kauffman, Tsippi. "Ha-shkhina ha-mitḥapeset: perek be-te'ologiya beshtianit." *Da'at* 78 (2015): 151–70.

———. "Hasidic Performance: Establishing a Religious (Non)Identity in the Tales About Rabbi Zusha of Annopol." *Journal of Religion* 95, no. 1 (2015): 51–71.

———. "Rabi barukh ve-shoshelet mezhibozh." *Tarbits* 87, no. 1 (2019): 99–143.

———. "Thoughts on the Seam Between Hasidic Literature and Haskalah Literature: The Works of Joseph Perl." *Prooftexts* 38, no. 2 (2020): 347–68.

Klausner, Yosef. *Historiyah shel ha-sifrut ha-'ivrit ha-ḥadasha.* 6 vols. Jerusalem: Aḥiasaf, 1960.

Klein, Joachim. "Herrscherlob. Panegyrische Dichtung und russischer Absolutismus." *Zeitschrift für Slavische Philologie* 70, no. 2 (2014): 257–93.

———, ed. "Special Issue." *Russian Literature* 75, nos. 1–4 (Winter 2014).

Klier, John D. "*Kievlianin* and the Jews: A Decade of Disillusionment, 1864–1873." *Harvard Ukrainian Studies* 5, no. 1 (March 1981): 83–101.

Kohn, Pinkhas. "Di fayerung lekoved stanislav oygust poniatovski in der vilner shtot shul (1764)." *Historishe Shriften* 1 (1929): 763–64.

Kolesnyk, Viktoriia. *Vidomi poliaky v istorii Vinnychchyny: Biohrafichnyi slovnyk.* Vinnytsia: VMHO "Rozvytok." 2007.

Konarski, Michał. "Wyjątki listów Pana Michała Konarskiego," *Dziennik Wileński* 118, no. 1 (1815): 181–87.

Kopylov, Serhii Anatoliiovych, and Andrii Zadorozhniuk, eds. *Opysy Podil's'koi hubernii kintsia XVIII – pochatku XIX st.* Kamianets-Podilskyi: Aksioma, 2011.

Koren, Y. H. "Kol 'ale nidaf, Kislon ben parnakh ha-par'atoni, mishpat 'ami." *Ha-kol* 32 (August 13, 1880): 486–87.

Kosenko, Ivan Oleksandrovych. "Materializatsiia obraziv Homerovoi *Odissei* v parkovykh kompozytsiiakh *Sofiivky* iak vershyna henial'nosti Liudvyha Mettselia." In *Ogrody Czartoryskich: Międzynarodowa Konferencja Naukowa Ogrody Rezydencji Magnackich XVIII-XIX Ww. w Europie Środkowej i Wschodniej Oraz Problemy Ich Ochrony*, 49–54. Warsaw: Ośrodek Ochrony Zabytkowego Krajobrazu, Narodowa Instytucja Kultury, 2001.

Krasko, Alla. *Zabytyi geroi voiny 1812 goda general-fel'dmarshal P. Kh. Vitgenshtein* Moscow: Tsentrpoligraf, 2012.

Kraszewski, Józef Ignacy. *Wspomnienia Odessy, Jedysanu i Budżaku*. Vol. 1. Vilnius: T. Glücksberg, 1845.

Krochmal, Naḥman. *Kitvei Rabi Naḥman Krokhmal*. Edited by Shim'on Ravidovits. 'Enot, 1924.

Kroen, Sheryl. *Politics and Theater: The Crisis of Legitimacy in Restoration France, 1815–1830*. Berkeley: University of California Press, 2000.

Kryvosheia, Iryna. *Shliakhta Umanshchyny v Impers'ku Dobu (kinets XVIII—persha Polovyna XIX St.)*. Uman: Vydavets "Sochinskyi," 2014).

Krzyżanowski, Stanisław Filip. *Tulczyn: Monografia*. Kraków: Wielogłowski, 1862.

Kuk, Yehudit. *Rabi naḥman mi-bratslav 'iyunim be-sipurav*. Jerusalem: Feldheim, 1994.

Kupfer, Efraim. "Ya'akov shemu'el bik le-'or te'udot ḥadashot." Gal-Ed 4–5 (1978): 535–47.

Kurzweil, Barukh. "'Al ha-satira shel yosef perl." In *Bema'avak 'al 'erkhey ha-yahadut*, 68–86. Jerusalem: Schocken, 1970.

Kuzmany, Boerries. *Brody: Eine galizische Grenzstadt im langen 19. Jahrhundert*. Vienna: Böhlau, 2011.

Lebedeva, Ekaterina. "Tul'chin chin vremeni dekabristov: Nezamechennye istochniki." *Istoricheskii kur'er* 6, no. 14 (2020): 9–29.

Leitner, Hermann. "Der geheime Dienst der Polizei in seinen Anfängen zur Zeit des österreichischen Absolutismus." PhD diss., University of Vienna, 1994.

Leszczyński, Jan. *Rządy rosyjskie w kraju Tarnopolskim*, 1809–1815. Kraków: Druk W. L. Anczyca, 1903.

Letteris, Me'ir. *Pelage mayim: . . . 'al mot . . . netsiv ha-aretz . . . frants freiherr von hoyer: et 'asher safad vayekonen 'alav* . . . Lemberg: Grosman, 1822.

———. *Sefer mikhtavei bnei kedem: kolel 'igrot u-mikhtavim be-leshon 'avar ve-'ashkenaz*. Vienna: Y. Shlosberg, 1866.

Levin, Shalom Duber. *'Igrot Kodesh*. Brooklyn: Kehot, 2002.

Lewis, Yizhak. *A Permanent Beginning: R. Nachman of Bratslav and Jewish Literary Modernity*. Albany: State University of New York Press, 2020.

Lipsker, Avidav. "'Ha-kala ve-shiv'at ha-kabtsanim': Le-she'elat me-korotav shel sipur ha-misgeret shel 'ma'aseh me-ha-zain betler.'" *Meḥkarei yerushalayim be-folklor yehudi* 13–14 (1991): 229–48.

Litvak, Olga. *Haskalah: The Romantic Movement in Judaism.* New Brunswick: Rutgers University Press, 2012.

Lobko, Oksana. "Pomishchyts'ki maietky Pravoberezhzhia v umovakh sotsial'no-ekonomichnoi transformatsii 1831–1917 rokiv (za materialamy volodin' hrafiv Potots'kykh)." PhD diss., Kyiv University, 2008.

Lob- und Danklied der Judengemeine zu Mohilow beym einzuge Ihrer Kayserlichen Majestät Katharina II, Selbstbeherrscherinn aller Reussen. N.p., 1780.

Lockhart, John Gibson. *Peter's Letters to His Kinsfolk: To Which Is Added, Postscript Addressed to Samuel T. Coleridge.* New York: Collins & Hannay, 1820.

Łojek, Jerzy. *Potomkowie Szczęsnego: Dzieje fortuny Potockich z Tulczyna, 1799–1921.* Lublin: Lubelskie, 1983.

Lukin, Benyamin (Veniamin). "Kagaly tainye i iavnye: Evreiskie obshchiny v voine 1812 goda." *Lechaim* 238 (2012).

——— "'Bditel'noe oko pravitel'stva': k istorii uchastiia rossiiskikh evreev v voine 1812 goda." *Lechaim* 248 (2012).

———. "'Sluzhba naroda evreiskogo i ego kagalov': Evrei i Otechestvennaia voina 1812 goda." *Lechaim* 187 (2007): 38–43.

Lukowski, Jerzy. *Liberty's Folly: The Polish Lithuanian Commonwealth in the Eighteenth Century, 1697–1795.* London: Routledge, 1991.

Lurie, Ilia. *Milḥamot lyubavitch, ḥasidut ḥabad be-rusiya ha-tsarit.* Jerusalem: Merkaz Zalman Shazar, 2018.

Lurie, Shalom. Introduction to *Ha-'ishon ha-katan = Dos kleyne mentshele,* by Shalom Ya'akov Abramovitsh, 30–31. Haifa: Hotsa'at Ha-sefarim Shel Universitat Ḥefa, 1984.

Macartney, Aylmer, ed. *The Habsburg and Hohenzollern Dynasties in the Seventeenth and Eighteenth Centuries.* New York: Harper & Row, 1970.

de Madariaga, Isabel. *Russia in the Age of Catherine the Great.* New Haven: Yale University Press, 1981.

Magid, Shaul. *Hasidism Incarnate: Hasidism, Christianity, and the Construction of Modern Judaism.* Stanford: Stanford University Press, 2015.

Mahler, Raphael. *Ha-ḥasidut ve-ha-haskala be-galitsya u-ve-polin ha-kongresa'it bamaḥatsit harishona shel ha-me'a ha-tesha 'esre.* Merḥavyah: Sifriyat po'alim, 1961.

———. *A History of Modern Jewry 1780–1815.* New York: Schocken Books, 1971.

———. *Russia in the Age of Catherine the Great.* New Haven: Yale University Press, 1981.

———. *Hasidism and the Jewish Enlightenment: Their Confrontation in Galicia and Poland in the First Half of the Nineteenth Century.* Philadelphia: Jewish Publication Society of America, 1985.

———. *Russia in the Age of Catherine the Great.* London: Phoenix, 2002.

Manekin, Rachel. "Ha-ḥerem be-lemberg bishnat 1816, ravrevanut maskilit ve-historiya yehudit." *Tsiyon* (2008): 173–98.

———. "Sefer ḥok le-yisrael ve-hitpashtut ha-ḥasidut: te'udah me'et yosef perl." In *Yashan mi-pnei ḥadash: Meḥkarim be-toldot yehudei mizraḥ eropa ve-tarbutam, shay le-'imanuel*

ʾ*etkes*, edited by David Assaf and Ada Rappaport, 2:345–55. Jerusalem: Merkaz Zalman Shazar, 2009.

———. "Hasidism and the Habsburg Empire, 1788–1867." *Jewish History* (2013): 271–97.

———. "Hasidism and the State." *Marginalia* (2018): https://themarginaliareview.com/hasidism-and-the-state-2/.

Malach, Eliezer Raphael. "Ha-bibliografya shel mendele." *Ha-toren* 4, no. 44 (January 18, 1918), 12.

Mantel, Martin Irving. "Rabbi Naḥman of Bratzlav's [*sic*] Tales: A Critical Translation from the Yiddish with Annotations and Commentary." Ph.D. diss., Princeton University, 1977.

Marisina, Irina. "'Smart Travels:' The Encounters of Grand Duke Nicholas with British Art and Artists, 1816–17." In *Courtly Gifts and Cultural Diplomacy: Art, Material Culture, and British-Russian Relations*, edited by Louise Hardiman, 253–69. Russian History and Culture 24. Paderborn: Ferdinand Schöningh, Brill Deutschland, 2023.

Mark, Rudolf. *Galizien unter österreichischer Herrschaft: Verwaltung, Kirche, Bevölkerung.* Marburg: Herder-Institut, 1994.

Mark, Yudl, "Di shprakh fun der komedye di genarte velt." *Yidishe Shprakh* (May–June 1943): 68–86.

Mark, Zvi. *Kol sipurei rabi naḥman mi-braslav, ha-maʿasiyot, ha-sipurim ha-sodiyim, ha-ḥalomot ve-ha-ḥezyonot.* Jerusalem: Mosad Bialik, 2014.

———. *Megilat setarim: Ha-ḥazon ha-meshiḥi ha-sodi shel r. naḥman mi-braslav.* Ramat Gan: Universitat Bar-Ilan, 2006.

———. *Mysticism and Madness: The Religious Thought of Rabbi Nachman of Bratslav.* New York: Continuum, 2009.

———. *The Scroll of Secrets: The Hidden Messianic Vision of R. Nachman of Breslav.* Boston: Academic Studies Press, 2010.

Marks, Alexander. "Mikhtav r. moshe meizelsh Le-eliʿezer ha-levi." *Zion: Meʿasef ha-ḥevra ha-ʿerets-yisraʿelit le-historya ve-ʿetnografya* 4 (1930): 39–43.

Martin, Erik. "Das Imperium und der Garten: Die metapoetische Rolle der Panegyrik in Stanisław Trembeckis *Sofijówka* (1806)." *Zeitschrift für Slavische Philologie* 77, no. 1 (2021): 97–121.

Mayzel, Nachman, ed. *Dos Mendele bukh: Briv un oytobiografishe notitsn.* New York: Ikuf, 1959.

Meir, Yonatan. *Ḥasidut meduma: ʿIyunim ni-ketavav ha-satiriyim shel yosef perl.* 3 vols. Jerusalem: Mosad Bialik, 2013.

Mendelsohn, Moshe (Moses) ben Menaḥem. *Yerushalaim.* Vienna: Perets ben moshe smolenskin, 1877.

Mevorakh, Barukh. *Napoleon u-tekufato: Reshumot ve-ʿeduyot ʿivriyot shel bnei ha-dor.* Jerusalem: Mosad Bialik, 1968.

Michałowska-Mycielska, Anna. "Jewish Autobiographical Writing: Memoirs of Moses Vasertsug (c. 1760–1832)." *Acta Poloniae Historica* 128 (2023): 249–76.

Miller, D. A. *The Novel and the Police*. Berkeley: University of California Press, 1988.

Miller, Michael. *Rabbis and Revolution: The Jews of Moravia in the Age of Emancipation*. Stanford: Stanford University Press, 2011.

Minkina, Olga, *"Syny Rakhili": Evreiskie deputaty v Rossiiskoi imperii, 1772–1825*. Moscow: Novoe literaturnoe obozrenie, 2011.

Miron, Dan. "Reshime fun publikatsyes un geshe'enishen, 1857–1869." In *Limdu heitev*, by Shalom Yankev Abramovitsh, edited by Dan Miron, 89–100. New York: YIVO, 1969.

———. *A Traveler Disguised: The Rise of Modern Yiddish Fiction in the Nineteenth Century*. New York: Schocken, 1973.

——— *From Continuity to Contiguity: Toward a new Jewish Literary Thinking*. Stanford: Stanford University Press, 2010.

———. "Lifnei sha'ar ha-ḥok." *Kivunim ḥadashim* 29 (December 2013): 136–82.

Mitchell, Timothy. "Society, Economy, and the State Effect." In *State/Culture: State-Formation After the Cultural Turn*, edited by George E. Marcus, 76–97. Wilder House Series in Politics, History, and Culture. Ithaca: Cornell University Press, 1999.

Molière. *Tartuffe: Comedy in Five Acts*. Translated by Richard Wilbur. New York: Harcourt, Brace & World, 1963.

Monas, Sidney. *The Third Section: Police and Society in Russia Under Nicholas I*. Cambridge: Harvard University Press, 1961.

Moshe Ḥaim Efraim of Sudlikow. *Degel maḥane efrayim*. Jerusalem: Makhon ha-Ktav, 1987.

Mukdoyni, A [pseud. Aleksander Kapel]. "Di ershte yidishe komedye." *Yidishe Kultur* 9 (September 1947): 42–43.

Müller, Eugeniusz. *Żydzi w Krakowie w drugiej połowie XIV stulecia*. Kraków: Druk. Czasu, 1906.

Murphy, Curtis. *From Citizens to Subjects: City, State, and the Enlightenment in Poland, Ukraine, and Belarus*. Pittsburgh: University of Pittsburgh Press, 2018.

Nacht, Joseph. "Ein unveröffentlichtes Aktenstück von Josef Perl." *Monatsschrift für Geschichte und Wissenschaft des Judentums* 7–8 (July–August 1927): 308–11.

Nadav, Mordekhai. *The Jews of Pinsk, 1506 to 1880*. Edited by Mark Mirsky and Moshe Rosman. Stanford: Stanford University Press, 2008.

Naḥman of Bratslav. *Sefer sipurei maʿasiyot she-zakhinu lishmoʿa mi-pi rabeynu ha-kadosh moharan zutsakal*. Ostraha: n.p., 1815.

———. *The Tales*. Translated by Arnold Band. New York: Paulist Press, 1978.

———. *Likutei moharan mahadura le-limud be-ʿiyun, hugʿa ʿal-pi defus moharnat, be-hashva'ah le-sha'ar defusim, kerekh meyuḥad li-khvod mata'im shanah le-histalkut rabeinu*. Jerusalem: n.p., 2011.

Naruszewicz, Adam Stanisław. *Dziennik podróży króla Stanisława Augusta na Ukraine i do innych ziem koronnych*. Warsaw: Instytut Badań Literackich PAN. Wydawnictwo, 2019.

Natanson, Bernard. *Sefer ha-zikhronot: Divrei yeme ḥayye yitzḥak ber levinzohn, tekhunat sefarav, merots ha-ʾigrot beno u-ven ḥakhmei doro be-nogeʿa le-haskalat ha-yehudim be-ʾartsot rusya*. Warsaw: Y. Goldman, 1890.

Natkovich, Svetlana. *Questionable People: Inventing Modern Jewish Selves in the Russian Empire, 1860–1890*. Judaic Traditions in Literature, Music, and Art. Syracuse: Syracuse University Press, 2025.

Neder, Wilhelm. "Die Übersetzungen von Gesetzen in der Habsburgmonarchie." Working Paper No. 7, Donau-Institut, Budapest, 2013.

Neschwara, Christian. "Zur Genese des österreichischen Strafgesetzes von 1803." In *Strafrechtsgeschichte im „langen" 19. Jahrhundert: Forschungen und Perspektiven*, edited by Martin P. Schennach, 37–60. Vienna: Verlag Österreich, 2020.

Netanel, Lilach. "Zman mendele: ʿAl ha-poetika shel ha-merḥak ha-ḥal ba-nusaḥ haʿivri shel ʿabramovitsh veʿad ha-roman ha-ʿivri-vinaʾi shel vogel." *ʿIyunim be-tkumat israel* 26 (2016): 1–21.

Nichols, Francis Morgan. *The Epistles of Erasmus from His Earliest Letters to His Fifty-First Year Arranged in Order of Time: English Translations from the Early Correspondence with a Commentary Confirming the Chronological Arrangement and Supplying Further Biographical Matter*. London: Longmans, Green, and Co., 1901.

Nigal, Gedalyah. *Ha-siporet ha-ḥasidit: Toldotehah ve-nosaḥeha*. Jerusalem: J. Marcus, 1981.

———. *The Hasidic Tale*. Oxford: Littman Library of Jewish Civilization, 2008.

Ogris, Werner. "The Habsburg Monarchy in the Eighteenth Century: The Birth of the Modern Centralized State." In *Legislation and Justice*, edited by Antonio Padoa-Schioppa, 313–34. Oxford: Oxford University Press, 1997.

Olechowski, Thomas. "Zur Entstehung des österreichischen Strafgesetzes 1852." In *Grundlagen der österreichischen Rechtskultur: Festschrift für Werner Ogris zum 75. Geburtstag*, edited by Alina Lengauer, Christian Neschwara, and Thomas Olechowski, 319–21. Vienna: Böhlau Verlag, 2010.

Opas, Tomasz. "Miasta prywatne a Rzeczpospolita." *Kwartalnik Historyczny* 78, no. 1 (1971): 28–47.

Pacholkiv, Svjatoslav. "Galizische Judengemeinden unter Maria Theresia und Joseph II." *Bulletin der Polnischen Historischen Mission* (2014): 93–123.

Pavel, Thomas. "Immersion and Distance in Fictional Worlds." *Itinéraires*, no. 1 (2010): 99–109.

Pelli, Moshe. "'La-menatse'aḥ ba-neginot maskil' – melekhet ha-shir u-tofa'at ha-shira ba-me'asef, ktav ha-ʿet ha-rishon shel ha-haskala ha-ʿivrit." *Dappim le-meḥkar be-safrut* 12 (1999–2000): 65–116.

———*Bikurei ha-ʾitim – Bikurei ha-haskala: An Annotated Index to Bikurei ha-ʾitim, the Hebrew Journal of the Haskalah in Galicia, 1820–1831*. Jerusalem: Magnes, 2005.

Perkins, Rollin M. "Ignorance and Mistake in Criminal Law." *University of Pennsylvania Law Review and American Law Register* 88, no. 1 (November 1939): 35–70.

Perl, Joseph. *Boḥen tsadik: Bo muvaʾ deʿot ʿal ha-sefer megale temirin*. Prague: M. J. Landau, 1838.

———. [pseud. Ovadia]. *'Mikhtav d'. Kerem Ḥemed* 3 (1838): 53–61.

———. *Yoysef perls yidishe ksovim*. Edited by Zelig Kalmanovitch. Vilnius: Yivo-Bibliotek, Filologishe Sektsye, 1937.

———. *Maʿasiyot ve-ʾigrot mi-tsadikim ʾamitiyim ume-ʾanshei shelomenu*. Edited by Chone Shmeruk and Shmuel Werses. Jerusalem: ha-ʾAkademya ha-Leʾumit ha-Yisraʾelit le-madaʿim, 1969.

——— *ʿAl mahut kat ha-ḥasidim*. Edited by Avraham Rubinshtayn. Jerusalem: ha-ʾAkademya ha-Leʾumit ha-Yisraʾelit le-Madaʿim, 1977.

———. *Revealer of Secrets*. Translated by Dov Taylor. Boulder: Westview Press, 1997.

———. *Megale temirin*. 3 vols. Edited by Jonathan Meir. Jerusalem: Mosad Bialik, 2013.

———. *Sound an Alarm! Joseph Perl's Revealer of Secrets, Megaleh Temirin, and Testing the Righteous, Boḥen Tsadik*, 2 vols. Translated by Dov Taylor. Cincinnati: Hebrew Union College Press, 2024.

Perrie, Maureen. "The Popular Image of Ivan the Terrible." *SEER* 56, no. 2 (1978): 275–86.

Petrenko, Oleksandr. "Bratslavs'ka huberniia i Bratslavs'ke namisnytstvo." *Kyivs'ka starovyna* 1 (2000): 44–61.

Petrushka, Simcha. "Makor polani le-sipurei maʿasiyot shel rabi naḥman mi-bratslav." *Ketuvim* 2, no. 42 (1928): 3.

Piekarz, Mendel. *Ḥasidut Bratslav: Perakim be-ḥayei me-ḥolela, bi-ktaveha uve-sefiḥeʾa*. Jerusalem: Mosad Bialik, 1972.

———. *Ha-hanhaga ha-ḥasidit: Samkhut ve-ʾemunat tsadikim be-ʾaspaklaryat sifurtah shel ha-ḥasidut*. Jerusalem: Mosad Bialik, 1999.

Plessis Richelieu, Armand-Emmanuel du. *Lettres d'Odessa du duc de Richelieu: 1803–1814*. Edited by Elena Polevchtchikova and Dominique Triaire. Ferney-Voltaire: Centre international d'étude du XVIIIe siècle, 2014.

Polnoe sobranie zakonov Rossiiskoi imperii, series 1. Vol. 23. St. Petersburg: n.p., 1830.

Polonsky, Anthony. *The Jews in Poland and Russia, vol. 1 (1350–1881)*, Oxford: Oxford University Press, 2010.

Polovynchak, Iuliia. *Hazeta "Kievlianin" i ukrainstvo: dosvid natsional'noi samoidentyfikatsii: Monohrafiia*. Kyiv: Natsionalna biblioteka imeni V.I. Vernadskoho NAN Ukrainy, 2008.

Potocki, Jan. *Principes de chronologie pour les temps antérieurs aux olympiades*. St. Petersburg: A. Pluchart et comp., 1810.

———. *Voyage dans les steppes d'Astrakhan et du Caucase: Histoire primitive des peuples qui ont habité anciennement ces contrées. Nouveau périple du Pont-Euxin . . . Ouvrages publiés et accompagnés de notes et tables*. Vol. 2. Paris: Merlin, 1829.

———. *Oeuvres*. Edited by François Rosset and Dominique Triaire. Louvain: Peeters, 2004.

Prokopovych, Markian. *Habsburg Lemberg: Architecture, Public Space, and Politics in the Galician Capital, 1772–1914*. West Lafayette: Purdue University Press, 2008.

Provinzial-Gesetzsammlung des Königreichs Galizien und Lodomerien für das Jahr 1823. Lemberg: Peter Piller, 1824.

Quilligan, Maureen. *The Language of Allegory, Defining the Genre*. Ithaca: Cornell University Press, 1979.

Raeff, Marc. *The Well-Ordered Police State: Social and Institutional Change Through Law in the Germanys and Russia, 1600–1800*. New Haven: Yale University Press, 1983.

Ram, Harsha. *The Imperial Sublime: A Russian Poetics of Empire*. Madison: University of Wisconsin Press, 2003.

Rapoport, Shelomo Yehuda Leib. *Kol nehi u-mispad mar: 'Al mot . . . landes-gouverneur fun galitsien frants freiherr von hauer be-yom 12 le-ḥodesh kislev 5583*. Lemberg: Schnaider Joseph, 1822.

———. "Mikhtav yud." *Kerem Ḥemed* 4 (1839): 45–57.

———. *Tekhunat 'ir pariz: Godla, maḥlakoteha, mispar yoshveha u-nimusehem, tekhunat 'armonoteha . . . reḥovoteha u-shvakeha, gam aklima, ve-ḥavrah lah gam tekhunat 'i 'alba godlo, yevulo ve-aklimo, mispar 'arav u-mivtsarav, mispar yoshavav, misḥaram ve-khol ma'ase yedeyhem*. Lemberg: Herz Grossman, 1814.

Rapoport-Albert, Ada. "He'arot le-ma'amaro shel yehuda *liebes*." *Tsiyon* 46 (1981): 346–51.

Raz-Krakotzkin, Amnon. *The Censor, the Editor, and the Text: The Catholic Church and the Shaping of the Jewish Canon in the Sixteenth Century*. Philadelphia: University of Pennsylvania Press, 2007.

Rebecchini, Damiano. "An Influential Collector: Tsar Nicholas I of Russia." *Journal of the History of Collections* 22, no. 1 (May 2010): 45–67.

Rędziński, Kazimierz. "Szkoła Józefa Perla w Tarnopolu (1813–1939)." In *Prace Naukowe Gliwickiej Wyższej Szkoły Przedsiębiorczości, Społeczne konteksty edukacji, Pedagogika*, edited by Kazimierza Rędzińskiego and Mirosława Łapota, 225–45. Gliwice: Gliwicka Wyższa Szkoła Przedsiębiorczości, 2009.

Robertson, Ritchie. "Freemasons Versus Jesuits: Conspiracy Theories in Enlightenment Germany." *Times Literary Supplement*, October 12, 2012.

Röskau-Rydel, Isabel. *Kultur an der Peripherie des Habsburger Reiches: Die Geschichte des Bildungswesens und der kulturellen Einrichtungen in Lemberg von 1772 bis 1848*. Wiesbaden: Harrassowitz, 1993.

Roskies, David. "The Master of Prayer: Rabbi Naḥman of Bratslav." In *God's Voice from the Void: Old and New Studies in Bratslav Hasidism*, edited by Shaul Magid, 67–102. Albany: State University of New York Press, 2002.

Rosman, Murray Jay (Moshe). *The Lords' Jews: Magnate-Jewish Relations in the Polish-Lithuanian Commonwealth During the Eighteenth Century*. Cambridge: Harvard University Press, 1990.

Rossi, Joseph. *Denkbuch für Fürst und Vaterland*. Vol. 2. Vienna: B. Wallishausser, 1814–1815.

Rostworowski, Emanuel. "Potocki Stanisław Szczęsny (Feliks) herbu Pilawa." In *Polski Słownik Biograficzny*, edited by Emanuel Rostworowski, 28:183–202. Warsaw: Zakład Narodowy im. Ossolińskich, Polska Akademia Nauk, 1984–1985.

Royal Academy of Arts. *The Exhibition of the Royal Academy, MDCCCXV*. London: B. McMillan, Bow-Street, Covent Garden, 1815.

Rozdolski, Roman. *Stosunki poddańcze w dawniej Galicji*. 2 vols. Warsaw: Państwowe Wydawn. Naukowe, 1962.

Rubinstein, Avraham. "Ktav hayad 'al mahut kat ha-ḥasidim'." *Kiryat Sefer* 38 (1963): 263–72, 415–24; 39 (1964): 117–36.

———. "Midrash ha-shemot shel yosef perl." *Tarbiz* 43 (1974): 140–57.

Sack, Johann Eduard. *Schloime Klappzümbels treuherzige Beschreibung der von der Lemberger Judenschaft abgehalten wordenen letzten Friedensfeier – Seinem innig geliebten Freunde Hersch Schmeckpuedele als ein Denkmahl des dabei genossenen unvergesslichen Freudengefühls dargebracht* (Lemberg: n.p., 1814).

———. *Schreiben des Rebb Jossel Pippik aus Anlass von Madame Catalani hier gegebenen Vokal Konzerte: An seinen Freund Rebb Simche Hoyker*. Lemberg: n.p., 1820.

Sadan, Dov. *A vort bashteyt: Shpatsirn tsvishn shprakh un literatur*. Tel Aviv: Farlag Y. L. Perets, 1975.

———. "Kal u-kaved: Le-darko shel pitgam." In *Studies in Jewish Bibliography, History, and Literature: In Honor of Edward kiev*, edited by Charles Berlin, 113–16. New York: Ktav Publishing House, 1971.

———. *Kheyn gribelekh: Tsu der biografie fun vort un vertl*. Buenos Aires: Altveltekher yidisher kultur kongres, 1971.

Sadowski, Dirk. *Haskala und Lebenswelt: Herz Homberg und die jüdischen deutschen Schulen in Galizien 1782–1806*. Göttingen: Vandenhoeck & Ruprecht, 2010.

———. "The Jewish German Schools in Galicia (1782–1806)—School Reality and Corporate Resistance." *Jewish Culture and History* 13, nos. 2–3 (2012): 153–72.

Sadowski, Dirk. "Maskilisches Bildungsideal und josephinische Erziehungspolitik: Herz Homberg und die jüdisch-deutschen Schulen in Galizien, 1787–1806." *Leipziger Beiträge zur jüdischen Geschichte und Kultur* 1 (2003): 145–68.

Sagiv, Gadi, and Ada Rapoport-Albert. 2017. "Ḥabad keneged ḥasidut 'polin': Le-toledotav shel dimuy." In *Ḥabad – historia, hagut ve-dimuy*, edited by David Assaf, 223–65. Jerusalem: Merkaz Zalman Shazar, 2017.

Sammlung aller k. k. Verordnungen u. Gesetze vom Jahre 1740 bis 1780, Die unter der Regierung des Kaisers Joseph des II. theils noch ganz bestehen, theils zum Theile abgeändert sind, als ein Hilfs- und Ergänzungsbuch zu dem Handbuche aller unter der Regie. Vienna: Mößle, 1787.

Sasportas, Jacob. *Tsitsat novel tsevi*. Edited by Isaiah Tishby. Jerusalem: Mosad Bialik, 1954.

Schabowski, Stanisław. "Przedstawiciele rodu Polignaców i ich dzienniki w zbiorach Muzeum Zamku w Łańcucie." *Studia Wilanowskie* 24 (2017): 115–28.

Scharf, Claus. *Katharina II Deutschland und die Deutschen*. Mainz: P. von Zabern, 1995.

Schechter, Ronald. *Obstinate Hebrews: Representations of Jews in France, 1715–1815*. Berkeley: University of California Press, 2003.

Schedrin, Vassili. *Jewish Souls, Bureaucratic Minds: Jewish Bureaucracy and Policymaking in Late Imperial Russia, 1850–1917*. Detroit: Wayne State University Press, 2016.

Schematismus des Königreiches Galizien und Lodomerien. Lemberg: Joseph Johann Piller, 1814.

Schembor, Friedriech. *Galizien im ausgehenden 18. Jahrhundert: Aufbau der österreichischen Verwaltung im Spiegel der Quellen*. Bochum: Verlag Dr. Dieter Winkler, 2015.

Schleicher, Marianne. *Intertextuality in the Tales of Rabbi Nahman of Bratslav: A Close Reading of Sipure Maʿasiyot*. Leiden: Brill, 2007.

Schmidt, Valentin Heinrich, and Daniel Gottlieb Gebhard Mehring. *Neuestes gelehrtes Berlin; oder literarische Nachrichten von jetztlebenden Berlinischen Schriftstellern und Schriftstellerinnen*. Berlin: Friedrich Mauer, 1795.

Schnitzler, Jean-Henry. *Secret History of the Court and Government of Russia Under the Emperors Alexander and Nicholas*. London: Richard Bentley, 1847.

Schwartz, Barry. "Hanoten teshuaʿ: The Origin of the Traditional Jewish Prayer for the Government." *Hebrew Union College Annual* 57 (1986): 113–20.

Schwarzfuchs, Simon. *Napoleon, the Jews and the Sanhedrin*. London: Routledge & Kegan Paul, 1979.

Scott, James C. *Seeing Like a State: How Certain Schemes to Improve the Human Condition Have Failed*. New Haven: Yale University Press, 1998.

Sealsfield, Charles (Karl Postl). *Austria as It Is; or, Sketches of Continental Courts by an Eyewitness*. London: Hurst, Chance, and Co., 1828.

Sefer shivḥei ha-besht. Kopys: Dfus Israel Yafe, 1815.

Seidman, Naomi. *A Marriage Made in Heaven: The Sexual Politics of Hebrew and Yiddish*. Contraversions 7. Berkeley: University of California Press, 1997.

Selig, Gottfried. *Lehrbuch zur gründlichen Erlernung der jüdisch-deutschen Sprache für Beamte, Gerichtsver-wandte, Advocaten und insbesondere für Kaufleute; mit einem vollständigen Hebräisch und jüdisch-deutschen Wörterbuche*. Leipzig: Votz und Leo, 1792.

Shaked, Gershon. *Mendele lifanav veʾaḥarav*. Jerusalem: Magnes Press, 2005.

Shapira, Yehuda Tsvi. *Ze sefer ha-derekh le-tsadik . . . ʿal ʿir ʾUman*. Jerusalem: n.p., 2000.

Sheler, Ahuva. "ʾAvraham Uri Kovner – reshita shel ha-bikoret ha-ʿivrit ha-ḥadasha." PhD diss., Tel Aviv University, 2003.

Shif, Ekaterina. *Mify i skazaniia v parke "Sofievka."* Kyiv: Mystetstvo, 2007.

Shifris, Nathan. *Shir ḥadash: Shelomo yehuda rapoport: rabanut, haskala, leʾumiyut*. Jerusalem: Merkaz Zalman Shazar, 2021.

Shmeruk, Chone. "ʾAlegorizatsiya yehudit shel yetsirot mi-folklor ha-ʿamim." *Ha-kongres ha-ʿolami ha-sheni le-madaʿei ha-yahadut* (1957): 3.

———. "Dvarim ke-havayatam u-devarim she-ba-dimyon be-megale temirin shel yosef perl." *Tsiyon* 21 (1957): 92–99.

———. "Ḥazono ha-maskili shel yosef perl." In Joseph Perl, *Maʿasiyot ve-ʾigrot mi-tsadikim ʾamitiyim u-meʾanshei shelomenu*, edited by Chone Shmeruk and Shmuel Werses, 36–42. Jerusalem: Ha-ʾAkademya ha-Leʾumit ha-Yisraʾelit le-Madaʿim, 1969.

———. Introduction to *Maʿasiyot ve-ʾigrot mi-tsadikim ʾamitiyim u-meʾanshei shelomenu*, by Joseph Perl, edited by Chone Shmeruk and Shmuel Werses. Jerusalem: ha-ʾAkademya ha-Leʾumit ha-Yisreʾelit le-Madaʿim, 1969,

———. *Keri'a lenavi, meḥkare historia vesafrut*. Jerusalem: Ha-merkaz le-Ḥeker Toldot Yehudei Polin ve-Tarbutam, 2000.

———. "Nosaḥ bilti yadu'a shel ha-komediya ha'anonimit 'Di Genarte Velt.'" *Kiryat Sefer* 54 (1979): 802–16.

———. *Sifrut yidish: Perakim le-toldoteha*. Tel Aviv: Mifʿalim Universita'iyim le-Hotsa'ah la-'or, 1978.

Shmidman, Avi. "'Dohere dolkim' ve'dohar eyna'im': *dahar* keleshon 'or bafaytanut hakeduma." *Leshonenu* 75 (1993): 37–54.

Shulman, Iakov Meerovich. *Goroda i liudi evreiskoi diaspory v Vostochnoi Evrope do nachala XX veka: Ukraina. Berdichev, Vinnitsa, Zhitomir, Kamenets-Podol'sk, Tul'chin*. Moscow: TLS Faktors, 2007.

Shur, Avraham Avish. "Yaḥas gedolei ha-ḥasidut la-shilton ve-ha-kesher bein ha-ʿaliya l-'erets isra'el le-halukat polin." *Kovets ḥitse giborim* 10 (April 2017): 1006–36.

Silber, Michael. "Shorshe ha-pilug be-yahadut hungariya: Tmurot tarbutiyot ve-ḥevratiyot mi-yemey yosef ha-sheni ʿad-ʿerev mahapekhat 1848." PhD diss., Hebrew University of Jerusalem, 1985.

Sinkoff, Nancy. *Out of the Shtetl: Making Jews Modern in the Polish Borderlands*. Providence: Brown University Press, 2004.

Sked, Alan. *Metternich and Austria, an Evaluation*. Basingstoke: Palgrave Macmillan, 2008.

Słotwiński, Konstanty. *Katechizm poddanych galicyjskich: O prawach i powinnościach ich względem Rządu, Dworu i samych siebie*. Lviv: n.p., 1832.

Smith-Peter, Susan. *Imagining Russian Regions, Subnational Identity, and Civil Society in Nineteenth-Century Russia*. Leiden: Brill, 2018.

S[okolov], N[aḥum]. "Ha-tsefira ve-ha-mevakrim mi-taʿam." *Ha-tsefira sefer ha-yovel* (1912): 8–10.

Sotrudniki Rossiiskoi natsional'noi biblioteki: Deiateli nauki i kultury; Biograficheskii slovar'. St. Petersburg: Izd-vo Rossiiskoi natsionalnoi biblioteki, 2005.

Sr. k.k. Majestät Franz des Ersten politische Gesetze und Verordnungen für Sämmtliche Provinzen des Österreichischen Kaiserstaates mit Ausnahme von Siebenbürgen. Vol. 34. Vienna: K.K. Hof- u. Staats-Aeralial- Druckerey, 1811.

Sternhartz, Nathan. *ʿAlim li-terufa*. Warsaw: Hotsa'at Braslav, 1930.

———. *Sefer ḥayei moharan: ḥayav ... shel rabi naḥman mi-bratslav ... ʿim hashmatot me-ha-rav [ʾalter] mi-teplik ve-hosafot me-ha-rav sh. horowitz*. Beyt Shemesh: Nekudotot Tovot, 2008.

———. *Tzaddik: A Portrait of Rebbe Nachman*. Translated by Avraham Greenbaum. Jerusalem: Breslov Research Institute, 2019.

———. *Yemei moharanat ʿim kuntras ha-tela'ot*. Beyt Shemesh: Nekuda Tova, 2010?

Stiles, William Henry. *Austria in 1848–49: Being a History of the Late Political Movements in Vienna, Milan, Venice, and Prague: With Details of the Campaigns of Lombardy and Novara: A Full Account of the Revolution in Hungary.* Vol. 1. London: Harper & Brothers, 1852.

Strakosch, Henry E. *State Absolutism and the Rule of Law: The Struggle for the Codification of Civil Law in Austria 1753–1811.* Sydney: Sydney University Press, 1967.

Stone, Daniel. *The Polish-Lithuanian State, 1386–1795.* Seattle: University of Washington Press, 2001.

Struve, Kai. *Bauern und Nation in Galizien: Über Zugehörigkeit und soziale Emanzipation im 19. Jahrhundert.* Schriften des Simon-Dubnow-Instituts 4. Göttingen: Vandenhoeck & Ruprecht, 2005.

Sulimierski, Filip, Bronisław Chlebowski, and Władysław Walewski. *Słownik geograficzny królestwa Polskiego i innych krajów Słowiańskich.* Warsaw: nakł. Filipa Sulimierskiego i Władysława Walewskiego, 1880–1902.

Tarler, Joseph (Peter). "Ya'alzu ḥasidim be-khavod." *Yerushalaim* 2 (1845): 95–96.

Taussig, Michael. *Defacement: Public Secrecy and the Labor of the Negative.* Stanford: Stanford University Press, 1999.

Teller, Adam. "The Legal Status of the Jews on the Magnate Estates of Poland-Lithuania in the Eighteenth Century." *Gal-Ed* 15–16 (1997): 41–63.

Teter, Magda. "Delegated Governance: Rethinking the Idea of Premodern Jewish Autonomy." *Shofar: An Interdisciplinary Journal of Jewish Studies* 43, no. 1 (2025): 215–29.

Thaden, Edward C. *Russia's Western Borderlands, 1710–1870.* Princeton: Princeton University Press, 1984.

Theyls, Ignatz. "Letter to Joseph Perl." *Shulamit* 2 (1812): 422–23.

Tilly, Charles. *Contention and Democracy in Europe, 1650–2000.* Cambridge: Cambridge University Press, 2004.

Tishby, Isaiah. *Pirkei zohar: Mivḥar ma'amarei ha-zohar me-turgamim le-'ivrit be-tseruf me-vo'ot ubi-urim.* 2 vols. Jerusalem: Mosad Bialik, 1969.

Topohrafichnyi opys Podil'skoi hubernii 1799 r.: Vinnyts'kyi, Iampil's'kyi, Bratslavs'kyi povity. Edited by Iurii Lehun. Vinnytsia: Nilan, 2017.

Trebitsch, Abraham. *Korot ha-'itim.* Brünn: Joseph Rossmann, 1801.

Trefilov, Evgenii, and Julia Leikin, "Proof of Sincere Love for the Tsar: Popular Monarchism in the Age of Peter the Great." *Kritika* 18, no. 3 (2017): 461–85.

Trembecki, Stanisław. *Sofijówka.* Edited by Jerzy Snopek. Warsaw: Instytut Badań Literackich, Pro Cultura Litteraria, 2000.

———. "Wyjątek z opisu Sofiówki przez Stanisława Trembeckiego." *Tygodnik Wileński* 1, no. 13 (1804): 182–86.

———. "Zofiówka." *Dziennik Wileński* (May 1806): 194–211.

———. *Zofiówka w sposobie topograficznym opisana przez Stanisława Trembeckiego.* Leipzig: n.p., 1806.

Tribe, Keith. *Governing Economy: The Reformation of German Economic Discourse, 1750–1840.* Cambridge: Cambridge University Press., 1988.

———. *Strategies of Economic Order*. Cambridge: Cambridge University Press, 2006.

Tronko, Petro Tymofilovych. *Istoriia mist i sil Ukrainy v konteksti rehional'nykh doslidzhen': Dosvid, problemy, perspektyvy*. Kyiv: Instytut istorii Ukrainy NAN Ukrainy, 1967–1973.

Tucker, Irene. *A Probable State: The Novel, the Contract, and the Jews*. Chicago: University of Chicago Press, 2000.

Unger, Menashe. "Yidishe verter in loshn koydeshn tekst fun sipurey mayses." *Yidishe shprakh* 28 (1967): 11–21.

Usenko, Pavlo. *Serpankova preliudiia "Sofiivky"—Pototski: pol's'kyi mozhnovladets' i hrets'ka superkrasunia v ukrains'komu prystanovyshchi zahal'noi istorii*. Kyiv: Instytut istorii Ukrainy NAN Ukrainy, 2010.

Uther, Hans-Jorg. *The Types of International Folktales: A Classification and Bibliography, Based on the System of Anttii Aarne and Stith Thompson*. 3 vols. Helsinki: Suomalainen Tiedeakatemia, Academia Scientiarum Fennica, 2004.

van Luit, Hendrika Johanna (Tehilah). "Paths of Modernity in Traditions' Strongholds: The German Jewish Schools as a Playground Between the Austrian Absolutist Welfare State and the Galician Kahal." PhD diss., Hebrew University of Jerusalem, 2011.

Vieusseux, Gian Pietro. *Journal-Itinéraire de mon voyage en Europe, 1814–1817: Con il carteggio relativo al viaggio*. Edited by Lucia Tonini. Florence: L. S. Olschki, 1998.

Vikul, Pavel. "Podol'skie arkhipastyri (1795–1895 gg.)." In *Trudy Podol'skago eparkhial'nago istoriko-statisticheskago komiteta*, 8:1–160. Kamianets-Podilskyi: Tipografiia podol'skago gubernskago pravleniia, 1897.

Vilenski, Mordechai. *Ḥasidim u-mitnagdim: Le-toldot ha-pulmus she-benehem ba-shanim tak–taka*. Vol. 1. Jerusalem: Mosad Bialik, 1990.

Viner, Meir. *Bibliologisher zamelbukh* 1 (1929): 140–47.

———, ed. *Di Genarte velt: Komedye fun an umbakantn avtor inem tsveytn yortsendlik funem nayntsntn yorhundert*. Moscow: Melukhe-farlag "Der Emes," 1940.

———. *Tsu der geshikhte fun der yidisher literatur in 19-tn yorhundert (etyudn un matiryaln)*. New York: Ikuf, 1945.

Volumina legum, przedruk zbioru praw staraniem XX: Pijarów w Warszawie od roku 1732 do roku 1782 wydanego. 12 vols. St. Petersburg: Ohryzko Jozafat, 1859.

von Mises, Ludwig. *Die Entwicklung des gutsherrlich-bäuerlichen Verhältnisses in Galizien (1772–1848)*. Vienna: Franz Deuticke, 1902.

von Sonnenfels, Joseph. *Grundsätze aus den Polizei Handlungs und Finanzwissenschaften*. 2 vols. Vienna: Joseph Edlen von Kurzbek, 1768–1786.

Vorobeytshik, Arn. "Tsu der frage vegen mendeles literarishe yerushe." In *Mendele un zayn tsayt: Materyaln tsu der geshikhte fun der yidisher literatur in XIX yorhundert*, edited by Arn Gurshteyn, 58–59. Moscow: Melukhe-farlag "Der Emes," 1940.

Vushko, Iryna. "Enlightened Absolutism, Imperial Bureaucracy and Provincial Society: The Austrian Project to Transform Galicia, 1772–1815." PhD diss., Yale University, 2008.

———. *The Politics of Cultural Retreat: Imperial Bureaucracy in Austrian Galicia, 1772–1867*. New Haven: Yale University Press, 2015.

Wakefield, Andre. *The Disordered Police State: German Cameralism as Science and Practice.* Chicago: University of Chicago Press, 2009.

Wandycz, Piotr S. *The Lands of Partitioned Poland, 1795–1918.* Seattle: University of Washington Press, 1974.

———. "The Poles in the Habsburg Monarchy." *Austrian History Yearbook* 3, no. 2 (1967): 261–86.

Wangermann, Ernst. "'By and By We Shall Have an Enlightened Populace': Moral Optimism and the Fine Arts in Late-Eighteenth-Century Austria." *Austrian History Yearbook* 30 (1999): 1–15.

———. *From Joseph II to the Jacobin trials: Government Policy and Public Opinion in the Habsburg Dominions in the Period of the French Revolution.* Westport: Greenwood Press, 1979.

Wasserzug. Mosche. *Memoiren eines polnischen Juden: Lebenserinnerungen von Mosche Wasserzug.* Edited by Heinrich Loewe. Berlin: n.p., 1911.

Weber, Max. *From Max Weber: Essays in Sociology.* Edited and translated by Hans Heinrich Gerth and Charles Wright Mills. New York: Oxford University Press, 1946.

Weinlos, Israel. "Yosl tarler einer von die ershten maskilim in galizien." *Morgen* (Lemberg), January 22, 1927, 3–4.

Weiss, Isaac Hirsch. *Zikhronotay me-yalduti 'ad melot li shemonim shanah.* Warsaw: Bi-dfus ha-aḥim shuldberg, 1895.

Weiss, Joseph George. *Meḥkarim be-ḥasidut braslav.* Jerusalem: Mosad Bialik, 1974.

———. "Mystical Hasidism and the Hasidism of Faith: A Typological Analysis." In *God's Voice from the Void: Old and New Studies in Bratslav Hasidism,* edited by Shaul Magid, 277–85. Series in Judaica. Albany: State University of New York Press, 2002.

Weisner, Jonas. *Der Bann in seiner geschichtlichen Entwicklung auf dem Boden des Judenhtums.* Leipzig: Leiner, 1864.

Weissberg, Meir (Max). "Die neuhebräische Aufklärungsliteratur in Galizien." *Monatsschrift für die Geschichte und Wissenschaft des Judentums* 36, nos. 1–2 (1928): 71–88.

———. *Die neuhebräische Aufklärungs-Literatur in Galizien: Eine Literar-Historische Charakteristik.* Leipzig: M. Breitenstein, 1898.

———. "Józef Kohn Zedek, Ostatni publicysta nowohebrajski galicyjskiej haskali." *Rocznik Żydowski* 6 (1906): 253–368.

Wendrinsky, Johann, ed. *Kaiser Josef II. Ein Lebens- und Charakterbild zur hundertjährigen Gedenkfeier seiner Thronbesteigung.* Vienna: Braumüller, 1880.

von Werdum, Ulrich. "Beyn Dimyon le-metsi'ut ba-maḥaze shel mendele *di takse.*" *Ḥulyot* 10 (Winter 2007): 11–23.

———. *Das Reisejournal des Ulrich von Werdum (1670–1677): Kritische Edition eines Reiseberichtes.* Edited by Silke Cramer. Frankfurt am Main: Peter Lang, 1990.

———. "Shive'im shenot ḥeker yetsirato u-foalo shel yosef perl." Ḥuliot 7 (2002): 321–38.

von Zeiller, Franz. *Commentar über das allgemeine bürgerliche Gesetzbuch: Für die gesammten deutschen Erbländer der österreichischen Monarchie.* Vienna: Geistinger, 1811.

Wiraszka, Marta. *Rozwój Przestrzenny I Zabudowa Miast Guberni Podolskiej w Czasach Imperium Rosyjskiego*. Warsaw: Neriton, 2008.

Wiskind-Elper, Ora. *Tradition and Fantasy in the Tales of Reb Nahman of Bratslav*. Albany: State University of New York Press, 1998.

Wisse, Ruth R. "The Jewish Informer as Extortionist and Idealist." In *Insiders and Outsiders: Dilemmas of East European Jewry*, edited by Richard I. Cohen, Jonathan Frankel, and Stefani Hoffman, 188–204. Portland: Littman Library of Jewish Civilization, 2010.

Witkowski, Przemyslaw B. "Jean Potocki et le théâtre de Tulczyn." In *Jean Potocki à nouveau*, edited by Émilie Klene, Emiliano Ranocchi, and Przemyslaw B. Witkowski. Amsterdam: Rodopi, 2010.

Wolf, Gershon. *Geschichte der Juden in Wien 1156–1876*. Vienna: A. Hölder, 1876.

Wolff, Larry. *The Idea of Galicia: History and Fantasy in Habsburg Political Culture*. Stanford: Stanford University Press, 2010.

———. "Revising Eastern Europe: Memory and the Nation in Recent Historiography." *Journal of Modern History* 78, no. 1 (March 2006): 93–118.

Wolfson, Eliott R. *Luminal Darkness: Imaginal Gleanings from Zoharic Literature*. Oxford: Oneworld, 2007.

Ya'akov Yosef mi-Polnoye, *Ben Porat Yosef*. Lemberg: n.p., 1866.

Yerushalmi, Yosef Hayim. *Servants of Kings and Not Servants of Servants: Some Aspects of the Political History of the Jews*. Tenenbaum Family Lecture Series in Judaic Studies. Atlanta: Emory University, 2005.

Zaiarniuk, Andrii. *Idiomy emansypatsii: "Vyzvol'ni" proiekty i halyts'ke selo v seredyni XIX stolittia*. Kyiv: Krytyka, 2007.

Zamoyski, Adam. *Phantom Terror: The Threat of Revolution and the Repression of Liberty 1789–1848*. London: William Collins, 2015.

Zdzisław, Kaczmarczyk, and Bogusław Leśnodorski, *Historia Państwa i Prawa Polski*, vol. 2. Warsaw: Państwowe Wydawn. Naukowe, 1965.

Ziegler, Ignaz. *Die Königsgleichnisse des Midrasch, beleuchtet durch die römische Kaiserzeit*. Breslau: S. Schottlaender, 1903.

Zinberg (Tsinberg), Israel. *A History of Jewish Literature*. Vol. 12. Cincinnati: Ktav Publishing House, 1978.

Zobel, Karolina. "Polizei: Geschichte und Bedeutungswandel des Wortes und seiner Zusammensetzungen." PhD diss., University of Munich, 1952.

Index

Page numbers in italics denote figures, and endnotes are indicated by "n" followed by the endnote number.

STANFORD STUDIES IN JEWISH HISTORY AND CULTURE

Jessica Marglin and Daniel Schwartz, Editors

This series features novel approaches to examining the Jewish past in the form of innovative work that brings the field into productive dialogue with the newest scholarly concepts and methods. Open to a range of disciplinary and interdisciplinary approaches, from history to cultural studies, this series publishes exceptional scholarship balanced by an accessible tone, illustrating histories of difference and addressing issues of current urgency. Books in this list push the boundaries of Jewish Studies and speak compellingly to a wide audience of scholars and students.

Chen Mandel-Edrei, *Hagiography in the Age of Mass Publishing: Hasidic Writing and the Making of Jewish Modernity*
2026

Jordan R. Katz, *Delivering Knowledge: Jewish Midwives and Hidden Healing in Early Modern Europe*
2026

Aya Elyada, *A Lingering Legacy: The Afterlife of Yiddish in German-Jewish Culture, 1818–1938*
2026

Sasha Senderovich and Harriet Murav, *In the Shadow of the Holocaust: Short Fiction by Jewish Writers from the Soviet Union*
2026

Michael Rom, *Brazilian Belonging: Jewish Politics in Cold War Latin America*
2025

Jacob Daniels, *The Jews of Edirne: The End of Ottoman Europe and the Arrival of Borders*
2025

John M. Efron, *All Consuming: Germans, Jews, and the Meaning of Meat*
2025

Elizabeth Imber, *Uncertain Empire: Jews, Nationalism, and the Fate of British Imperialism*
2025

Paris Papamichos Chronakis, *The Business of Transition: The Jewish and Greek Merchants of Salonica, 1882-1919*
2024

Naomi Seidman, *Translating the Jewish Freud: Psychoanalysis in Hebrew and Yiddish*
2024

Ariel Evan Mayse, *Laws of the Spirit: Ritual, Mysticism, and the Commandments in Early Hasidism*
2024

Immanuel Etkes, *The Invention of a Tradition: The Messianic Zionism of the Gaon of Vilna*
2024

Viola Alianov-Rautenberg, *No Longer Ladies and Gentlemen: Gender and the German-Jewish Migration to Mandatory Palestine*
2024

Susan Rubin Suleiman, *Daughter of History: Traces of an Immigrant Girlhood*
2023

Sandra Fox, *The Jews of Summer: Summer Camp and Jewish Culture in Postwar America*
2023

David Biale, *Jewish Culture Between Canon and Heresy*
2023

Alan Verskin, *Diary of a Black Jewish Messiah: The Sixteenth-Century Journey of David Reubeni through Africa, the Middle East, and Europe*
2023

Aomar Boum, Illustrated by Nadjib Berber, *Undesirables: A Holocaust Journey to North Africa*
2023

Dina Porat, *Nakam: The Holocaust Survivors Who Sought Full-Scale Revenge*
2023

Christian Bailey, *German Jews in Love: A History*
2023

Matthias B. Lehmann, *The Baron: Maurice de Hirsch and the Jewish Nineteenth Century*
2022

Liora R. Halperin, *The Oldest Guard: Forging the Zionist Settler Past*
2021

Samuel J. Spinner, *Jewish Primitivism*
2021

For a complete listing of titles in this series, visit the Stanford University Press website, www.sup.org.

The authorized representative in the EU for product safety and compliance is:
Mare Nostrum Group
B.V Doelen 72
4831 GR Breda
The Netherlands

www.ingramcontent.com/pod-product-compliance
Ingram Content Group UK Ltd.
Pitfield, Milton Keynes, MK11 3LW, UK
UKHW041839160726
473357UK00004B/128
* 9 7 8 1 5 0 3 6 4 7 9 8 5 *